DOING

Visual Ethnography

Images, Media and
Representation in
Research

SARAH PINK

SAGE Publications

London ● Thousand Oaks ● New Delhi

ISBN 0-7619-6053-8 (hbk)
ISBN 0-7619-6054-6 (pbk)
© Sarah Pink 2001
First published 2001
Reprinted 2002, 2003, 2004, 2005

SAGE Publications Ltd
1 Oliver's Yard
55 City Road
London EC1Y 1SP

SAGE Publications Inc
2455 Teller Road
Thousand Oaks
California 91320

SAGE Publications India Pvt. Ltd
B–42 Panchsheel Enclave
PO Box 4109
New Delhi 110 017

British Library Cataloguing in Publication data
A catalogue record for this book is available from the British Library

Printed on paper from sustainable sources

Typeset by Mayhew Typesetting, Rhayader, Powys
Printed and bound in Great Britain by
Athenaeum Press Limited, Gateshead, Tyne & Wear

Contents

Acknowledgements

Writing this book has been a personal project that has enabled me to draw together my interests in research methodology, visual cultures and visual representations. However, it was also inspired by my experiences of using images in research with informants and of working with other visual anthropologists, sociologists and photographers. This work would have been impossible without the support of the many people who have collaborated in my research, allowing me to photograph or video them in Spain, the UK and Guinea Bissau. In particular I would like to thank Alberto Martinez, Tomas and Antoine Mendes in Guinea Bissau and Encarni Lucena Solís in Spain.

For the combination of technical visual and ethnographic training that has informed this work I am indebted to the staff of the Granada Centre for Visual Anthropology at the University of Manchester and the Centre for Anthropology and Computing at the University of Kent. I would also like to thank Olivia Silva and Barbara Hind whose work has developed my understanding of photographic practice, and Sandra Revill, Isabelle Badinand and Chris Owen from whom I learnt about digital media at the University of Derby. Many other people have given me important advice and practical support and I would also especially like to thank Linda Swanson, Louise Richards and Sage's anonymous reader.

Introduction

Photography, video and electronic media are becoming increasingly incorporated into the work of ethnographers: as cultural texts; as representations of ethnographic knowledge; and as sites of cultural production, social interaction and individual experience that themselves form ethnographic fieldwork locales. Visual images and technologies now form the areas, methods and media of ethnographic research and representations as well as the topics of university courses in visual anthropology, visual sociology or visual cultures. Simultaneously, the benefits of an ethnographic approach are being realized in visual arts and media studies with developments such as 'media ethnography' (see Crawford and Hafsteinnson 1996), and the use of ethnographic research methods and anthropological theory to inform photographic practice and representation (e.g. Olivia da Silva, Barbara Hind). In this contemporary context, ethnography and visual studies have much to contribute to one another. While photographic and film theory can inform our understanding of the potential of visual media in ethnographic research and representation, an ethnographic approach can also support the production and interpretation of visual images. This book is primarily for ethnographers who wish to incorporate the visual into their ethnographic work, but it is also for photographers and video makers who wish to gain a deeper understanding of how ethnographic research may inform their artistic practice.

During the last ten years I have worked with rapidly changing technologies and theoretical paradigms to use photography, video and electronic media in my own ethnographic work in Europe and West Africa. My involvement began in the late 1980s when proponents of the 'new ethnography' introduced ideas of ethnography as fiction and emphasized the centrality of subjectivity to the production of knowledge. Anthropology experienced a 'crisis' through which positivist arguments and realist approaches to knowledge, truth and objectivity were challenged. These ideas paved the way for the visual to be increasingly acceptable in ethnography as it was recognized that ethnographic film or photography were essentially no more subjective or objective than written texts. During the 1990s new innovations in visual technology, critical 'postmodern'

Figure 1   Master Caravela © Olivia da Silva.
Olivia da Silva is a photographer who uses anthropological methods to inform her
photographic practice. Master Caravela is a member of the fishing community in
Matosinhos (Portugal) that Olivia da Silva has researched using participant
observation, interviewing and a study of local photographic cultures and family
photography collections to produce her photographic project *In the Net* (2000).

theoretical approaches to subjectivity, experience, knowledge and
representation, a reflexive approach to ethnographic fieldwork methodology, and an emphasis on interdisciplinarity have invited exciting new
possibilities for the use of photographic technologies and images in
ethnography. I shall draw together some of these themes to examine their
methodological implications and explore the possibilities they offer for
practical work with video, photography and electronic media.

An approach to theory, method and the visual in ethnography

The relationship between theory and method is important for understanding any research project. Similarly, an awareness of the theoretical
underpinnings of 'visual research methods' is crucial for understanding

Figure 2   Blessing the travellers as they set off for their home at Darhan, north of
Ulaanbaatar (Arhangal, Summer, 1997 © Barbara Hind). A relative of the family
commented 'motorbikes are very popular in the countryside'.
Barbars Hind's photograph of Mongolians are informed by her reflexive approach to
her own participation in their lives and a sensitive awareness of their culture.

how those images and the processes through which they are created are
used to produce ethnographic knowledge. The existing literature on
visual research methods has rightly been criticized for being 'centred
on how-to manuals of method and analysis working within a largely
unmediated realist frame (e.g. Collier and Collier 1986)' (Edwards 1997a:
53). Such manuals, like Prosser's notions of 'an image-based research
methodology' (1996), propose problematically prescriptive frameworks
that aim to distance, objectify and generalize, and therefore detract from
the very qualities and potentials that the ambiguity and expressivity (see
Edwards 1997a) of visual images offers ethnography. Such criticisms
highlight the need for a literature that will depart from this scientific and
realist paradigm to develop a new approach to making and understanding ethnographic images.

However, my intention has not been to write another recipe book for
successful visual research, but to offer an alternative. It is frequently
emphasized that methodologies are developed for/with particular
projects, they are interwoven with theory and 'as most good researchers
know, it is not unusual to make up the methods as you go along. The
methods should serve the aims of the research, not the research serve

the aims of the method' (McGuigan 1997: 2). Moreover, as Josephides points out, 'our ethnographic strategies are also shaped by the subjects' situations, their global as well as local perceptions, and their demands and expectations of us'. Therefore, 'There can be no blueprint for how to do fieldwork. It really depends on the local people, and for this reason we have to construct our theories of how to do fieldwork *in the field*' (Josephides 1997: 32, original italics). The same applies to the use of visual images and technologies in fieldwork; specific uses should be creatively developed within individual projects. Therefore, rather than prescribing 'how to' do 'visual research' I draw from my own and other ethnographers' experiences of using images in research and representation to present a range of examples and possibilities. These are intended as a basis, or even point of contrast, from which new practices may be developed.

Different and competing methodologies, linked to specific theoretical approaches co-exist in academic discourse. This forms a theme of this book as I consider the relationship between scientific-realist and what I shall call 'reflexive' approaches to the visual in ethnography. Scientific approaches to social research still abound and students who wish to use visual methods should have a good knowledge of the debates that surround the use of the visual in social research. The theoretical agendas to which particular methods and practices are attached should be made explicit and questioned, and it is for this reason that scientific-realist and reflexive approaches are frequently contrasted in this book. In my opinion the approach of those visual sociologists who aim to incorporate a visual dimension into an already established methodology based on a 'scientific' approach to sociology (e.g. Grady 1996; Prosser 1996; Prosser and Schwartz 1998) does not allow the potential of the visual in ethnography to be realized. Their proposal that visual images should support the project of a scientific sociology suffers from the problems of perspectives like equality feminism: it must subscribe the dominant discourse in order to be incorporated. The advocates of this conservative strategy are thus obliged to prove the value of the visual to a scientific sociology that is dominated by the written word, thus effectively evaluating the worth of images to research on the terms of a sociological agenda that has rejected the significance of visual meanings and the potential of images to represent and generate new types of ethnographic knowledge.

In this book I shall take the contrasting view, that to incorporate the visual appropriately, social science should, as MacDougall has suggested, 'develop alternative objectives and methodologies' (1997: 293) rather than attaching the visual to existing methodological principles and analytical frames. This means abandoning the possibility of a purely objective social science and rejecting the idea that the written word is essentially a superior medium of ethnographic representation. While images should not necessarily replace words as the dominant mode of research or representation, they should be regarded as an equally meaningful element of ethnographic work. Thus visual images, objects, descriptions should be incorporated when it is appropriate, opportune or enlightening to do so. Images may not necessarily be *the* main research method or topic, but through their relation to other sensory, material and discursive elements of the research images and visual knowledge will *become* of interest. As Stoller reminds us, 'it is representationally as well as analytically import-ant to consider how perception in non-western societies devolves not simply from vision . . . but also from smell, touch, taste and hearing' (1997: xv–xvi). In some projects the visual may become more important than the spoken or written word, in others it will not. In this book I shall therefore argue that there is no essential hierarchy of knowledge or media for ethnographic representation. Academic epistemologies and conven-tional academic modes of representation should not be used to obscure and abstract the epistemologies and experienced realities of local people. Rather, these may complement one another as different types of ethnographic knowledge that may be experienced and represented in a range of different textual, visual and other sensory ways.

Disciplinary concerns and ethnographic research

Anthropology, sociology, cultural studies, photographic studies and media studies are the key disciplines to which I shall refer. With their shared interests in material culture, practices of representation, the interpretation of cultural texts and comprehending social relations and individual experience, each discipline offers its own understanding of the visual in culture and society. While different disciplines use visual images and technologies in ethnography to serve their own epistemo-logical and empirical agendas, and should of course be at liberty to do so, recently a number of significant interdisciplinary links have been implied.

Some have argued that the once uncomfortable relationship between anthropology and cultural studies should be developed into a more productive alliance. According to Harvey 'many of those [anthropolo-gists] who attack the cultural studies approach focus on the differences between studying texts and studying people, between representation and situated practice' (Harvey 1996: 14). She points out the irony of this criticism given that Geertz, an anthropologist, was one of the most prominent proponents of the textual approach, and this approach has been criticized in cultural studies. Harvey critiques an anthropology that objectifies culture (such as art), separating it from everyday life and (citing McRobbie's 1992: 730 critique) a cultural studies that treats people as textual subjects rather than as agents. She notes that an 'awareness of a tension between text and everyday life is not exclusively anthropologi-cal' (1996: 14) and argues that 'the discipline of anthropology cannot ignore the contributions from cultural studies' (1996: 15). An interlinking of cultural studies and anthropological approaches seems particularly pertinent to an ethnography that incorporates visual images and techno-logies. This approach recognizes the interwovenness of objects, texts, images and technologies in people's everyday lives and identities. It aims not simply to 'study' people's social practices or to read cultural objects or performances as if they were texts, but to explore how all types of material, intangible, spoken, performed narratives and discourses are interwoven with and made meaningful in relation to social relationships, practices and individual experiences.

The idea of crossing disciplinary boundaries has also been proposed by Edwards (1997a) who has demonstrated how anthropological and photographic theories of representation may be combined to produce a deeper understanding of the expressive possibilities of photography for anthropological representation (see Chapter 6). Meanwhile, some photographers like Olivia da Silva and Barbara Hind have developed an ethnographic approach to their photographic practice (see Chapter 3). In contrast, sociological approaches to ethnographic uses of photography and video are often more insular, tending to look inwards to their own discipline. Concepts of 'validity', sampling and triangulation abound in sociological methods texts on ethnography (see, for example, Hammer-sely and Atkinson 1995: 227–32; Walsh 1998: 231). Correspondingly, many visual sociologists have attempted to incorporate these conditions into their use of visual images, making their visual ethnographic 'data' succumb to the agenda of a scientific and experimental sociology (e.g. Grady 1996; Prosser 1996; Prosser and Schwartz 1998). This 'traditional' sociological approach fails to develop the full potential of the visual in ethnography. However, other visual sociologists, such as Chaplin (1994), have developed more interdisciplinary approaches that incorporate feminist, anthropological, cultural studies and other critical approaches.

A second motive for taking an interdisciplinary approach to the visual in ethnography is the idea that ethnography is an *aspect* of research and representation. Ethnography is rarely the sole means or end of a research project; different disciplinary uses of it are likely to situate ethnography differently within their processes of research and representation. One could argue that no project is ever purely ethnographic, but that it will draw from ethnography and other methods to varying extents. Ethnography may be combined with textual, historical, narrative, statistical or a whole range of other research practices which may intertwine and overlap or link conceptually as the research proceeds. Some of these connections will be flagged up in this book. For example, in Chapters 3 and 4 I discuss how studying local photographic and media cultures and histories can inform our understanding of contemporary ethnographic photography and video. Moreover, statis-tical sources or analysis of existing visual texts may be used to inform the design and interpretation of visual research. Similarly, in Chapters 6, 7 and 8 I emphasize the importance of understanding the media that are used for ethnographic representation through a consideration of how photographic, video and electronic texts communicate and are interpreted.

Vision and images in social science: methodologies and theories

Ethnographers have long since used photography, film and more recently video in research and representation. However, historically and in different disciplines they have done so with varying degrees of acceptance and continuity. Moreover, both between and within disciplines the development of 'visual research methods' has been informed by different theoretical approaches. A review of some of these developments traces the distinctiveness of anthropological, sociological and cultural studies approaches to photography and video.

Developments in visual anthropology

Ethnographic uses of the visual have usually been shrouded in some controversy. From the 1960s to the early 1980s debates focused on whether visual images and recordings could usefully support the observational project of social science (see, for example, Collier and Collier 1986; Hockings 1975, 1995; and Rollwagen 1988). During this period many social scientists resisted the use of the visual in ethnography, claiming that as a data collection method it was too subjective, unrepresentative and unsystematic. Ethnographers like Mead, Collier and Becker set out to prove otherwise, in both their theoretical arguments and their practical applications of film and video. Visual ethnographers were forced to confront the accusation that their visual images lacked objectivity and scientific rigour. Mead's response was that cameras left to film continuously without human intervention produced 'objective materials' (Mead 1995 [1975]: 9–10). Others, suggesting that the specificity of the photographed moment rendered it scientifically invalid (see, for example, Collier 1995 [1975]: 247), endeavoured to compensate for this. For instance, Becker followed Ruby (1972) to propose that the photographs anthropologists and sociologists might take during fieldwork 'are really only vacation pictures' (Becker 1986: 244), indistinguishable from those of the anthropologist's – or anyone else's – vacation. He advocated a systematic approach to photography as the social scientists' key to success (Becker 1986: 245–50) in an echo of Collier, who warns that '[t]he photographic record can remain wholly impressionistic UNLESS it undergoes disciplined computing' (1995 [1975]: 248). Thus some disputed the validity of the visual on the grounds of its subjectivity, bias and specificity. Others responded that, under the right controls, the visual could contribute to a positivist social science as an objective recording method.

One of the most influential publications of this era is Collier's (1967) *Visual Anthropology: Photography as Research Method* (revised and reprinted in 1986). The most comprehensive textbook on the use of photography and video in ethnographic research and representation, this remains the basis of some contemporary approaches to the visual (e.g. Prosser 1996; Prosser and Schwartz 1998). Collier and Collier advocate a systematic method of observation in which the researcher is supported by visual technology. They assert that 'good video and film records for research are ultimately the product of observation that is organized and consistent. The equipment, except in specialized circumstances, cannot replace the observer' (Collier and Collier 1986: 149). This approach depends on a realist interpretation of still and moving images and, as I note above, has been criticized on this basis (for example, by Edwards 1997a). For Collier and Collier, the research plan is key to the ethnographer's project of recording an appropriate version of the reality he or she is able to observe. Therefore they distinguish between the fiction of the '"shooting scripts" often used in the photographic and film world' and research plans that purport to record reality. On their terms ethnography is an observation of reality, as opposed to the constructedness of the narrative-based communication 'stories' of scripted films (Collier and Collier 1986: 162).

In the same year as Collier and Collier's book, in the now landmark collection, *Writing Culture* (1986), Clifford suggests that, to the contrary, ethnographies themselves are constructed narratives: in a word, 'fictions'. He uses the term 'fiction', not to claim that ethnographies are 'opposed to the truth' or are 'false', but to emphasize how ethnographies cannot reveal or report on complete or whole accounts of reality; that they only ever tell part of the story (1986: 6). For Clifford, not only is ethnography a constructed version of truth, but 'Ethnographic truths are . . . inherently *partial* – committed and incomplete' (1986: 7, original italics). This can be applied to both research and representation. Clifford's ideas question Collier and Collier's claim that research shooting guides differ from 'fictional' shooting scripts because the 'systematic selectivity' of 'field shooting or observation guides' is concerned 'with defining procedure, structure, and categories for recording that produce data on which later research analysis and summations are built' (1986: 162). Clifford's very point is that 'cultural fictions are built on systematic, and contestable, exclusions' (1986: 6). This suggests that the selectivity, predetermined categories and precautions that Collier and Collier assume will prevent ethnography from being a 'fiction' rather than a realist observation are in fact the very corner stones upon which Clifford's ethnographic 'fictions' are constructed. Collier and Collier recognize that the 'whole' view of a situation cannot be recorded on video, they urge the research photographer to confront 'the challenge of gathering a semblance of the whole circumstance in a compressed sample of items and events observed in time and space' (1986: 163). They do not account for the possibility that any attempt to represent a 'whole view' itself constitutes a 'partial truth' or, in Clifford's terms, a 'fiction' based on 'systematic exclusions'.

In the 1980s Clifford's ideas helped to create a favourable environment for the visual representation of ethnography. The emphasis on specificity and experience, and a recognition of the similarities between the constructedness and 'fiction' (in Clifford's sense of the term) of film and written text, created a context where ethnographic film became a more acceptable form of ethnographic representation (Henley 1998: 51; Ruby 1982: 130). However, initially, little attention was paid to re-thinking the theoretical implications of photography and video as research methods. There were of course some exceptions. For example, Larson (1988) used photography and images reflexively to learn about her informant's views of reality through collaborative photography (see Chapter 3). But the greater focus on the mediation of meaning between anthropologists and informants was developed in the reflexive ethnographic film style of David and Judith MacDougall and their contemporaries (see Loizos 1993).

In the 1990s a new literature has approximated the historical debates and developments of the relationship between photography, film and the observational approaches of both anthropology and sociology (e.g. Chaplin 1994; Edwards 1992; Harper 1998a, 1998b; Henley 1998; Loizos 1993; Morphy and Banks 1997; Pink 1996, 1998b). Edwards's (1992) and Morphy and Banks's (1997) volumes signify an intentional departure from the scientific-realist paradigm but recognize that the contemporary context is one in which '[m]any anthropologists still feel caught between the possibility of conceptual advances from visual anthropology and the more conservative paradigms of a positivist scientific tradition' (MacDougall 1997: 192). Rather than attempting to fit visual anthropology into a scientific paradigm, whereby visual research methods could support and enhance an objective anthropology, MacDougall proposes a significantly different approach that would 'look at the principles that emerge when fieldworkers actually try to rethink anthropology through use of a visual medium' (1997: 192). This implies a radical transformation of anthropology itself that would 'involve putting in temporary suspension anthropology's dominant orientation as a discipline of words and rethinking certain categories of anthropological knowledge in the light of understandings that may be accessible only by non-verbal means' and 'a shift from word-and-sentence-based anthropological thought to image-and-sequence-based anthropological thought' (1997: 292). Therefore, rather than attempting to incorporate images into a word-based social science, MacDougall advocates that since '[v]isual anthropology can never be either a copy of written anthropology or a substitute for it . . . [f]or that very reason it must develop alternative objectives and methodologies that will benefit anthropology as a whole' (1997: 292–3).

Developments in visual sociology

While from the late 1970s visual anthropologists, turning their attention to ethnographic film and video, began to question the notion of visual realism, visual sociologists (e.g. Wagner 1979) continued to develop their use of photography within the realist paradigm (Harper 1998a: 27; see also Pink 1998d). Some sociologists have responded to feminist and postmodern critiques, in some cases developing interdisciplinary approaches to the sociology of visual culture (e.g. Crawshaw and Urry 1997) and the implications of photography for sociological under-standings of the individual and self-identity (Lury 1998). However, many of those who call themselves visual sociologists seem to have engaged little with social theory or debates over reflexivity and sub-jectivity in research. Many sociologists continue to reject the use of visual images in research and representation (see Prosser 1996), arguing that their subjectivity and specificity renders them invalid for the scientific project of sociology. The sub-discipline of visual sociology has, perhaps in response to this, also been correspondingly slow to accept the idea that the visual may have a contribution beyond its use as a 'recording method' and 'support' for a word-based discipline. For instance, Prosser and Schwartz do not engage with the potential of the visual to challenge existing approaches but consider how photography may be incorporated into 'a traditional qualitative framework rather than adopt ideas emanating from postmodern critique' (1998: 115). Gold's approach similarly maintains a close alliance with existing sociological methods. He argues that visual sociologists must address the problem that visual sociology is divided into two camps that deal with either the interpretation or the creation of visual images. Gold defines this as a 'theory/method split' – and 'a major obstacle in the further development of visual sociology' and proposes that theory and method may be brought together through the established 'grounded theory' approach (Gold 1997: 4).

Harper (1998a, 1998b), in contrast to Prosser and Schwartz (1998), argues that visual sociology should take on board the postmodern critiques of ethnography and of documentary photography to develop 'a newly integrative visual sociology'. He calls for a redefinition of the relationship between the researcher and the informant in the form of a collaborative approach developed in the 'new ethnography' and the incorporation of the postmodern approach to documentary photography that 'begins with the idea that the meaning of the photograph is con-structed by the maker and the viewer, both of whom carry their social positions and interests to the photographic act' (1998a: 34–5, 1998b: 140). However, Harper does not propose a radical departure from existing sociological approaches to the visual since he recommends that visual sociology should 'begin with traditional assumptions and prac-tices of sociological fieldwork and sociology analysis' that treat the photograph as 'data', and that it should open up to integrate the demands of the 'new ethnography' (1998a: 35).

Chaplin has been the main critic of traditional approaches to the visual in sociology. In her book *Sociology and Visual Representations* (1994), Chaplin engages with post-feminist, and post-positivist agendas to suggest a way forward for a 'visual sociology'. She advocates a collaborative approach that reduces the distance between the discipline and its subject of study. Thus, unlike Harper, she argues that rather than the visual being the 'data' that is subjected to a verbal 'analysis', the potential of the visual as sociological knowledge and critical text should be explored (Chaplin 1994: 16). While there is some evidence to suggest that visual sociologists are realizing the potential that Chaplin has indicated in their work (e.g. Barndt 1997; Barnes et al. 1997, whose work will be discussed in the following chapters), much visual sociology remains firmly rooted in existing sociological theory and method. Chaplin (like MacDougall, Edwards and Morphy and Banks in anthropology) takes a step further than most visual sociologists by engaging with the visual not simply as a mode of recording data or illustrating text, but as a medium through which new knowledge and critiques may be created. The methodological implications of this stress collaboration, not solely between researcher and informants, but also between the visual and textual and the producers of images and words. These ideas form the basis of the discussions of the potentials of photography, video and hypermedia in research and representation in the following chapters.

The visual in cultural studies

Cultural studies approaches to photography and video have largely focused on the study of visual representation and visual cultures (including digital culture, see Chapters 6 and 8). For example, Hall's key text uses 'a wide range of examples from different cultural media and discourses, mainly concentrating on *visual* language' (1997: 9, original italics). It considers issues related to the negotiation of visual meanings, emphasizing the contested nature of meaning and 'the practices of representation' (1997: 9–10). However, the focus in cultural studies is on interpreting existing images and objects and the social and cultural conditions within which they are produced, rather than on how images and their production form part of ethnographic practices (see also, for example, Cooke and Wollen 1995; Evans and Hall 1999; Jenks 1995). Given the interest that cultural studies has paid to 'visual cultures', representations and visual symbolism, as well as its increasing use of ethnography, it has incorporated these forms of representation correspondingly little in its own research practices.

As an interdisciplinary subject cultural studies does not identify with the development of a particular methodological tradition in the way that

social anthropology, for example, is identified with participant observation: 'it still remains difficult to say quite what cultural studies
amounts to methodologically'. Instead 'cultural studies is eclectic in the
methods it uses, drawing liberally from across the humanities and social
sciences', it thus deals with *methodologies* rather than a single
methodology (McGuigan 1997: 1). Alasuutari similarly notes: 'Cultural
studies methodology has often been described by the concept of *bricolage*:
one is pragmatic and strategic in choosing and applying different
methods and practices' (Alasuutari 1995: 2). This may explain why
cultural studies guides to the use of visual images and technologies in
ethnography are few and varied. Alasuutari suggests that 'to record non-
verbal communication one needs a movie or video camera, and in a
group discussion situation there should probably be several of them'
(1995: 43), and recommends that video or tape recordings be made of
interviews that may later be transcribed (1995: 179). Alasuutari's
comments on the use of video in cultural studies research are not concerned with the development of the visual as a new form of knowledge,
but are firmly embedded in a realist paradigm. Thomas's discussion of
her study of a youth and community dance group in south-east London
(1997: 142) represents a more useful demonstration of the potential of
video in cultural studies research. Thomas follows Geertz and Clifford in
asserting that ethnography is 'not about making truth claims'. Instead,
she sees 'the construction of ethnographic descriptions' as 'an imaginative act which should bring us into touch with the lives of strangers'
(Thomas 1997: 143). She describes a reflexive research process that
involved the use of video with dancers rehearsing, performing and in a
group interview. This work was based in an appreciation of feminist film
theory, developing a participatory approach and aiming to avert the
oppressive 'masculine gaze' (see Chapter 4).

Common theoretical threads: the transformative potential of the visual

Across the disciplines that use ethnographic methods the use of visual
images in research and representation is becoming more frequently
written about and more rigorously theorized. Many researchers appear
willing to scrutinize reflexively their own methods through explorations
of how subjectivity, individual experience and negotiation with informants figure in the production of ethnographic knowledge. However,
these developments are occurring at an uneven pace both between and
within the disciplines and not all are prepared to engage with the
transformative potential of the visual for ethnographic research and
representation.

    These changing disciplinary approaches to the visual can also be
situated in relation to broader theoretical shifts. Recent work has

situated the image and the camera as key elements in an intersection between modernity and a critique of modernity (McQuire 1998) and the relationship between photography and notions of the individual, memory and identity in Euro-American societies (e.g. Lury 1998). Both McQuire and Lury see photography not only as a product of particular social and cultural environments, but also as a force that has itself encouraged shifts in ways of understanding and 'seeing'. McQuire argues that the ambiguity of the meaning of images not only questions the modern notion of truth, but destabilizes the basic premises of modernity. He proposes that the uncertainty of meaning implied by the camera questions the idea that there can be an 'ultimate goal' of a single, pure or 'untouched' meaning and this 'entrains a profound epistemological shift in which the meaning of meaning has itself been irreversibly transformed (McQuire 1998: 47). McQuire emphasizes the 'promiscuity' and ambiguity of the image: its simultaneous appearances of objectivity and subjectivity that became the basis upon which anthropologists rejected or accepted it and debated its usefulness to the social sciences in the 1970s. In McQuire's version of the history of the visual in modernity, he attributes power to the camera as an agent of change that overturns the realist paradigm. This implies that an appropriate application of visual images and technologies in ethnography may be developed as a force that will bring new meaning(s) to ethnographic work and social science. Suggesting, as MacDougall has proposed for anthropology, a rethinking of social science 'through a visual medium' (1997: 293). Moreover, as Lury's exploration of how 'the photographic image may have contributed to novel configurations of personhood, self-knowledge and truth' (1998: 2) suggests, the visual has implications not only for the discourses of modernity and ethnographic practice, but also for our understandings of the individuals who are the subjects of ethnography. Lury proposes that 'the photograph, more than merely representing, has taught us a way of seeing (Ihde, 1995), and that this way of seeing has transformed contemporary self-understandings' (1998: 3).

Approaches to the visual in anthropology, sociology and cultural studies have developed in rather different ways and have been informed by different understandings of the visual. However, recent reassessments of the relationship between vision, observation and 'truth' have influenced the ways in which the visual is approached across the disciplines, emphasizing the arbitrariness of visual meanings and the potential of the visual for the representation of ethnographic knowledge. It has been suggested that photographic and video images can act as a force that has a transformative potential for modern thought, culture and society, self-identity and memory and social science itself. Therefore by paying attention to images in ethnographic research and representation it is possible that new ways of understanding individuals, cultures and research materials may emerge.

The book

The first chapter outlines the theoretical approach of the volume, situating visual images and technologies in relation to a reflexive approach to ethnography that focuses on subjectivity, creativity and self-consciousness. It incorporates recent ideas about the individual in society from anthropology, with cultural theories of the visual and an exploration of consumption and material culture, to consider how visual images and technologies are interwoven with not only the cultures ethnographers study but also the academic cultures to which they belong. The more practical uses of photography and video in ethnographic research and representation are the main foci of the following chapters, extending to a consideration of the potential of hypermedia representation in the final chapter.

Before going on to discuss the particular technologies and representations in the field, in Chapter 2 the more practical aspects of preparing for visual fieldwork are discussed, alongside project design, ethical considerations and gender issues. The following two chapters focus on different technologies and images in the research process. First, photography, which has been employed much more extensively by visual sociologists than in other ethnographic disciplines, is explored in Chapter 3. Ethnographic film, which has dominated the practice and literature of visual anthropology (e.g. Heider 1976; Loizos 1993; Rollwagen 1988) is not my main concern here. Rather, I draw from this literature to discuss video in Chapter 4. Chapter 5 focuses on the organization and interpretation of visual materials, while Chapters 6, 7 and 8 discuss the production of different types of text and how visual, written and other materials may be combined and interlinked in different representations. Electronic technologies have recently opened up new and fascinating possibilities for the use of visual images in research and representation. However, these new potentials also raise a series of new issues of representation, interpretation and the authoring of knowledge that need to be addressed at the outset of their use rather than retrospectively (see Pink 1998c).

PART 1

THINKING ABOUT VISUAL RESEARCH

Visual research and representation may sometimes unexpectedly become part of an ethnographic project that is already in progress. In other scenarios use of the visual will be part of a carefully prepared plan, although, as the examples in Chapters 3 and 4 indicate, new visual aspects of a project may develop. It is always important to be well prepared in the theoretical and practical possibilities raised by visual research methods. Part 1 offers a grounding in theoretical, practical and ethical issues that can inform a researcher whose uses of the visual in ethnography are either planned or (like many moments in ethnography) serendipitous.

CHAPTER 1

The Visual in Ethnography: Photography, Video, Cultures and Individuals

Images are 'everywhere'. They permeate our academic work, everyday lives, conversations (see Pink 1997a: 3) and dreams (see Edgar 1997). They are inextricably interwoven with our personal identities, narratives, lifestyles, cultures and societies, as well as with definitions of history, space and truth. Ethnographic research is likewise intertwined with visual images and metaphors. When ethnographers produce photographs or video, these visual texts, as well as the experience of producing and discussing them, become part of their ethnographic knowledge. Just as images inspire conversations, conversation may invoke images; conversation visualizes and draws absent printed or electronic images into its narratives through verbal descriptions and references to them. In ethnography images are as inevitable as sounds, words or any other aspect of culture and society. Nevertheless, ethnographers should not be obliged to make the visual *central* to their work (see Morphy and Banks 1997: 14), but to explore its relation to other senses and discourses.

The visual has recently received much critical attention from scholars of the social 'sciences' and humanities. It is now commonly recognized that it is time to, as Crawford (1992: 66) recommended, depart from notions of 'pure image' and 'pure word' and instead to emphasize the constructedness of this distinction. In this sense even the term 'visual research methods' (see Banks n.d.), that refers to uses of visual technologies and images in research, places an undue stress on the visual. 'Visual research methods' are not purely visual. Rather, they pay particular attention to visual aspects of culture. Similarly, they cannot be used independently of other methods; neither a purely visual ethnography nor an exclusively visual approach to culture can exist. This chapter focuses on this interlinking of the visual with ethnography, culture and individuals.

Ethnography and ethnographic images

What is ethnography? How does one 'do' ethnography? What is it that makes a text, photograph or video ethnographic? Handbooks of 'traditional' research methods tend to represent ethnography as a mixture of participant observation and interviewing. For example, Hammersley and Atkinson define ethnography as 'a particular method or set of methods' that:

> involves the ethnographer participating, overtly or covertly, in people's daily lives for an extended period of time, watching what happens, listening to what is said, asking questions – in fact, collecting whatever data are available to throw light on the issues that are the focus of the research. (1995: 1)

Such descriptions are limited on two counts. First, they restrict the range of things ethnographers may actually do. Secondly, their representations of ethnography as just another method or set of methods of 'data collection' wrongly assumes that ethnography entails a simple process of going to another place or culture, staying there for a period of time, collecting pieces of information and knowledge and then taking them home intact.

　　Instead, I shall define ethnography as a methodology (see Crotty 1998: 7); as an approach to experiencing, interpreting and representing culture and society that informs and is informed by sets of different disciplinary agendas and theoretical principles. Rather than being a method for the collection of 'data', ethnography is a process of creating and representing knowledge (about society, culture and individuals) that is based on ethnographers' own experiences. It does not claim to produce an objective or 'truthful' account of reality, but should aim to offer versions of ethnographers' experiences of reality that are as loyal as possible to the context, negotiations and intersubjectivities through which the knowledge was produced. This may entail reflexive, collaborative or participatory methods. It may involve informants in a variety of ways at different points of the research and representational stages of the project. It should account not only for the observable, recordable realities that may be translated into written notes and texts, but also for objects, visual images, the immaterial, and the sensory nature of human experience and knowledge. Finally, it should engage with issues of representation that question the right of the researcher to represent 'other' people, recognize the impossibility of 'knowing other minds' (Fernandez 1995: 25) and acknowledge that the sense we make of informants' words and actions is 'an expression of our own consciousness' (Cohen and Rapport 1995: 12).

　　There is, likewise, no simple answer or definition of what it is that makes an activity, image, text, idea, or piece of knowledge 'ethnographic'. No single action, artifact or representation is essentially in itself 'ethnographic', but will be defined as such through interpretation and context. Anthropologists have noted the absence of concrete boundaries between ethnographic and fictional texts (see Clifford and Marcus 1986), and between ethnographic, documentary and fictional film (see Loizos 1993: 7–8). Similarly, there is no clear-cut way of defining an individual photograph as, for example, a tourist, documentary or journalistic photograph (see Chapter 3), or of deciding whether a piece of video footage is a home movie or ethnographic video (see Chapter 4). The same applies to the arbitrary nature of our distinctions between personal experience and ethnographic experience, autobiography and anthropology (see Okely 1996; Okely and Callaway 1992) and fieldwork and everyday life (Pink 1999a). Any experience, action, artifact, image or idea is never definitively *just one thing* but may be redefined differently in different situations, by different individuals and in terms of different discourses. It is impossible to measure the 'ethnographicness' of an image in terms of its form, content or potential as an observational document, visual record or piece of 'data'. Instead, the 'ethnographicness' of any image or representation is contingent on how it is situated, interpreted and used to invoke meanings and knowledge that are of ethnographic interest.

Reflexivity and subjectivity

In their critique of natural science approaches, authors of 'traditional' research methods texts have emphasized the constructedness of ethnographic knowledge (e.g. Burgess 1984; Ellen 1984), usually coupled with a stress on the central importance of reflexivity (see also Fortier 1998; Walsh 1998). A reflexive approach recognizes the centrality of the subjectivity of the researcher to the production and representation of ethnographic knowledge. Reflexivity goes beyond the researcher's concern with questions of 'bias' or how ethnographers observe the 'reality' of a society they actually 'distort' through their participation in it. Moreover, reflexivity is not simply a mechanism that neutralizes ethnographers' subjectivity as collectors of data through an engagement with how their presence may have affected the reality observed and the data collected. Indeed, the assumption that a reflexive approach will aid ethnographers to produce objective data represents only a token and cosmetic engagement with reflexivity that wrongly supposes subjectivity could (or should) be avoided or eradicated. Instead, subjectivity should be engaged with as a central aspect of ethnographic knowledge, interpretation and representation.

Postmodern thinkers have argued that ethnographic knowledge and text can only ever be a subjective construction, a 'fiction' that represents only the ethnographer's version of a reality, rather than an empirical truth. Some, like Walsh, proposed that such approaches take reflexivity too far. Walsh argues that the 'social and cultural world must be the ground and reference for ethnographic writing, and reflexive ethnography should involve a keen awareness of the interpenetration of reality and representation'. He insists that researchers should not 'abandon all forms of realism as the basis for doing ethnography' (Walsh 1998: 220).

Walsh's argument presents a tempting and balanced way of thinking about the experienced reality in which people live and the texts that ethnographers construct to represent this reality. Nevertheless it is also important to keep in mind the centrality of the subjectivity of the researcher to the production of ethnographic knowledge. Cohen and Rapport's point that our understandings of what informants say or do is solely 'an expression of our own consciousness' (see above), problematizes Walsh's proposition. If the researcher is the channel through which all ethnographic knowledge is produced and represented, then the only way reality and representation can 'interpenetrate' in ethnographic work is through the ethnographer's textual constructions of 'ethnographic fictions'. Rather than existing objectively and being accessible and recordable through 'scientific' research methods, reality is subjective and is known only as it is experienced by individuals. By focusing on how ethnographic knowledge about how individuals experience reality is produced, through the intersubjectivity between researchers and their research contexts, we may arrive at a closer understanding of the worlds that other people live in. It is not solely the subjectivity of the researcher that may 'shade' his or her understanding of 'reality', but the relationship between the subjectivities of researcher and informants that produces a negotiated version of reality (see, for example, Fortier 1998).

In relation to this, researchers should maintain an awareness of how different elements of their identities become significant during research. For example, gender, age, ethnicity, class and race are important in the way researchers are situated and situate themselves in ethnographic contexts. Ethnographers ought to be self-conscious about how they represent themselves to informants and they ought to consider how their identities are constructed and understood by the people with whom they work. These subjective understandings will have implications for the knowledge that is produced from the 'ethnographic encounter' between researcher and informants. For example, as I found during my research in Guinea Bissau, there were at the time many 'rich white development workers' in the area where I worked and I was classified as part of this group by many Guinea Bissauans (see Pink 1998a). Clearly their understandings of my identity and status had implications for the way I was able to interact with local people and the specific knowledge that our interactions produced. In this particular research context economic inequalities unavoidably formed a back-drop to my relationships with Guinea Bissauans (see, for example, Pink 1999b). My use of photography and video (technologies that are prohibitively costly for most Guinea Bissauans) therefore had to be situated in terms of the wider economic context as well as my own identity as a researcher. Similarly, as I describe in Chapter 3, during my fieldwork in Southern Spain, being 'a woman with a camera' was a significant aspect of my gendered identity as a researcher (see Pink 1998b, 1999c). Gendered and economic power relations implied in and by images and image production have an inevitable influence on how visual images and technologies can be used in ethnographic research.

Gendered identities, technologies and images

In the 1990s gender became a central theme in discussions of ethnographic research methodology. This included a focus on the gendered identity of the researcher, the intersubjectivity of the gendered negotiations that ethnographers have with their informants, the sensuous, sexualized and erotic aspects of fieldwork and the gendered nature of the ethnographic research process, or of the 'ethnographic narrative' (see especially Bell et al. 1993; Kulick and Willson 1995). A consideration of gender and other aspects of identity also has implications for ethnographic research with images.

Recent developments in gender theory have had an important impact on ethnographic methodology. A stress on the plural, rather than binary, nature of gendered identities and thus on *multiple* femininities and masculinities (see, for example, Connell 1987, 1995; Cornwall and Lindisfarne 1994; Moore 1994) has meant that differences *among* as well as *between* men and women are accounted for. Moreover, the fixity of both gender and identity have been questioned as researchers and theorists have begun to explore how the same individual may both experience and represent his or her masculinity or femininity differently in different contexts and in relation to different people (see Pink 1997a). It has been argued that the gendered self is never fully defined in any absolute way, but that it is only in specific social interactions that the gender identity of any individual comes in to being *in relation to* the negotiations that it undertakes with other individuals. In this sense, as Kulick (1995: 29) has summarized, the gendered self is only ever completed in relation to other selves, subjectivities, discourses, representations or material objects. If we apply this to the fieldwork context, it implies that precisely how both researcher and informant experience themselves and one another as gendered individuals will depend on the specific negotiation into which they enter. If visual images and technologies are part of the research project, they will play a role in how both researcher and informant identities are constructed and interpreted. As part of most contemporary cultures photography, video and other media also form part of the broader context in which researcher and informant identities are situated.

An understanding of gender relations as relations of power and a concurrent gendering of power relations has been developed in existing literatures on visual image production, representation and ethnographic research. In some instances gendered power relations become an explicit aspect of fieldwork experience. Barndt demonstrates this through a memorable example: 'Ever since that moment in 1969 when I took my first people picture and got threatened by my subject/victim (who in self-defense, wielded over me the butcher knife she had been using to carve her toe nails), I have understood that the act of photography is imbued with issues of power' (Barndt 1997: 9). In another project, photographing the staff of a sociology department, Barndt found also that the gendered and hierarchical power relations within the department corresponded with the access she had to different people:

> It seemed much harder to get into the space of the powerful than into the space of the less powerful: the (primarily female) secretaries in the departmental office were easier prey, for example, than the (usually male) full professors; you had to pass through two doors and get their permission before you could photograph them. (1997: 13)

An understanding of the intersection between image production, image-producing technologies and the ethnic, racial, gendered and other elements of the identities of those who use or own them is crucial for a reflexive approach. In more abstract discussions it has been argued that the modern or 'conventional' ethnographic research process itself constitutes a masculine pursuit that oppresses a feminine approach to knowledge. Kulick has likened the traditional narrative structure of ethnography as an exploitative and repressive act where the masculine ethnographer penetrates the feminized 'field' generalizing, abstracting and oppressing the 'feminine' objects of his study. He has argued for a different (and more feminine) approach to ethnography that focuses on negotiation and intersubjectivity (Kulick 1995). This perspective thus develops a model of masculinity as exploitative and repressive. This does not mean that all types of masculinity are always repressive or exploitative; in everyday life and experience many different types of masculinity ·exist (see Connell 1995). Rather, the abstracted models of feminine and masculine approaches to ethnography are important in that they stand as metaphors for particular approaches to ethics, epistemology and subjectivity.

These gendered models of ethnography as masculine, exploitative, observational and objectifying or feminine, subjective, sensuous, negotiating and reflexive have parallels in film studies and photography. In particular, notions of the gendered gaze, as developed by Mulvey (1989) in film studies, and of the 'archive' developed by Sekula (1989) in photography, have suggested that women, or the less powerful, are oppressed by an objectifying masculine gaze that is implied by the way they are represented visually in both film and photography. Borrowed originally from Foucault, these ideas have been re-appropriated to discuss visual representations in other cultures (e.g. Pinney 1992a) and historically in western culture. For example, studies of colonial photography have characterized the 'colonial gaze' on other less powerful cultures as an exploitative and objectifying project to catalogue and classify the colonized (see Edwards 1992, 1997b). As a response to this, feminist approaches to the production of ethnographic knowledge and of ethnographic images and the uses of technology have been developed in Chaplin's work with photography (1994) and Thomas's research with video (1997). These collaborative approaches that confront and attempt to resolve the gendered power relations of technology and representation are discussed further in Chapters 3 and 4.

Unobservable ethnography and visual culture

In the Introduction I have described the realist view of visual technologies as tools for creating visual records. This view persists in some social science research methods text books. For example, Flick refers to 'the use of visual media for research purposes' as 'second-hand observation' (1998: 151). While this may prove a useful means of undertaking some forms of social research, this 'observational' approach depends on the problematic assumption that reality is visible, observable and recordable in video or photography. However, as writers such as Fabian (1983) have suggested, the epistemological and ethical principles of the observational approach should be rethought. In particular two issues need to be addressed. First, is it possible to observe and record 'reality'? For instance, just because something appears to be visible, this does not necessarily mean it is true. Second, the observational approach implies that we can observe and extract objective information (data) about our informants. This can be problematized as an 'objectifying' approach that does research *on* but not *with* people.

The relationship between the visual, the visible and reality has been a recent theme in cultural studies as well as anthropology. As Jenks has argued, while material objects inevitably have a visual presence, the notion of 'visual culture' should not refer only to the material and observable, 'visible' aspects of culture (Jenks 1995: 16). Rather, the visual also forms part of human imaginations and conversations. As Strecker emphasizes, images play a central role in the human mind and in human discourse which is 'metaphorically grounded' (Tyler 1987; Lakoff and Johnson 1980, quoted in Strecker 1997). The 'material' and 'visual cultures' that we encounter when we do ethnographic fieldwork may therefore be understood from this perspective: material objects are unavoidably visual, but visual images are not, by definition, material. Nevertheless, the intangibility of an image that exists as verbal description or is imagined makes it no less 'real'. This approach to images presents a direct challenge to definitions of 'the real in terms of the material, which can be accessed through the visible' (Slater 1995: 221). This rupture between visibility and reality is significant for an ethnographic approach to the visual because it implies that reality cannot necessarily be observed visually. Therefore, rather than recording reality on video tape or camera film, the most one can expect is to represent those aspects of experience that are visible. Moreover, these visible elements of experience will be given different meanings as different people use their own subjective knowledge to interpret them.

Strecker criticizes existing treatments of images in ethnography, pointing out that ethnographers have tended to 'stand between' their informants and audiences/readers by translating images into words. In doing so ethnographers impose one (their own) interpretation on the images, thus dismissing the possibility that the images may have more than one potential meaning. Instead, Strecker proposes that since ethnography is 'largely to do with the interpretation of images' it should pay greater attention to 'the rhetorical contexts in which they are embedded' (Strecker 1997: 217). This theme is taken up again in the following chapters (especially Chapter 5) as I consider how visual images are given new meanings in a range of different contexts. Just as reality is not solely 'visible' or observable, images have no fixed or single meanings and are not capable of capturing an objective 'reality'. The most one can expect is that observation and images will allow one only to interpret that which is visible.

Photography and video do nevertheless bear some relationship to 'reality'. However the connection between visual images and experienced reality is constructed through individual subjectivity and interpretation of images. As Wright points out, this may be because '[a]s products of a particular culture, they [in this case photographs] are only perceived as real by cultural convention: they only *appear* realistic because we have been taught to see them as such' (Wright 1999: 6 original italics). As ethnographers, we may suspend a belief in reality as an objective and observable experience, but we should also keep in mind that we too use images to refer to certain versions of reality and we treat images as referents of visible and observable phenomena: 'As Alan Sekula (1982: 86) has pointed out, it is the most natural thing in the world for someone to open their [sic] wallet and produce a photograph saying "this is my dog"' (Wright 1999: 2). Such 'realist' approaches to photography and video are embedded in the experience and everyday practices of most ethnographers. Indeed, as I argue later in this book, in some cases realist uses of photographic and video images may be appropriate in ethnographic research and representation. However, realist uses of the visual in ethnography should be qualified by a reflexive awareness of the intentions behind such uses and their limits as regards the representation of 'truth'.

Images, technologies, individuals

Photography and video have been appropriated in varying forms and degrees by many individuals in almost all cultures and societies.

However, visual images and technologies are not only elements of the cultures that academics 'study', they also pertain to the academic cultures and personal lifestyles and subject positions from which contemporary ethnographers approach their projects. As Chaplin has argued for sociology, ethnographic disciplines should not distance themselves from the topics they study (1994: 16). This means thinking not simply of 'the sociology *of* visual representation' but of sociology *and* visual representations as elements of the same cultural context. Thus ethnographers should treat visual representation as an aspect of the material culture and practice *of* social scientists as well as a practice and material culture that is researched *by* social scientists.

Most ethnographers, and an increasing number of informants (depending on the fieldwork context), own or have some access to still and video cameras. The inevitable interlinking between personal and professional understandings, agendas and intentions means that ethnographers' professional approaches to visual images and technologies cannot essentially be separated from their personal approaches and a reflexive approach to one's own visual practices is important for ethnographic and artistic work. Rather than there being a single corporate 'ethnographic approach' that all ethnographers take on, the practices of individual ethnographers are attached to a combination of personal and professional elements. Recent work in anthropology (e.g. Kulick and Willson 1995; Okely 1996; Okely and Callaway 1992) has stressed the inseparability of personal from professional identities and the importance of autobiography and personal experience in the production of ethnographic knowledge. Some existing work develops this in practice, showing that there are inevitably continuities between the different personal and professional uses to which visual images and technologies may be put. For example, Okely has written anthropological text that uses autobiographical information as what she has called 'retrospective fieldwork'. This article, based on Okely's experiences of attending a boarding school, uses her memories and photographs from this period of her life (1996: 147–74). Likewise, Strecker and Lydall's ethnographic film *Sweet Sorghum*, about their daughter's childhood experiences of living with the Hamar people in Ethiopia while her parents were doing fieldwork, cuts their own old 'home movie' footage with a recently shot interview with their daughter. In such ways personal uses and experiences of visual technologies as well as actual images may later become part of a piece of professional work. Here a reflexive awareness of not only the visual dimensions of the culture being researched, but also of ethnographers' own cultural and individual understandings and uses of visual images and technologies, is important.

In my own fieldwork I have had to recognize that I have been just as much a 'consumer' of photographic images and technologies as my informants (although maybe in different ways). Consumption and style have recently become the focus of multidisciplinary projects (e.g. Miller

1995; and preceding this Appadurai 1986), usually about the practices of
'other' people. However, ethnographers' subjectivity and fieldwork
styles may be theorized similarly: ethnographers are also consumers and
apply certain practices of consumption to their visual technologies and
images. Ethnographers' photography or video making may be related
equally to their professional fieldwork narratives or personal biographies. Moreover, photography and photographs can represent an explicit
meeting point (or continuity) between personal and professional
identities; as material objects they pass through, and are invested with
new meanings in, situations where individuals may wish to express
different aspects of their identities. For example, when is a photograph of
one's informants/friends kept in a 'research archive'? And when does it
remain in one's personal collection? When I first returned from fieldwork
in Southern Spain in 1994 I had two sets of photographs: one of friends
and one of 'research'. As time passed these photographs shifted between
categories. They moved out of albums and eventually into a series of
envelopes and folders. The personal/professional visual narratives into
which I had initially divided them gradually became dissolved into other
categories as I worked through the experience of fieldwork in an attempt
to translate it into ethnographic knowledge. Thus my anthropological
analysis began to appropriate my personal experience and possessions.
Concurrently my informants and friends, both in 'the field' in Andalusia
and 'at home' in the UK, appropriated my 'anthropological' and personal photographs, incorporating them into, and making them meaningful in terms of, their own material and visual cultures as they
included them in their own photograph albums.

Consuming technology and practising photography

Photographers and video makers, whether or not they are ethnographers, are individuals with their own intentions working in specific
social and cultural contexts. In order to understand the practices of both
ethnographers and informants as image-makers it is important to
consider how relationships develop between individuals, visual technologies, practices and images, society and culture. Bourdieu (1990)
made an early attempt to theorize photographic practices and meanings
to explain why individuals tend to perpetuate existing visual forms and
styles in their visual work. Bourdieu proposed that while everything is
potentially photographable, the photographic practice of individuals is
governed by objective limitations. He argues that 'photography cannot
be delivered over to the randomness of the individual imagination' but
instead 'via the mediation of the *ethos*, the internalization of objective
and common regularities, the group places this practice under its
collective rule' (Bourdieu 1990: 6). According to this interpretation,
images produced by individual photographers and video makers

would inevitably express the shared norms of that individual's society. Thus, Bourdieu argues 'that the most trivial photograph expresses, apart from the explicit intentions of the photographer, the system of schemes of perception, thought and appreciation common to a whole group' (1990: 6).

Individuals undoubtedly produce images that respond and refer to established conventions that have developed in and between existing 'visual cultures'. However, the implication of this is not necessarily that individual visual practices are dictated by an unconsciously held common set of beliefs. Bourdieu's explanation represents a problematic reduction of agency, subjectivity and individual creativity to external objective factors. It is difficult to reconcile with more recent and more convincing theories of agency and self-hood, such as Cohen's proposition that individuals are 'self-driven' (1992: 226) 'thinking selves' and the creators of culture (1994: 167), thus viewing 'society as composed of and by self-conscious individuals' (1994: 192). This focus on individual creativity (as opposed to Giddens's notion of the individual as the product of structure) has recently been brought to the forefront in some anthropological work. In particular, Rapport has argued in favour of a recognition of the individual 'as a seat of consciousness, as well-spring of creativity, as guarantor of meaning' as opposed to 'the *dissolved, decentered, deconstructed* individual actor and author as he or she appears in Durkheimian, Structuralist and Post-Structuralist schools of social science' (Rapport 1997a: 7, original italics). This suggests that while it is likely that individuals will reference known visual forms, styles, discourses and meanings through the content and form of their own visual images, this does not mean that they have internalized and are reproducing these formats. It is also probable that, as Evans and Hall have noted (1999: 3), their practices will intersect with camera and film manufacturing industries and developing and processing companies. Thus in creating images that reproduce or reference 'conventional' compositions and iconographies, individuals draw from personal and cultural resources of visual experience and knowledge. They thus compose images that they intend to represent particular objects or meanings; moreover they do so in particular social and material contexts. In the following chapters I emphasize the importance of attending to the intentionality of ethnographic photographers and video makers as creative individuals.

Images and image producers: breaking down the categories

Existing social scientific literature on photography tends to distinguish between family, snapshot, amateur and professional photographies. Similarly, distinctions are made between home movies and professional videos. For photographers themselves these categories and the distinctions between them can be important. To mistakenly put a photographer/amateur/snapshotter in the 'wrong' category can imply problematic assumptions about his or her knowledge of both photographic technique and his or her subject matter. For instance, in Spain bullfight *aficionados* associate different types of bullfight photography with particular gendered identities and corresponding understandings of the bullfight (see Pink 1997a). Work on photography in North American and European cultures implies that similar categories of image and image producers often appear to be assumed by both informants and researchers, and are not usually questioned (e.g. Bourdieu 1990; Chalfen 1987; Pink 1997a; Slater 1995). However these, like all categories, are in fact culturally constructed, and individually understood and experienced. Individual photographers, video makers or visual images may not fit neatly into just one of the identities that is implied by the distinction between categories such as domestic, amateur, professional (or ethnographic) images and producers. No photographic or video image need have one single identity and, as I have noted above, no images are, for example, essentially 'ethnographic' but are given ethnographic meanings in relation to the discourses that people use to define them.

The categorization of different types of photography and photographer also raises issues concerning professional identity for ethnographers who use still photography or video. For example, if categories of 'domestic', 'tourist', 'documentary' or 'ethnographic' are used to define a fieldwork photograph, each implies different types of knowledge and intentionality for the photographer. Some criticisms of the value of ethnographers' photography have suggested that it is 'unlikely to be professional', 'mere vacation photography', 'unsuitable for exhibition' or less relevant as 'representation' than images produced by professional, commissioned photographers (all comments I have heard social scientists voice). These opinions assume there is an essential difference between professional ethnographic and personal leisure photographs or video. However, during ethnographic fieldwork the distinction between leisure and work is frequently ambiguous, for both ethnographers (especially anthropologists, for whom it raises the question is one ever 'off duty'?) and 'informants' who may find it difficult to regard some 'research' activities as 'work'. Often an ethnographer's research is structured by other people's leisure time (among other things). Correspondingly, a proportion of 'ethnographic' photography may be centred on leisure activities in which the ethnographer participates. I found that in Spain, when photographing the professional and social life of bullfighting culture, many of my photographs and much of my photographic activity was structured simultaneously by my own work and leisure or my informants' leisure (see also Chapter 5). Thus the photographs I took at birthday parties, bullfights and official receptions were simultaneously ethnographic, anthropological, family and leisure photographs. While fixed categories imply that if an ethnographer's photography or video is classified as 'tourist' or 'leisure' images, then they are not 'ethnographic'. My experiences indicate that a fieldwork photograph or video need never be fixed in any single category and that it would be mistaken to distinguish categorically between leisure and professional images and situate ethnographers' images accordingly. Ethnographers' own photographs are often worked into a range of different personal and professional narratives and subject positions (of ethnographers and their informants). They do not belong in any one fixed category and may be incorporated differently as the same individuals re-negotiate their gendered identities in different situations (see Chapter 2).

Fieldwork photographs often simultaneously belong to the different but connected material cultures of visual anthropology or sociology and of the culture being 'studied' (see Chapter 5). This may raise certain issues. For instance, what happens when ethnographers start to produce the very material culture they are studying; what impact do ethnographers have when they participate in and contribute to the visual discourses they are analysing; and what are the effects of informants' appropriations of ethnographers' images. I explore some of these scenarios in the following chapters.

Summary

Ethnographers themselves are members of societies in which photography and video are already practised and understood in particular ways. The ways in which individual ethnographers approach the visual in their research and representation is inevitably influenced by a range of factors, including theoretical beliefs, disciplinary agendas, personal experience, gendered identities and different visual cultures. Fundamental to understanding the significance of the visual in ethnographic work is a reflexive appreciation of how such elements combine to produce visual meanings and ethnographic knowledge.

CHAPTER 2

Planning and Practising Visual Methods: Appropriate Uses and Ethical Issues

Why use 'visual methods'?

It is impossible to predict, and mistaken to prescribe, precise methods for ethnographic research. Similarly, it would be unreasonable to 'require that visual methods be used in all contexts'. Rather, as Morphy and Banks suggest, 'they should be used where appropriate, with the rider that appropriateness will not always be obvious in advance' (1997: 14). In practice, decisions are best made once researchers are in a position to assess which specific visual methods will be appropriate or ethical in a particular research context, therefore allowing researchers to account for their relationships with informants and their experience and knowledge of local visual cultures. Nevertheless, certain decisions and indicators about the use of visual images and technologies in research usually need to be made before commencing fieldwork. Often research proposals, preparations and plans must be produced before fieldwork begins; the fieldwork may be in an area where technologies are difficult to purchase or hire; if the project is to be funded and equipment purchased from a research grant, technological needs must be anticipated and budgeted for.

The appropriateness of 'visual methods'

Banks divides visual research methods into three broad activities: 'making visual representations (studying society by producing images)'; 'examining pre-existing visual representations' (studying images for information about society); 'collaborating with social actors in the production of visual representations' (Banks n.d.). These can generally be planned and developed before fieldwork. However, more specific uses of visual images and technologies tend to develop as part of the social relationships and activities in which ethnographers engage during fieldwork. Some of these will be purposefully thought out and strategically applied. In Chapters 3 and 4 the specific applications of general models of visual research methods are discussed in detail. In other cases unanticipated uses of the visual may be discovered by accident and retrospectively defined as 'visual methods'. Ethnographers might repeat such activities (sometimes in collaboration with informants), thus developing and refining the method throughout the research. However, methods developed within one research context may not be transferable to, or appropriate in, others. For example, when I started to research Spanish bullfighting culture I began photographing people at the many public receptions held to present trophies, exhibitions and book launches. After my first reception I showed my photographs to the organizers and participants and they asked me for copies of certain photos, some of which they gave to their colleagues. By keeping note of their requests and asking questions about the images I gained a sense of how individuals situated themselves in relation to other individuals in 'bullfighting culture'. As I attended more receptions I consciously repeated this 'method' and developed my use of the camera and the photographs in response to the relationship that developed between my informants, the technology, the images and myself as photographer (see Chapter 3; Pink 1998b, 1999c).

This method of researching with images was appropriate in bull-fighting culture partly because it imitated and was incorporated into my informants' existing cultural and individual uses of photography. When I began to photograph during my next fieldwork in West Africa, I considered using a similar method. However I quickly realized that in Guinea Bissau I was working in an economic system where photographs were costly prestige items. For instance, commercially, a studio photograph would cost the price of ten loaves of bread – a large dent in most local people's budgets. Here I could not participate in local people's photographic culture in the same way, as any use of photographic equipment and images implied economic inequalities. In this context, other new methods had to be developed (see Chapter 3; Pink 1998d, 1999b).

Before attempting visual research it is useful to read up on visual methods used by other ethnographers. However, it is also crucial to evaluate their appropriateness for a new project. This includes considering how visual methods, images and technologies will be interpreted by individuals in the cultures where research will be done, in addition to assessing how well visual methods suit the aims of specific projects. In some situations visual methods appear inappropriate. For example, in Guinea Bissau I undertook a research project to assess people's willingness and ability to pay for health services and medicines in the region in which I was living. This included a series of focus group discussions in rural areas and a European colleague suggested I video record the discussions and interviews. I recalled a case study in which Freudenthal (1992) describes how he used video recordings of group discussions with rural villagers in a development research project in

Figure 2.1 When I first asked these Guinea Bissauan bread sellers if I could photograph them, they said 'no', thinking that I was a commercial photographer who would charge them for the images. When I explained that I was not and that I wanted the photographs for my work they were happy to pose. In Guinea Bissau one studio or location photograph taken by a local commercial photographer costs several times the price of one locally baked fresh loaf of bread.

Tanzania. His method succeeded in creating a participatory approach to the production of knowledge about the evaluation of a small local forestry project. However, basing my opinion on my prior knowledge of the culture I was working with and the limited time that I would spend in each village (approximately two days) I felt using video would be inappropriate. I discussed the methods with a local health director who agreed that the time and resources available to the project were insufficient to allow us to develop an appropriate context of trust and collaboration for the use of video.

Researchers should not have fixed, preconceived expectations of what it will be possible to achieve by using visual research methods in a given situation. Sometimes visual methods will not support the researcher's aims. Hastrup's (1992) description of her attempt as a woman anthropologist to photograph an exclusively male Icelandic sheep market demonstrates this well. She describes the difficulty and discomfort she experienced while photographing this event but notes that having accomplished the task she felt a sense of satisfaction 'to have been there and to have been able to document this remarkable event' (1992: 9). She had left with the sensation that she 'even had photos from the sacred grove of a male secret society' (1992: 9). However her photographic method was not appropriate for recording the type of information she had anticipated and she writes of the disappointment she experienced on later seeing the printed photographs: 'they were hopeless. Ill-focused, badly lit, lopsided and showing nothing but the completely uninteresting backs of men and rams' (1992: 9). She emphasizes the difference between her experience of photographing and the end results. While I was taking them I had the impression that I was making an almost pornographic record of a secret ritual. They showed me nothing of the sort but bore the marks of my own inhibition, resulting from my transgression of the boundary between gender categories' (1992: 9). Hastrup's expectations of what she may obtain by using this visual research method were not met. She anticipated that her photographs would represent ethnographic 'evidence' of her experience of the event: 'a record of a secret ritual'. To assess why this was not achieved she generalizes that 'pictures have a limited value as ethnographic "evidence"', and the 'secret' of informants' experiences can only be told in words (1992: 9). While I would agree that as ethnographic 'evidence' photographs indeed have limited value (see Chapter 1), this does not necessarily indicate that one may only represent ethnographic knowledge with words (see especially Chapters 6–8). The potential of photography or video as a realist recording device or a way of exploring individual subjectivities and creative collaboration will be realized differently in every application.

Sometimes using cameras and making images of informants is inappropriate for ethical reasons (see below). In some situations photographs or videos of informants may put them in political danger, or subject them to moral criticism. The appropriateness of visual methods should not simply be judged on questions of whether the methods suit the objectives of the research question and if they fit well with the local culture in which one is working. Rather, such evaluations should be informed by an ethnographic appreciation of how visual knowledge is interpreted in a cross-cultural context. Therefore decisions about the particular methodologies and modes of representation to be used should pay attention to intersections between local visual cultures, the ways in which the visual is treated by wider users or audiences of the research and ethnographers' own knowledge, experience and sensitivity. By thinking through the implications of image production and visual representation in this way ethnographers should be able to evaluate how their 'ethnographic' images would be invested with different meanings by different political, local and academic discourses.

Planning visual research

Without good knowledge of the context in which one is planning to do ethnographic research it is very difficult to predict how and to what extent visual images and technologies may be used. Similarly, the basis upon which one may judge if visual methods will be ethical, appropriate, or a useful way to participate or collaborate with the people with whom one is working, will be contingent on the particular research context. Plans to use visual methods made before commencing the research may appear unnecessary or out of place once the research has begun. For example, my original proposal to do research about women and bullfighting in Southern Spain anticipated the extensive use of video. However, once in the field I found my informants only occasionally used video cameras. I was working in a culture where photography was a dominant source of knowledge and representation about bullfighting. In this situation it was usually more appropriate to participate in local events as a 'photographer' than as a 'video maker'. Since some of my informants also participated in their 'bullfighting culture' as amateur photographers, I was able to 'share' an activity with them as well as producing images which interested them. At the time photography fitted the demands of the project. However, retrospectively, I was able to identify ways in which video could have supported the research, fitted into the local bullfighting culture and also served my informants' interests. Such insights could be used as the basis of future research plans.

Usually ethnographers with some experience of working in a particular culture and society already have a sense of the visual and technological cultures of the people with whom they plan to work. Ethnographers should have an idea of how their photographic/video research practices will develop in relation to local practices, and a sense of how they may learn through the interface between their own and local visual practices. Such background knowledge makes it easier to present a research proposal that defines quite specifically how and to what ends visual technologies and images are to be employed. This may entail developing insights from prior research in the same culture, doing a short 'pilot study', or researching aspects of visual cultures from library and museum sources, ethnographic film and the internet. This need not be solely a 'traditional' literature review about visual culture. The first stage of the research process may be an interactive exploration of websites and e-mail contacts where elements of the visual culture of a research area are represented. For instance, if I was to begin research into the visual representations of bullfighting culture now, at the beginning of 2000 rather than the early 1990s, an ideal starting point from my base in the United Kingdom would be an exploration of the now numerous bullfighting websites and on-line magazines. Similarly, before beginning fieldwork in Guinea Bissau, few internet resources were available. However in summer 1998, one year after my return, a website with photographic images and text had been built. E-mail communications and electronic exchanges of digital images are also options for researchers working with informants who are technology users themselves. The internet should not be ignored as an aspect of some contemporary ethnographic fields (see Pink 1999a).

Pre-fieldwork surveys of literature, electronic and other visual texts and examples of how other ethnographers have successfully worked with visual images and technologies in specific cultures can indicate the potential for using visual methods in particular fieldwork contexts. Combined with some considered guesswork about people's visual practices and discourses, this can form a basis from which to develop a research proposal. However, neither a researcher's own preparation, nor other ethnographers' accounts can predict how a 'visual method' will develop in a new project. Just as ethnography can only really be learnt in practice, ethnographic uses of visual images and technologies develop from practice-based knowledge. Moreover, as projects evolve novel uses of photography or video may develop to explore and represent unexpected issues. Chapters 3 and 4 are intended to represent sources of examples, ideas and inspirations through which ethnographers may develop their own styles.

Choosing the technology for the project

Like images, and any material object, technologies are also interpreted differently by individuals in different cultures. If possible, ethnographers should explore the meanings informants give to different visual technologies before purchasing equipment.

The selection of a digital or 'traditional' camera, a semi-professional video camera or the cheapest hand-held VHS model may be related to economic factors, but should also account for how the equipment one uses will become part of one's identity both during fieldwork and in academic circles. Individuals constantly re-situate themselves and construct their self-identities in relation to not only other individuals but also to material objects and cultural discourses. The visual technologies that ethnographers use, like the images they produce and view, will be invested with meanings, inspire responses and are likely to become a topic of conversation. Some informants may have a 'shared' interest in photography or video (in some cases they will have better cameras and skills than the researcher). For example, in Spain my amateur interest in bullfight photography was shared with several local people. This led us to discuss technical as well as aesthetic aspects of bullfighting photography, such as the best film speeds, zoom lenses and seating in the arena. In a recent video interviewing project in the United Kingdom and Spain, interviewees appeared relaxed with my domestic digital video camera simply seeing it as one of the latest pieces of new video technology. In comparison to solitary field diary writing, photography and video making can appear more 'visible', comprehensible activities to informants, and may link more closely with their own experience. Photographs and video-tapes themselves become commodities for exchange and the sites of negotiation, for example, among informants, between researchers and informants, between researchers and their families and friends 'at home' and among researchers. In short, the visual technologies and images associated with ethnographers will also be implicated in the way other people construct their identities and thus impact on their social relationships and experiences.

Therefore, when selecting and applying for funding for technology it is important to remember that a camera will be part of the research context and an element of the ethnographer's identity. It will impinge on the social relationships in which he or she becomes involved and on how informants represent themselves. Different technologies impact on these relationships and identities in different ways. In some cases image quality may have to be forsaken to produce images that represent the type of ethnographic knowledge sought. For example, the relationship between ethnographer and subjects that can develop in a photographic or filmic situation created by the use of professional lighting and sound equipment will differ from when the ethnographer is working alone with just a small hand-held camcorder or stills camera. The images may be darker and grainier, the sound less sharp, but the ethnographic knowledge they invoke may be more useful to the project.

In tandem with the social and cultural implications of the use of visual technologies, practical and technical issues also arise. How will a camera and other equipment be powered and transported? (Will there even be electricity?) What post-production resources will be available? Finally, what resources will be available for showing the images to informants? In some locations cameras can be connected to TV monitors and video recorders. In others, a solar-powered lap-top computer might be used to screen digital still and video images. When purchasing equipment it is important to keep track of technological developments and also of post-fieldwork equipment requirements. Will it be necessary to have the technology to transfer digital images on to a computer for analysis, or on to another tape format for editing? As Ratcliffe (n.d.) points out, most up-to-date information on video and photographic technology can be found in specialist consumer report magazines. These can be purchased in most high-street newsagents. Both equipment and production can be costly and it is important to budget realistically for the cost of tape transfer using editing facilities, printing and computing equipment.

Ethics and ethnographic research

A consideration of the ethical implications of ethnographic research and representation should underpin any research project. Most guides and courses on research methods dedicate a section to ethics. Such texts usually cover a standard set of issues such as informed consent, covert research, confidentiality, harm to informants, exploitation and 'giving something back', ownership of 'data', and protection of informants.

These indisputably relevant issues are critically reviewed later in this chapter. However, the issue of ethics in ethnographic work refers to more than simply the ethical conduct of the researcher. Rather, it demands that ethnographers develop an understanding of the ethical context(s) in which they work, a reflexive approach to their own ethical beliefs, and a critical approach to the idea that *one* ethical code of conduct could be hierarchically superior to all others. Because ethics are so embedded in the specific research contexts in which ethnographers work, like decisions about which visual research methods to employ in a project, ethical decisions cannot be concluded until the researcher is actually in the field.

In practice, ethics are bound up with power relations between ethnographers, informants, professionals, sponsors, gatekeepers, governments, the media and other institutions (see Ellen 1984: 134). Ethical decisions are ultimately made by individual ethnographers, usually with reference to personal and professional codes (often laid out by professional organizations) of ethical conduct and the intentionalities of other parties. The personal dimension of ethnographic research, the moral and philosophical beliefs of the researcher and his or her view of reality impinges greatly on the ethical practices that he or she applies in research and representation.

Ethics are also bound up with the epistemological concerns of academic disciplines – they both inform and are informed by theory and methodology. For instance, a research methodology that is informed by a relativist approach requires that ethics becomes not simply a matter of ensuring that research is done in an ethical way (i.e. conforms to a fixed ethical code or set of rules), but that ethics becomes an area of philosophical debate in itself. If difference denotes plurality and equality rather than hierarchy, then it would seem unreasonable to argue that one ethical code would be superior to another. This problematizes the idea that there is one set of rules that defines *the* ethical way to undertake ethnographic research and challenges the assumption that ethnographic research may be guided by one code of ethical conduct rather than by another. However, such a relativist approach to ethics raises difficult questions. For instance, how relativist can ethnographic research and representation afford to be in relation to ethics while remaining an 'ethical' activity? Should ethnographers accept all ethical codes as being equally permissible? Clearly there are some activities that ethnographers would wish to render 'unethical'.

Rapport has suggested that the inadequacy of a relativist approach for dealing with ethics may be resolved by a focus on the individual. He argues that '[i]nstead of relativistic making of allowances for different cultures maintaining different traditions – whatever the consequences to their individual members – I want to outline a liberal basis for social science which recognises individuals as universal human agents above whom there is no greater good, without whom there is no cultural tradition' (Rapport 1997a: 181). For Rapport the ethical approach of social science should be one that responds against 'the violation of individual integrity, the threat to the individual's conscious potential, the ideological prioritising of community above and beyond the individuals who at any one moment constitute it' (1997a: 181). Therefore he is able to argue that social scientists should be able to see a number of practices (such as 'Naziism, religious fundamentalism, female circumcision, infanticide and *suttee*') as unethical 'because of the hurt they cause to individuals, because of the harm which accrues in those social milieux where an ethic of interpersonal tolerance is not managed' (1997a: 181).

Rapport's principle offers a basis upon which ethnographers may evaluate the ethical practices of themselves as researchers, their informants and other individuals, agencies and institutions with whom they come into contact during research. Ultimately, the decision will be a personal one for each ethnographer has to decide whether his or her research practices and representations are ethical before these are held up to the scrutiny of others who will then interpret this question for themselves. Similarly, the question of the ethics of those whom we study, and the ethics of studying and/or making moral judgements about them, is one that individual ethnographers must address for themselves at some stage in their research. It will also be addressed by those who read or view their representations at another stage. During my research about bullfighting I was often confronted with the question 'was bullfighting morally right or wrong?' While carrying out this research I felt morally able to 'stand on the fence'. I did not commit myself to a moral judgement either way, and still maintain that I don't. However, I was aware that some of my Spanish informants and some acquaintances in the United Kingdom felt that not only bullfighting, but also my research and my participation in bullfighting culture by attending (and sometimes enjoying) bullfights was unethical. They felt that by researching and writing on the subject I was effectively condoning what they regarded an unethical practice. On occasion I could empathize with their subject position, but I felt I was doing nothing more than shifting subject positions; I was never making a personal commitment to either standpoint. Aware that some people, especially animal rights activists, would judge my informants' practices as unethical, and having heard their views that bullfighting fans were 'blood thirsty', 'violent' and 'barbaric', I felt obliged to 'protect' my informants by attempting to represent them as sensitive and moral human beings and to describe their understanding of bullfighting in a way that indicated they did not fit the unethical profile others had associated with them. The ethics that guide ethnographers may be a critical discourse on the ethics of the people they study, or of an individual or institution who has power over them. Rapport admits that his perspective on ethics (see above) is personal. Similarly, my own approach to the ethics of bullfighting was based on a personal conviction. Another ethnographer might argue that any activity that causes harm or hurt to animals is unethical, thus taking a different approach to the representation of ethnographic work on bullfighting.

As Pels has pointed out for anthropology, in the contemporary world:

> Globalising movements have resulted in a situation in which the ethics of anthropology can no longer be thought of simply in term of the dyad between researcher and researched: anthropology is placed squarely within a more complex field of governmentality, cross-cultural conflict and global mobility. Some of these developments seem threatening to anthropology, others seem to provide new opportunities, and all raise novel questions about the ethics of anthropological research. (Pels 1996: 18)

It is not solely ethnographers and informants who are implicated in the ethical issues researchers confront during fieldwork. Indeed, there may be a whole range of other interested parties and agendas that shape the ethical conduct of ethnographers and their informants either by enforcing their own guidelines, or by posing a threat to the safety of those represented in ethnographic work. Ethnographers therefore need to understand how plural moralities are at play in any ethnographic situation, and the extent to which these different ethical codes are constructed and interpreted in relation to one another. Ethnographers should seek to identify where the ethics of the research fit in with these other ethical codes with which it intersects. Ultimately, ethics in ethnography is concerned with making decisions based on interpretations of the moralities and intentionalities of other people and the institutions they may represent.

Visual research methods and ethical ethnography

The theoretical underpinning of my approach to ethics and visual research methods is based on the relationship between vision and reality discussed in Chapter 1. This emphasizes the specificity of the visual meanings that operate in the different cultures and societies in which ethnographers work and in the different ways ethnographers' images can be interpreted by other bodies such as academics, informants, professionals, sponsors, gatekeepers, governments, the media and other institutions. However conscious ethnographers are of the arbitrary nature of photographic meanings, ethnographic images are still likely to be treated as 'truthful recordings' or 'evidence' by non-academic viewers. Ethnographers should pay particular attention to how different approaches to the visual and different meanings given to the same images may coincide or collide in the domains in which we research and represent our work.

Below I critically review existing approaches to ethics in ethnographic research methodology, to consider their implications for the use of visual images.

Covert research and the question of informed consent

As a scientific-realist strategy, covert research was assumed to enable ethnographers to better observe an 'objective truth'. In the case of the covert use of video recording and photography the same principle was applied: the use of a hidden camera was thought to allow researchers to produce images of an objective reality, less 'distorted' by their own subjectivity (see Chapter 1). In Chapter 1 I have noted that such objectivity can never actually be achieved. Moreover, in my opinion, any type of covert research requires a careful consideration of ethics. This does not mean all covert research is necessarily unethical (see, for example, Hammersley and Atkinson 1995: 263–8), but that ethical decisions should be made according to the specific research context.

The approach to photography and video in ethnographic research I propose in Chapters 3 and 4 emphasizes the idea of collaboration between researcher and informant. Covert research implies the researcher videoing and photographing the behaviour of informants in a secretive rather than collaborative way, for example, using a hidden camera or using the camera under the guise of a role other than that of researcher. A collaborative method, in contrast, assumes that researcher and informant are consciously working together to produce visual images and specific types of knowledge through technological procedures and discussions. However, there may be occasions where covert image-making becomes part of a collaboration, for example, if an ethnographer collaborates with informants to photograph others who are not aware they are being photographed. The ethical implications of such work need to be reviewed for each project and on the terms of each individual researcher. If a researcher considers the very act of recording covertly a violation of the integrity of their informants, and thus unethical, then covert work will be ruled out. In other situations an ethnographer may feel that to record or photograph an activity secretly is ethical because he or she will be able to take personal responsibility for the images and not to violate the integrity of those covertly recorded.

The distinction between overt and covert research is, however, further complicated by challenging the notion of 'informed consent'. First, because cross-culturally consent may take different forms, involve different individuals and relationships and have different meanings. Secondly, informants may be keen to collaborate without actually engaging fully with *why* a researcher would want to video record certain activities. Even if informants collaborate or participate in the production of ethnographic video and photography, it is unlikely that their understanding or intentions *vis-à-vis* the project will coincide exactly with the ethnographer's. In such cases it could be argued that even if consent is given, it is not *informed* consent, and the researcher is (even if unintentionally) keeping his or her real agenda hidden from the informants.

The ethical implications of covertly shot video or photography vary at different stages of the project at which the images may become accessible to different parties. If the ethnographer is to publish covertly produced images, this raises a range of new issues (see below).

Permission and the 'right' to photograph/video at public events

It is good practice to ask permission to photograph in any public context or event, as well as seeking the consent of the individuals photographed, and in some situations official permission is required. Permission to photograph and video at public events may be granted in a variety of ways. During my fieldwork in Spain, like many of my informants, I often photographed the bullfight. While it was not allowed to video record a bullfight without formal permission, photography was usually freely permitted. Much of this involves photographing individual performers, however their permission is rarely asked and their fans tend to assume their right to photograph a public figure. Bullfighters are frequently photographed before and after as well as during their performances. Fans queue up at their hotels, hoping for a chance to pose with the performer, while the arena is packed with many aspiring bullfight photographers with a range of different types of camera and skills. In this research context public photography was freely permitted and acceptable. In other field contexts formal permission is needed before photographing in any public place or event. During my first weeks of fieldwork in Guinea Bissau I began to research the forthcoming carnival. With the idea of eventually photographing aspects of carnival, I started researching local people's photographs of previous carnivals and seeking out public photographic records or exhibitions. I later photographed some of my neighbours preparing their hair for carnival and the carnival masks that had won previous competitions. My informants told me that to photograph or video carnival in the capital city, Bissau, a photography or video permit must be purchased. Knowing this, I approached the regional office of the Ministry of Culture in Canchungo, the town I was living in; it seemed polite to ask the head of the local office for per-mission to photograph in the town. He told me that as far as he was concerned I was allowed to photograph during carnival and instructed me that if anyone challenged me I should tell them he had given me permission. This raised several issues for me, since it seemed that I had been given permission to photograph carnival participants without their consent. In practice, I photographed only those individuals who agreed to be photographed (usually people I already knew), or those parti-cipating in activities that they knew were likely to be photographed.

The question of whether an ethnographer has permission to photo-graph or video differs from situation to situation and according to whom we listen. Often it seems obligatory initially to negotiate official per-mission to video or photograph with institutional gatekeepers. However,

permission to video or photograph individuals in their capacity as participants in events is usually best negotiated with each individual or
group. The ethics of obtaining permissions vary in different research
contexts, according to project aims and the agendas of researchers,
informants and other interested parties.

Harm to informants

While ethnographic research is unlikely to cause harm as, for example,
drugs trials may, it can lead to emotional distress or anxiety
(Hammersley and Atkinson 1995: 268). Sensitivity to how individuals
in different cultures may experience anxiety or stress through their
involvement in research is important in any ethnographic project.
However, rather than prescribing actual methods of preventing harm to
informants in visual research, my intention is to suggest a way of
thinking about how research, anxiety and harm are understood and
experienced in different ethnographic contexts. General methods of
preventing harm to informants may not be locally applicable. First, there
are culturally different ways of understanding harm and of causing it
with images. Therefore, in order to prevent harm being caused, a
researcher needs a good understanding of local notions of harm and
anxiety, how these may be experienced and how they relate to images.
Secondly, the idea that informants may find the research process
distressing is usually based on the assumption that the informants are
having the research *done to them*. In this scenario the researcher is
supposed to be in control of the research situation and therefore also
assumes responsibility for the potential harm that may be done to the
informants. This approach requires that in taking responsibility to
protect their informants, researchers should be sensitive to the visual
culture and experience of the individuals with whom they are working.
For instance, ethnographers need to judge, or ask (if appropriate), if
there are personal or cultural reasons why some people may find
particular photographs shown to them in interviews or discussions
offensive, disturbing or distressing, or if being photographed or videoed
themselves would be stressful.

Anxiety and harm to informants can often be avoided through a
collaborative approach to visual research and joint ownership of visual
materials. Here researchers and informants should maintain some
degree of control over the content of the materials and their subsequent
uses.

Harm, representation and permission to publish

Above I have discussed the issue of permission to video or photograph
during ethnographic research. The publication of the research raises new
issues. Sometimes this is already a concern when the images are shot,
especially if the ethnographer's project is to produce a documentary or

photographic exhibition. These intentions should be made clear to the subjects of the images. Some ethnographic filmmakers ask the subjects of their films to sign consent forms (see Barbash and Taylor 1997). However, if this is not done, moral and legal issues of ownership of the images and of consent may arise. If the images were produced covertly, without the permission of their subjects, the moral right of the video maker or photographer to publish them could be questioned. Moreover, it cannot be assumed that people have consented to being in a publicly screened video or to have large images of themselves exhibited in a gallery simply because they have allowed the images to be taken or have responded to the camera. This raises questions such as should the subjects of photographs and video be allowed to see printed or edited copies before they consent to their images entering a public domain? Different filmmakers, photographers and ethnographers have their own opinions and practices regarding this. Much of ethnography is about making private aspects of people's lives public. Therefore, who should be responsible for deciding the content of the visual representation of other people's lives?

Questions of harm to individuals, or institutions become pressing when it comes to publication. For photography and video this is particularly important since it is usually impossible to preserve anonymity of people and places. Ethnographers have to make choices regarding if and how video footage will be incorporated into the final publication of the research. This requires a serious consideration of ethical issues and possibly the participation of the informants or the subjects of the images. The publication of certain photographic and video images may damage individuals' reputations; they may not want certain aspects of their identities revealed or their personal opinions to be made public. People express certain things in one context that they would not say in another, and in the apparent intimacy of a video interview an informant may make comments that he or she would not make elsewhere. Institutions may also be damaged by irresponsible publication of images. The public front of any institution is often a veneer that holds fast the conflicts and organizational problems that are part of its everyday order.

Finally, once visual and other representations of ethnographic work have been produced and disseminated publicly neither author nor subjects of the work can control the ways in which these representations are interpreted and given meanings by their readers, viewers or audiences. In Chapters 6, 7 and 8 these issues are raised in a discussion of the visual representation of ethnographic work.

Exploitation and 'giving something back'

Usually ethnographers stand to gain personally from their interactions with informants, through an undergraduate or masters degree project, PhD thesis, consultancy project or other publication that will enhance their career. In contrast, informants may not accrue similar benefits from their participation in research projects. Conventional responses to this ethical problem focus on how ethnographers may 'give something back'; how the participants in the research may be empowered through their involvement in the project, or that research should be directed at the powerful rather than the weak (Hammersley and Atkinson 1995: 274–5). None of these responses, however, provide satisfactory solutions to the exploitative nature of research (see Hammersley and Atkinson 1995).

The idea of 'giving something back' implies that the ethnographer extracts something (usually the data) and then makes a gift of something else to the people from whom he or she has got the information. Rather than making research any less exploitative, this approach merely tries to compensate for it by 'giving something back'. Ironically, this may benefit the ethnographer, who will feel ethically virtuous, while the informants may be left wondering why they have been given whatever it was they 'got back', and what precisely they got it in return for. Rather than try to redress the inequalities after the event, it would seem better advised to attempt to undertake ethnography that is less exploitative. If ethnography is seen as a process of negotiation and collaboration with informants, through which they too stand to achieve their own objectives, rather than as an act of taking information away from them, the ethical agenda also shifts. By focusing on collaboration and the idea of 'creating something together', agency becomes shared between the researcher and informant. Rather than the researcher being the active party who both extracts data and gives something else back, in this model both researcher and informant invest in, and are rewarded by, the project. Recent work with video and photography shows how these media can be used to develop very successful collaborative projects. In some cases this has empowered informants/subjects and can serve to challenge existing power structures that impinge on the lives of informants and ethnographers. In a project developed by Barnes, Taylor-Brown and Weiner (1997), a group of HIV-positive women collaborated with the researchers to produce a set of video-tapes which contained messages for their children. This use of video allowed the women to represent themselves on video-tapes to be screened in the future. Simultaneously, the agreement allowed the researchers to use the tapes as research materials (see Chapter 4).

As I have suggested above, the concept of 'giving something back' often depends on the idea of ethnography as a 'hit and run' act: the ethnographer spends a number of months in the field gathering 'data' before leaving for home where this data will be written up. Very little remains once ethnographers leave their field sites, apart from (in the case of overseas fieldwork) those domestic and other things that did not fit into a suitcase. Field notes and papers are of little use or interest to most informants, and at any rate researchers may feel these are personal documents. However, video-tapes and photographs are usually of interest to the people featured in them and the people who were involved in their production. If an ethnographer is working on the 'giving something back' principle, copies of video and photography of individuals and activities that informants value could be an appropriate return for the favours they have performed during fieldwork. However, a collaborative approach to ethnographic image production may do more to redress the inequalities that inevitably exist between informants and researchers. Engelbrecht's collaborative work with ethnographic film shows how visual work can become a product in which both informants and ethnographer invest. Engelbrecht (1996) describes a number of filmmaking projects that involved the collaboration of local people in both filmmaking and editing. In some cases people wanted their traditional festivities or rituals to be documented, and were pleased to work with the filmmakers to achieve these ends. Others realized the commercial potential of their participation in film projects. For example, Engelbrecht notes how the artisans who were represented in her film *Copper Working* participated actively in the film and 'were also thinking of the potential of film as a marketing instrument [for their copper artifacts]' (1996: 167). In this case, the subjects of the film had their own agenda and were able to exploit the project of the filmmakers for their own purposes: 'it was agreed upon that one copy of the film should be given to the local museum exhibiting the best of the recent copper work of the village so as to use it for tourist information' (1996: 167).

A further problem with the notion of 'giving something back' is that it neglects the interlinkages between the researcher's personal autobio-graphical narrative and the research narrative. Fieldwork, everyday life and writing-up may not necessarily be separated either spatially or temporally in the ethnographer's life and experience (see Chapter 1). Ethnographic research may not entail the researcher going somewhere, taking something away and being morally obliged to 'give something back'. Instead, the ethnography may be part of a researcher's everyday interactions. There may be a continuous flow of information and objects between the ethnographer and informants. This might include the exchange of images, of ideas, emotional and practical exchanges and support, each of which are valued in different ways.

Ownership of research materials

In some cases visual research materials are jointly owned by a set of different parties such as the researcher, informants/subjects, funding bodies, bodies involved in post-production and other institutions and universities or organizations. While researchers may consider their own practices to be ethical, this may be challenged by any joint owners of the photographs or tapes. Such problems may arise if a project is sponsored by an institution that claims ownership of the data, or the project has involved team-work and photographs or video-tapes are joint possessions of the members of the project team. Moreover, if video or photographic images have been produced in collaboration with informants, the collaborators may wish to use the images in ways that the researcher feels are unethical. To attempt to avoid such problems it is advisable to clarify rights of use and ownership of video and photographic images before their production. This will inevitably bear on the ethical decisions taken during the research and may influence the types of images that are produced. In some cases it is appropriate to use a written agreement that states who will use the video or photographic materials; the purposes for which it will be used; and whether the participants have consented to its use.

Summary

Preparing for ethnographic research is a complex task. It is impossible to predict exactly how fieldwork will proceed and many decisions about using visual methods and the ethical questions they raise are taken during research. Often ethnographers cannot answer the questions that inform the use of photography and video in particular social and cultural contexts, until they have experience of the visual culture and social relationships with which they will be working.

PART 2

PRODUCING KNOWLEDGE

Actually doing fieldwork is a unique and personal experience and while ethnographers may purport to be using the same methods, they will in fact be doing so in different ways. In Chapters 3 and 4 I draw from some of my own and other ethnographers' experiences of doing research with photography and video to offer some ideas and possibilities for a reflexive approach to visual methods. Analysis can take place at any point in the research process, and may be combined with some of the methods described in Chapters 3 and 4. In Chapter 5 I focus more specifically on the storage, analysis and interpretation of research materials.

CHAPTER 3

Photography in Ethnographic Research

Photography has a long and varied history in ethnography. Supported by different methodological paradigms, a camera has been an almost mandatory element of the 'tool kit' for research for several generations of ethnographers. During the colonial period in the late nineteenth and early twentieth centuries, photography, seen as an objective recording device, flourished as a method for the 'scientific' documentation of cultural and physical difference (see Edwards 1992, 1997b). For example, Major Powell-Cotton, an explorer and hunter, produced a large collection of photographs in Africa and Asia, some of which are exhibited at http://www.era.anthropology.ukc.ac.uk/index.html. At the end of the nineteenth century Haddon, a British anthropologist, used photography and film (see Chapter 4) in his anthropological research. These materials are exhibited on-line at www.rsl.ox.ac.uk/isca/haddon/HADD_home.html. Later, in the mid twentieth century, the anthropologists Mead and Bateson used photography as a method of recording and representing Balinese culture (Bateson and Mead 1942; and see Chaplin 1994: 207ff). Since the 1970s photography has been employed to fit the needs of, first, scientific-realist and, later, reflexive approaches to ethnography. In this chapter I draw from my own and other ethnographers' experiences to explore two aspects of the relationship between photography and ethnography: the study of local photographic cultures and uses of photographic images and technologies in ethnographic research.

The study of photographic 'cultures', technologies and practices has developed in anthropology, sociology and cultural studies. In the 1990s anthropologists turned their critical gaze on the history of their own discipline, highlighting the ethnocentric, oppressive agendas in which scientific anthropological uses of photography during the colonial period were implicated (see Edwards 1992, 1997b). Other critiques have revealed the primitivizing agenda of later photography in, for example, ethnographic representations of Spain of the 1950s to 1970s (Brandes 1997). Studies of photographic practices have focused on photography in consumer culture (see Chapter 1) (e.g. Bourdieu 1990 [1965]), family photography (e.g. Chalfen 1987), tourist photography (e.g. Chaney 1993; Crawshaw and Urry 1997; Edensor 1998; Hutnyk 1996; Urry 1990), the relationship between digital and 'traditional' photography (e.g. Lister 1995; T. Wright 1998) and ethnographic studies of local or ethnic photographic cultures such as Pinney's (1997) work on photography in India and my own on the photographic culture of bullfighting (Pink 1996, 1997b, 1998b and 1999c). Recent projects about photographic culture have also been produced in the form of ethnographic films. For example, *Photo Wallahs* (MacDougall and MacDougall 1991) represents photography in an Indian hill town, while *Future Remembrance* (Wendl and Du Plessis 1998) is a study of studio photography in Ghana. These two films represent existing photographic practices in specific localities. In contrast, Martinez Perez's *Cronotopo* (1997) represents the photographic activities and images of individuals invited to photograph a street in Madrid called the Gran Vía as part of an ethnographic research project.

In Chapter 2 I proposed that visual research methods should be informed by ethnographers' knowledge of the visual cultures in which they work, including knowledge about local and academic uses of photographs. In my opinion, using photography in ethnographic research is not simply a matter of studying visual culture on the one hand, and on the other adding to disciplinary and personal resources of visual materials by photographing exotic situations and persons. Instead, ethnographic photography can potentially construct continuities between the visual culture of an academic discipline and that of the subjects or collaborators in the research. Thus ethnographers can hope to create photographic representations that refer to 'local' visual cultures and simultaneously respond to the interests of academic disciplines. To do so involves a certain amount of research into uses and understandings of photography in the culture and society of the fieldwork location. In some cases this could mean using recent theoretical studies such as Lury's (1998) work on photography, identity and memory in modern western societies (see Chapter 1) or studies like those cited above. However, researchers may often find that the photographic dimension of the culture they are working in has been virtually undocumented.

The 'ethnographicness' of photography

Anthropologists and sociologists have argued that no image or photographic practice is essentially ethnographic 'by nature', but the 'ethnographicness' of photography is determined by discourse and content (see Chapter 1). Edwards has noted how 'an anthropological photograph is any photograph from which an anthropologist could gain useful, meaningful visual information' (Edwards 1992: 13). She emphasizes how viewers subjectively determine when or if a photograph is anthropological, pointing out that '[t]he defining essence of an anthropological photograph is not the subject-matter as such, but the consumer's classification of that knowledge or "reality" which the photograph appears to convey' (1992: 13). Similarly, using as his example the categories of visual sociology, documentary photography and photo-journalism, Becker notes that the definition of the genre of a photograph depends more on the context in which it is viewed than it pertaining to any one (socially constructed) category (Becker 1995: 5).

Therefore the same photograph may be put to a range of different personal and 'ethnographic' uses; it may even be invested with seemingly contradictory meanings. As Edwards notes, '[m]aterial can move in and out of the anthropological sphere and photographs that were not created with anthropological intent or specifically informed by ethnographic understanding may nevertheless be appropriated to anthropological ends' (1992: 13). Similarly, a photograph created by a researcher with a particular ethnographic agenda in mind may travel out of 'the research' and into the personal collections of informants or other individuals, therefore being appropriated for *their* own ends (see Pink 1996; 1998b). For example, one photographic slide that I took of Encarni, a friend and informant during fieldwork, was duplicated as a print and used in a variety of ways, in her personal collection and family album, in my discussions with other informants, in my PhD thesis (Pink 1996), my book (Pink 1997a), in a conference paper (Pink 1996), as well as being part of my own personal collection of photographs of friends (see Chapter 5). Similarly, as I show in the CD ROM *The Bullfighter's Braid* (Pink 1998b), the photograph of the same name was an 'ethnographic photograph' that appeared on the front cover of my book *Women and Bullfighting* (1997a). This photograph also won a prize for artistic journalistic photography, was used to publicize the visit of a female bullfighter to Córdoba and became part of the personal collections and wall displays of my informants. Therefore, during the fieldwork this photograph had no single meaning, but it was re-appropriated and given new significance and uses in each context. As I outline in Chapter 5, the diversity of meanings invested in these two images was fundamental to my subsequent analysis of them and informed the academic meanings I gave to them.

Thus there are no fixed criteria that determine which photographs are ethnographic. Any photograph may have ethnographic interest, significance or meanings at a particular time or for a specific reason. The meanings of photographs are arbitrary and subjective; they depend on who is looking. The same photographic image may have a variety of (perhaps conflicting) meanings invested in it at different stages of ethnographic research and representation, as it is viewed by different eyes and audiences in diverse temporal historical, spatial and cultural contexts. Therefore it seems important that ethnographers seek to understand the individual, local, and broader cultural discourses in which photographs are made meaningful, in both fieldwork situations and academic discourses (see Chapter 6). Photographs produced as part of an ethnographic project will be given different meanings by the subjects of those images, local people in that context, the researcher, and other (sometimes critical) audiences. Edwards's work on historical photography (1992, 1997b) is a good example of this. The contributors to her edited collections discuss mainly colonial archival photography. They critically deconstruct the theories, philosophies and political agendas that informed the intentions of those who produced and used these images. By revealing the historical meanings that these photographs were given, the authors thus give them new meanings by embedding them in new discourses. At the turn of the twentieth century such images were assumed to represent objectively-collected scientific knowledge about 'inferior', dominated peoples. Almost 100 years later, the contributors to Edwards's collections largely view them as documents that represent the subjectivity of a particular theoretical 'scientific' perspective on reality and the ethnocentric, racist and oppressive ramifications of this. Re-situated, the images have been made to represent a critique of the intellectual and 'scientific' environment and framework of beliefs in which they were produced (see also Chapter 5).

However, it is not only historically that the meanings given to photographs may be renegotiated. When I showed a class of students a series of slides of a woman bullfighter's performance, some members of the group reacted by interpreting them in terms of an anti-bullfighting discourse. The meanings they invested in them were quite different from the ways in which they were interpreted by bullfight *aficionados*, who focused on the details of the bullfighter's technique and her female body. Other students in the group situated the images in another moral discourse. Taking a more relativist approach, they argued that we should try to understand what the photographs would mean in a Spanish cultural context. For me, however, the slides are also ethnographic photographs. They were shot as part of ethnographic fieldwork with dual intentions that related to my research; as an attempt to document the performance of a woman bullfighter and as part of my project to learn the art of bullfight photography.

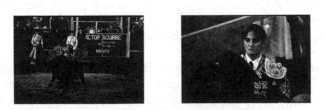

Once she had finished performing with the pink cape Cristina switched to the red *muleta* and sword.

She tossed her hat over her head to signify that she was dedicating her bull to the audience.

Then she performed with the red *muleta* . . .

. . . using the same cape passes and poses that are practised by her male colleagues . . .

. . . and holding the audience's attention.

Just before the end of the performance Cristina's cape was caught by the bull's horns, she was tossed in the air, and fell to the ground . . .

. . . but got up, kicked off her shoes and went on successfully to kill the bull.

In recognition of her success she was awarded one of the bull's ears as a
trophy . . . and was thrown flowers from the audience.

Figure 3.1 These slides were taken at Cristina Sanchez's performance in
Valdemorillo in 1993. They are usually projected in sequence. Bullfight *aficionados*'
interpretations of them would focus on the women bullfighter as performer – her
poses, her performance skills and achievements – thus understanding them in
terms of specific gendered narratives on bullfighting. Some UK viewers invested
quite different meanings in the images, understanding them in relation to a narrative
on animal rights and cruelty. One viewer situated this further in terms of her
personal narrative as a vegetarian. Each viewer used his or her own cultural and
experienced-based knowledge and moral values to give meanings to the images. For
bullfight *aficionados* this was often concerned with the question of whether or not
women should be bullfighters; for others it referred to whether bullfighting should be
allowed at all.

Ethnographer as photographer

When ethnographers take photographs, like any professional or 'lay'
photographer, they do so with reference to specific theories of photography and in the context of particular social relationships. As Wright has
pointed out, 'anyone who uses a camera or views a photograph, will most
probably be subscribing, albeit unwittingly, to some or other theory of
representation' (1999: 9). A reflexive approach to ethnographic photography means researchers being aware of the theories that inform their
own photographic practice, of their relationships with their photographic
subjects, and of the theories that inform their subjects' approaches to
photography. This is an important issue for portrait photography, as Lury
notes (citing Homberger 1992), 'at the heart of the photographic portrait is
a contract between the subject and the photographer, a contract in which
the former negotiates the term of the latter's appropriation of his or her
property rights in the self' (Lury 1998: 45). Yet the nature of this 'contract'
varies. For example, Lury describes, on the one hand, the commercial
contract whereby the photographer 'makes especially clear the rights of
the individual to self-possession created in portraiture: so for example the
individual has the right to accept or reject the portrait' (1998: 45). On the
other hand, in different circumstances 'other epistemological and judicial
principles . . . provided the authority for the abandonment of the contract

and undermined the function of the uniqueness of the self as a possession of the individual' (1998: 46). These principles were those that operated in the construction of the photographic archives (see Chapter 5) of government bureaucracies and colonial systems.

Therefore, it is useful to pay attention to the subjectivities and intentionalities of individual photographers, coupled with the cultural discourses, social relationships and broader political, economic and historical contexts to which these refer and in which they are enmeshed. Edwards's (1992) volume contains historical examples of this (e.g. Hockings 1992; Tayler 1992). Macintyre and Mackenzie demonstrate how in Papua New Guinea the 'cultural distance' between different colonial photographers and their local subjects varied according to 'the range of photographic genres and the varying degrees of control exerted by those behind the lens' (Macintyre and Mackenzie, 1992: 163). Their comments remind us that for both historical and contemporary photography, '[t]he experience, the motivations and the social positions of the photographers are intrinsic to the images' (1992: 163). Archival research about vintage photographs should therefore investigate not solely the content of the image, but also the personal and professional intentions of photographers and of other institutions and individuals with whom they negotiated. Ethnographic research into local photographic cultures should refer to the same principles. Therefore, when possible, analysis of the content or iconography of photographs should be informed by a consideration of the photographers' personal and professional intentions, the institutional agendas to which they were obliged to respond, how they have used photography to refer to specific cultural discourses and construct particular aspects of self identity, and the theories of representation that informed their practice. Ethnographic photographers may create their own photographs as a critical response or vindication of the power relations represented in such existing bodies of photographic work.

In Chapter 1 I discussed the difficulty of distinguishing between ethnographers' personal and professional lives and activities. It is similarly problematic to define a researcher's intentions as being 'purely ethnographic'. The photographs I take during fieldwork are usually neither distinctly 'research' or 'personal' photographs but could easily fit in to both categories. Since it is often difficult to distinguish between parts of one's life that are strictly 'research', 'leisure' or 'social life', it is hard to say whether such photographs were taken during 'work' or 'leisure'. Much of my fieldwork in Córdoba in Southern Spain was at social events, festivities and celebrations, where it was difficult for my informants to comprehend what I was doing as 'work'. Thus I frequently took 'ethnographic' photographs while socializing. For me these photographs are ethnographic because I was interested in people's visual self-representation, and I usually photographed informants on their request. These photographs were simultaneously visual representations of my own social experience and personal documents that belong to both

Figure 3.2 Conversation between a Kazakh herdsman and a Mongolian camel man. The situation is represented as neither exotic nor degenerate, but of the everyday and 'co-eval' (Fabian 1983) with the time of the photographer. (Bayan-Olgii, Summer 1994 © Barbara Hind).

Barbara Hind's photography seeks to represent Mongolians in ways that depart from the exoticism and objectifying approaches of historical and colonial representations.

my own collection and those friends for whom I copied them. Ethnographers can have dual (or multiple) intentions when photographing during fieldwork. For example, these intentions could be personal, artistic or ethnographic, and could combine to determine the content of the image, possibly in collaboration with the subjects of the photograph. To understand how these personal and professional intentions intersect, inform each other and combine to produce and represent ethnographic knowledge visually, a reflexive approach is necessary. This involves: first, developing a consciousness of how ethnographers play their roles as photographers in particular cultural settings, how they frame particular images, and why they choose particular subjects; second, a consideration of how these choices are related to the expectations of both academic disciplines and local visual cultures; and third, an awareness of the theories of representation that inform their photography. Sometimes it is useful to keep a reflexive diary about the development of one's photographic practice and the intentions and ideas that informed taking each image.

Below I consider some 'classic' uses of photography as a research method: photography as a visual recording method; photographic interviewing; and collaborative photography. These 'methods' may interlink and overlap at different stages of a research project.

Photography as a recording device: the potential of the photographic survey

The photographic survey has a long history in social science, from the colonial archive and the archives of photographs of criminals produced in the early twentieth century, to more recent studies where ethnographers have collaborated with informants photographically to document aspects of their culture. The creation of photographic records has often been based on the assumption that the artifacts photographed have finite, fixed symbolic meanings. For example, Collier and Collier propose a 'cultural inventory', where, for example, by producing a systematic photographic survey of visual aspects of the material content and organization of a home, one may answer questions relating to the economic level of the household, its style, decor, activities, the character of its order and its signs of hospitality and relaxation (Collier and Collier 1986: 47–50). Collier and Collier's approach provides a way of visually comparing specific material aspects of different households or even cultures. However, such photographic records are limited because they do not indicate how these objects are experienced or made meaningful by those individuals in whose lives they figure. In recent years this photographic survey approach has been employed mainly by visual sociologists. For example, Secondulfo's (1997) study of the symbolism of material items within the home and Pauwels's (1996) study of the material environment of the Brussels office of a Norwegian chemical multinational. Pauwels has sought to contexualize his visual survey through interviews and an analysis of other aspects of office life. However, in my opinion, these studies, based on a realist approach to photographic representation, do not fully develop the potential of survey photography for ethnographic work because they seek to document visual facts and in doing so neglect the idea that photographs are in fact subjective representations.

Schwartz's (1992) approach to photographic survey work in the North American Waucoma farming community is an example of closer collaboration with informants. Schwartz defines her survey photographs as neither 'objective visual documents' nor 'photographic truth'. Rather, they 'represent a point of view' – in this case her 'initial inferences about life in Waucoma' (1992: 14). She used her survey images of the Waucoma physical environment, together with old photographs of the same places, in interviews with local people. Rather than basing her analysis of the images on their content, her interpretation 'is informed by insights gained through ethnographic fieldwork and informant's responses to them'. In this work Schwartz assumed that her photographs 'would prompt multiple responses'. She 'sought to study the range of meaning they held for different members of the community' (1992: 14). Therefore, she made the idea that visual meanings are arbitrary a key element of her research method.

Photographic surveys or attempts to represent physical environments, objects, events or performances can form part of a reflexive ethnography. However, such photographs should be treated as representations of *aspects* of culture; not recordings of whole cultures or of symbols that will have complete or fixed meanings. This also has implications for the way ethnographers store, categorize and analyse photographs (see Chapter 5).

Participatory and collaborative photography

Ethnographers collaborate with informants to produce photographs in a variety of ways. Existing examples involve working alone with a single informant (e.g. Collier and Collier 1986), with groups involved in a particular set of creative (e.g. Chaplin 1994) or ceremonial (e.g. Larson 1988) activities, or in eclectic ways at different occasions and events as part of a wider ethnographic project (e.g. Banks n.d.; Pink 1998b). If photographs are produced 'collaboratively', they combine the intentions of both ethnographer/photographer and informant and should represent the outcome of their negotiations.

Collaborative photography usually involves ethnographers engaging in some way with the photographic culture of their informants. In some cases this could involve an attempt to reproduce the kinds of images that are popular in informants' photographic cultures. In other projects, ethnographers may want to produce photographs that refer to local photographic conventions, but that also conform to the demands of an academic discipline. The intentions and objectives of researchers and informants combine in their negotiations to determine the content of the photographs in ways that of course vary in different projects. For instance, informants may seek family photographs, images that will provide legal evidence, documentation of local 'traditions' or of work processes, artistic exhibits, souvenirs or photographs that may be used for publicity. Ethnographers may wish to produce images that they can publish with academic text or exhibit. They may wish to learn local photographic styles, conform to the conventions of their academic discipline, or produce images that follow a particular photographic tradition, such as realist documentary, expressive or art photography.

Existing ethnographic examples indicate that people are usually quick to teach a potential photographer what kinds of images they would like to have taken. Sometimes the photographs informants request challenge the assumptions behind the ethnographer's original intentions and initiate a shift in the anticipated use of photography as a research method. For instance, my Guinea Bissauan neighbours were keen for me to photograph them and often asked me when I was going to their houses to take a picture. But when I arrived at their verandas during the morning, when the light was good, they were not prepared to have their photographs taken. Busy working, the local women were wearing their old clothes and had not arranged their hair. 'Later, later', they would put me off, telling me that they would come to my house when they had dressed up for the photography. My neighbour arrived at my house one evening, having changed the torn African dress (that she had been wearing to carry water) for a smart imported European T-shirt and skirt, wearing her gold earrings and having combed her hair. She sat at the table in my house, where I had been writing my 'field diary' a few minutes earlier, and (as I had never seen her before) posed holding my pen as if writing in my notebook. I could not take the 'documentary' images of everyday life that I had anticipated; instead, I learned how local women wanted to represent themselves, through a particular local style of portraiture practised in photographic studios and at public events and festivities (similar to that practised in Ghana, see *Future Remembrance* (Wendl and Du Plessis 1998)). This method of photographing taught me about the prestige items that women valued locally, and how people represented their aspirations though their visual self-representations.

Pinney also describes how, during his first fieldwork in India in 1982, he learnt how local people wanted to be represented through his attempts to photograph his informants in terms of his own aesthetic designs. He notes how he took a photograph of his neighbour that fitted the type of image he wanted to produce: 'candid, revealing, expressive of the people I

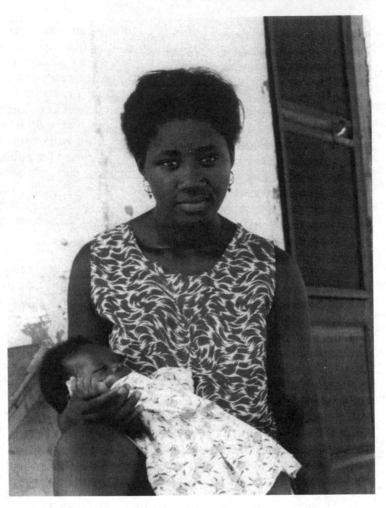

Figure 3.3 When I was doing fieldwork in Guinea Bissau my neighbour, Jacqueline, had been asking me to take a photograph of her new baby ever since she had been born. When I stepped out of my house one day with my camera I spotted them sitting on the veranda and offered to take the photograph. Jacqueline said she could not be photographed as she had no gold earrings or good clothes to wear for the photograph, but she still wanted a photo of her baby. She called over Potcho, another neighbour, who was always well dressed, and asked her to pose with the baby. This, like many other instances, became part of my experience of learning about the way local women felt comfortable about representing themselves visually in photographs.

was living among' (Pinney 1997: 8). This photograph was a half-length image taken around 5pm in the fields: 'a good time to catch the mellowing sun' (1997: 8). But his informant was not satisfied with the image. He 'complained about the shadow and darkness it cast over his face and the absence of the lower half of his body. The image was of no use to him' (1997: 9). Pinney's informants wanted a different type of photograph, one that was taken according to another procedure. These photographs 'could not be taken quickly since there were more lengthy preparations to be made: clothes to be changed, hair to be brushed and oiled (and, in the case of upper-caste women, the application of talcum powder to lighten the skin)' (1997: 9). Moreover, their content and symbolism conformed to different expectations: 'These photos had to be full-length and symmetrical, and the passive, expressionless faces and body poses symbolised for me, at that time, the extinguishing of precisely that quality I wished to capture on film' (1997: 9).

In these examples the portraits indicated informants' existing expec-tations of photography and their personal and cultural uses of images. In my research I began to pay greater attention to the personal photograph collections women showed me in order to interpret how they wanted me to photograph them. My adoption of local people's photographic expec-tations *vis-à-vis* portrait photography guided my own photographic practice. For example, I realized if I developed my photographs in the costly (about three times more expensive than in the United Kingdom) Taiwanese shop in Bissau, the capital city, my informants' images would be over-exposed, representing them with the lighter skins that they desired (as seemed to be the laboratory's policy). Thus my 'visual research method' was shaped out of my interactions with the local people and institutions, rather than being preconceived.

Ethnographers often photograph ritual or other cultural activities. For example, Banks found that during his fieldwork in urban India much of his photography was at communal ritual events. Sometimes his informants actively 'directed' his photography. Banks describes how at one event his informants insisted that he 'took a pre-posed photograph of the woman who had paid for the feast, ladling a dollop of a rich yoghurt-based dessert on to the tray of one of the feasters' (Banks n.d.). Interpreting this photographic event, Banks shows how this collaborative photography was informed by his own and his informants' knowledge, writing that

> It was composed and framed according to my own (largely unconscious) visual aesthetic and is part of my own corpus of documentary images of that feast. But it is also a legitimization and concretization of social facts as my friends saw them: the fact that the feast had a social origin in the agency of one person (the feast donor) as well as by virtue of the religiously and calendrically prescribed fasting period that preceded it; the fact that this was a good feast during which we ate the expensive and highly-valued yoghurt desert (Banks n.d.).

Figure 3.4 This photograph was taken of me with Cristina Sanchez by the Director of the Bullfighting Museum. I was accompanying him, Cristina Sanchez, her father and a bullfight journalist, to photograph her day in Córdoba. When the Director took my camera to take this photograph for me, it confirmed the knowledge I had already been developing about the images that bullfight *aficionados* tend to collect. This image was the photograph I was meant to want to have: an image that situated me in relation to the 'star'.

For Banks, the 'directed' photography became a way of visualizing and reinforcing his existing ethnographic knowledge because 'I "knew" these social facts, because I had been told them on other occasions, but by being directed to capture them on film I was made aware not only of their strength and value but of the power of photography to legitimize them' (Banks n.d.).

Although in some situations researchers may ask informants to 'direct' the photography, in others 'directed' photography develops through informants' initiatives. While I was researching in Spain, the Director of Museums invited me to accompany him during a woman bullfighter's official visit to the city. My role was to photograph their day in Córdoba and the Director often told me what to photograph. Once he asked for my camera to photograph me sitting in a bar with the woman bullfighter. He took the photograph that, according to the usual standards of the visual culture of bullfighting photography, I should have wanted to have (see Pink 1997a).

Like Banks, I connected this photography to my existing knowledge. I had already studied bullfighting fans' personal photographic collections and knew that this was a recurring image composition. Later in the day,

(a)

(b)

Figure 3.5 A group of students from the University Aula Taurina (photo (a)) asked me to take their photograph with the woman bullfighter, Cristina Sanchez (centre). In the photograph they are holding copies of the journal edited by the Aula Taurina, which has my photograph, 'The Bullfighter's Braid', on the back cover. In photo (b) Cristina Sanchez is signing the photograph.

at an evening reception for the woman bullfighter, I was asked to take
more photographs of a similar kind.

On another occasion I was in the audience of a bullfight with a young
woman informant. During the performance she instructed me which
standard stages I should photograph, as well the stages of her person-
alized narrative of the event such as when her favourite bullfighter
waved to the part of the ring where she and the other members of his
supporters' club were sitting. During his performance, she asked for my
camera to photograph him performing the kill herself. Most bullfight
fans regard the kill as the most important stage of the performance, and
thus also the key photographic moment. Through her actions my
informant had not only shown me the importance of this, but had also
used the camera to express her own knowledge of the bullfight. In these
two situations my informants had already imagined the photographs
they wanted me to take and those they wanted to take themselves: they
were constructing them in response to an existing visual culture, the
discourses of which they were conversant in. By analysing the context
in which the images were taken and the local photographic conventions
to which their composition complied, I gained a deeper understanding
and a more informed visual representation of the significance of particular social relationships, representations of self, and of stages of the
bullfight.

Collaborating with informants to produce images need not involve the
ethnographer taking the lead as photographer. 'Native' photography has
also been used in some studies where ethnographers have asked
informants to photograph for or with them. The sociologist Cavin has
used children's photography to research 'children's perspectives' by
giving children Polaroid cameras with which to produce images. Cavin
points out it is not so much the content of the images that indicates how
children see the world (as the images tended to represent 'the world
blurrily at odd angles'), but that a child's use of the camera would be
'based on a clearly defined and consistent framing of the world' (Cavin
1994: 39). Martinez Perez also used 'native' photography in her project
about the Gran Vía in Madrid. As her film *Cronotopo* (1997) shows
Martinez Perez asked her informants to photograph this street and then
discuss their images with her.

Getting started: taking the first picture

The question of when to take the first photograph varies from project to
project. Sometimes photographing can form a way of getting the research
off the ground and establishing relationships with informants. In other
situations researchers may have to wait several months before beginning
to photograph. I have stressed above the importance of developing
knowledge about the visual culture in which one works. This knowledge

should inform such decisions. For ethical reasons ethnographers should consider not only where their photography fits into local visual cultures, but also how their photographic practices may affect local economies and other individuals (see Chapter 2).

Several examples demonstrate how photography may serve as a way to initiate and support research. Collier and Collier (1986) write about the idea of the camera as a 'can-opener' in two ways, both of which they see as means of establishing rapport with one's informants. First, they note how playing a 'photographer' role can put researchers in an ideal position to 'observe' the culture or groups they are researching. Secondly, showing photographs to their subjects can provide both feedback on the images and their content while also forging connections with members of the 'community'. This can provide excuses for further meetings and photography and may be a reason to visit informants in their homes. While it will not always be appropriate to use photography in this way, ethnographers often find that photographing and photographs provide a useful method of representing their own identities and communicating with informants at the early stages of fieldwork. Taking the first images with a Polaroid or a digital camera may speed up the process, allowing informants to gain an idea of what the ethnographer is doing almost instantly, and (hopefully) to engender their trust and interest.

Sometimes, in order to be able to photograph the activities in which they are interested, ethnographers will first have to establish themselves locally as someone who is trusted to take photographs. Shanklin (1979) describes how she worked as ethnographer/photographer during research in rural Ireland. She had intended to take photographs of people at work that she could subsequently discuss with her informants, but initially she found this impossible. However, she learnt, through her observations of her informants' displays of family photography in their homes, that photographing children would be an appropriate activity that would provide parents with valued images: 'Just as I had to learn something about patterns of social interaction in order to become more a member of the culture I studied, so too I had to learn something about their use of photographs in order to integrate my own picture taking into the roles to which I had been assigned' (Shanklin 1979: 143). Once she had established herself as someone who took photographs within the local community, she found that she was then able to proceed and photograph agricultural workers at work and combine this with the interviews as she had originally intended.

In some projects photographing may come first and can be a means of making contact with local people. This was the case in Schwartz's (1992) research. Following Collier she began her research by photographing the physical environment of Waucoma, the town that she was studying. On arrival, she began to photograph buildings to let the residents know of her presence, and at the same time to observe the goings on of everyday life. This provided her with a good entry into local interaction as seeing a stranger photographing the town made many people curious enough to approach her and ask what she was doing. The local people became interested in and supportive of Schwartz's work and the photographic aspect of the project became a key point of communication between her and her informants.

In my research in Spain I was able to begin to photograph as soon as I made contact with the groups I was interested in working with. My initial photographic work in Spain provided me with an appropriate activity to be involved in at the beginning of my research into bullfighting culture. As an unaccompanied woman at bullfighting receptions and public occasions and, at the time, still learning the language and unable to engage in any detailed conversation, I was grateful to have a role as 'photographer'. My photography was endorsed by the organizers and was not problematic for participants since at any such public event a number of press photographers were expected to be present. Once my photographs of the receptions were printed, I showed them to the organizers and other participants with whom I was in contact. We discussed the event and the people who were present, and my informants often asked me for copies of particular images, usually of themselves with particular people, so that they could pass them on to their friends, colleagues or contacts within the bullfighting world. In this way I was able not only to gain feedback about the events that I had participated in as a photographer, but also to get a sense of the way that social relationships and alliances were mapped out and constructed within the bullfighting world. I did this by studying who wanted to be photographed with who during the events, and by tracking the collection and distribution of the copies of the images that my informants asked for (see Pink 1998b).

Building on the success of this way of making local contacts at the beginning of my research in Spain, I tried to use photography to make links with local people on my arrival in Guinea Bissau. During my first visit of two weeks in Canchungo, the town in which I lived for eight months, I asked two of the women market traders who had been friendly to me if I could photograph them, promising that I would give them the photos when I returned to Guinea Bissau two weeks later. They were pleased that I had really returned and fulfilled my promise and from then on I always had a friend in the market. However, as I have noted in Chapter 2, in Guinea Bissau it was not appropriate for me to use this method as extensively as I had in Spain.

Viewing ethnographers' photographs: interviewing with images

In this section I explore the roles that photographs may play in interviews or conversations. In Chapters 1 and 2 I argued that visual images are made meaningful through the subjective gaze of the viewer, and that each individual produces these photographic meanings by relating the

(a)

(b)

Figure 3.6 When I attended receptions, still unable to speak good Spanish, my camera became a means of being occupied, photographing details of who was present, the sequence of events, and taking the photos that people asked for. In this way I was able to produce a set of images that allowed me to represent the sequence and participants of the event and to collaborate with some of the subjects of my photographs to produce images in which they represented particular social relationships. Once the photographs were developed, I discussed them with certain key informants. This helped me to learn more about the participants in the event, their social networks and how they situated themselves in the 'bullfighting world'. When people asked for copies of certain photographs, both for themselves and to give to other participants in the event, I was able to learn about their own social networks and the links that an individual may be trying to forge or strengthen by passing an image of himself or herself with another participant to that person.

image to his or her existing personal experience, knowledge and wider
cultural discourses. This approach critiques the assumption that
'photographs can be *tools* with which to *obtain* knowledge' (Collier and
Collier 1986: 99, second italics are mine) in order to argue that photographs are visual objects through which people reference aspects of their
experience and knowledge. Therefore, when photographs become the
focus of discussion between ethnographers and informants, certain
questions arise. For instance, how do ethnographers and informants
situate themselves and each other in relation to the photograph? How
does the intersubjectivity between ethnographers, informants and the
material/visual images 'complete' the identity of an informant during an
interview? How do informants create narratives with and around photographs and ethnographers? It is not simply a matter of asking how
informants provide 'information' in 'response' to the content of images.
Rather, ethnographers should be interested in how informants use the
content of the images as vessels in which to invest meanings and through
which to produce and represent their knowledge, self-identities, experiences and emotions.

In the past the term most used to refer to photographic interviewing
has been the rather problematic 'photo-elicitation'. This concept implies
using photographs to elicit responses from informants, to 'draw out' or
'evoke' an 'admission, answer *from* a person' (*Concise Oxford Dictionary*
1982, my italics). Collier provides good examples of this technique.
Researching farming families who were also employed in urban fac-
tories, Collier used his photographs of both work locations as reference
points in photographic interviews to examine his informants' attitudes to
city life, factory work and migration to the city. His work provides a
useful example of how his informants talked about the images and of
how a photographic research project may evolve over time. However,
Collier's analysis is based on the assumption that 'the facts are in the
pictures' (Collier and Collier 1986: 106) and the idea that I have questioned above that the ethnographer may elicit knowledge about the
visual content from informants.

More recently, Harper has developed a new approach that attempts to
integrate photo-elicitation with the 'new ethnography' by redefining it as
'a model of collaboration in research' (1998a: 35). For Harper, photographs are not simply visual records of reality, but are representations
that are interpreted in terms of different understandings of reality. When
informants view photographs taken by an ethnographer they will actually be engaged in interpreting the ethnographer/photographer's visual-
ization of reality. In a photographic interview, therefore, ethnographer
and informant will be able to discuss their different understandings of
images, thus collaborating to determine each other's views. Schwartz has
developed a similar approach. She identifies her own photographs of a
Waucoma community as representations of her own vision of the physical and social environment. Basing her analysis on the principle that 'the

photograph prompts personal narratives generated by the content of the image', she describes how her use of photographs in interviews 'was informed by the unique and contradictory nature of the medium . . . photographs elicit multiple perceptions and interpretations' (Schwartz 1992: 13). Photographic interviews can allow ethnographers and inform-ants to discuss images in ways that may create a 'bridge' between their different experiences of reality. A photograph may become a reference point through which an informant can represent aspects of his or her reality to an ethnographer and vice versa.

In Guinea Bissau I used photographs in this type of creative dialogue with informants. A set of photographs that I had taken of Tomas, a local weaver, his son and Alberto Martinez, who was working as a VSO Maths and Science teacher in Guinea Bissau became central to a series of conversations between Alberto, Tomas and I (some of which I video recorded (see Chapter 4)). During Tomas's five-week stay of weaving traditional cloth in our garden, I took five films of colour prints, mainly of him and his son at work. We often spent evenings looking through and talking about the photographs and the events, activities and indi-viduals they represented. This case study is represented with video clips, transcripts and photographs in the CD ROM *Interweaving Lives* (Pink 1998d). Elsewhere (Pink 1999b) I have interpreted the conversations that Alberto and Tomas had about/with these photographs as a series of ongoing negotiations. In these conversations the photographs become reference points in which both men interpret and invest meanings in terms of their own realities. My analysis of these photographic con-versations or interviews examined how individuals interpret the content of images differently and how they used the photographs to construct continuities between their different realities. For example, one evening, we discussed my photographs of a chameleon. In response to these images, Tomas explained an element of his view of reality. His story made us aware of the differences between our respective beliefs and attitudes to this small animal. The photographs of the chameleon also served as a common point of reference through which our different interpretations, beliefs and experiences could be connected.

> Tomas: What is this you have got here? a chameleon?
> Alberto: This is a real chameleon. Its nice isn't it?
> Tomas: Very nice, very nice, it has gone up a stick.
> Alberto: I had the stick in my hand.
> Tomas: Ah, in your hand.
> Alberto: After that I put it here.
> Tomas: Oh Alberto! How did you dare?
> Alberto: It doesn't do any harm.
> Tomas: It may not do anything, but me! Catch it, put it in my hand, I wouldn't dare.
> Alberto: Why not?
> Tomas: I am scared of them.

(a)

(b)

Figure 3.7

Alberto: But it is very small.

Tomas: People say that if you see the chameleon's house you get very rich.

Alberto: Why?

Tomas: Because if you know where he lives, where he has his children, you can rest in this world, you will be very rich . . . you will have a lot of money. . . . The money would fill the whole room.

Alberto: And all this because of the chameleon? Tomas, are you making fun of me?

Tomas: No! It's true!

The photographic image, embedded in this conversation, connected our different realities. Tomas linked it to his reality of chameleon wealth. He used the image to construct continuity between the reality of the wealth associated with the chameleon and the theme of wealth in our previous conversations (see Pink 1999b).

Figure 3.8 These photographs of Cristina Sanchez (above) and *Finito de Córdoba* (below) became part of the way I discussed bullfighting during my fieldwork in Spain. Informants used these photographs to comment on the bullfighters' performance skills and on the development of my own skills in learning to take the photograph at the 'right' moments of the bullfight. In doing so, they were able to represent their own expert knowledge of the bullfight. From these discussions I was able to learn about the knowledge that was meant to inform appropriate bullfight photography as well as the values and knowledge that my informants used to inform their commentaries on the images.

During fieldwork in Spain I made a different use of my own bull-fighting photography. By attempting to learn how to photograph the bullfight myself, I produced photographs that allowed my informants to comment on my knowledge of the bullfight and at the same time express their own.

Viewing informants' photographs: interviewing with images

Conversation is filled with verbal references to images and icons. People use verbal description to visualize particular moralities, activities and versions of social order (or disorder). Sometimes informants refer to absent images (including photographs) or they might introduce material images or objects into a conversation. During my fieldwork in Europe and Africa people have often brought or shown me photographs as part of the stories they have been telling me about their lives. During my first

fieldwork in Northern Ireland, I sat with a Protestant woman, at the time
in her forties, talking at her kitchen table. Long before we had met, she
had married a man who had converted his own religion from being a
Catholic to becoming a Protestant. He had remained friends with some
Catholics and because of the religious tensions in Northern Ireland this
made some complications in their social life. His wife was seeking a way
to express this religious divide to me and, although she had not been
speaking of their wedding at the time, she told me she would show me a
wedding photograph. As I waited for her to fetch the photograph I
expected to see a 'white wedding' – the couple and the confetti – but she
handed me a photograph taken from the back of a church. One side of
the photograph was filled with people but the other was empty. She
explained how her husband's family couldn't attend the Protestant
service because they were Catholics, so his side of the church was empty.
They were waiting outside the church and after the service all went to
the reception. It seemed that this beginning had become symbolic of a
continuing state of affairs for her. She had not been talking about her
wedding, or showing her wedding photos, but they had become a visual
reference point in a narrative about other boundaries and the way her
life was currently affected by the religious divisions that the photograph
symbolized so powerfully for her.

Other researchers have had similar experiences. For example, Riches
and Dawson (1998) found that bereaved parents often showed them
photographs of their dead child during interviews. The parents tended to
incorporate the photographs of their dead child into personal narratives
of their experiences of the death and used images as ways of representing
self-identities. As Riches and Dawson demonstrate, their informants'
uses of photographs in the interviews linked with their existing practices,
whereby photographs become 'an object of personal internal conversation *with* the deceased and . . . a vehicle for conversations between
surviving relatives and others *about* the deceased' (1998: 124).

Okely describes how her informants' own photograph collections
became an important part of her research about the 'changing conditions
and experience of the aged in rural France' (Okely 1994: 45). When an
elderly woman informant in a nursing home led her to her room and took
out a box of old photographs Okely 'found a route to her past through
images' that stood for 'profound recreations of her past' (1994: 50). For
Okely, these images were not merely illustrations of her informant's oral
narrative, but themselves were evocative descriptions and comments. She
argues that the introduction of the photographs into their conversation
enhanced the sensory dimension of the interview: 'A mere tape recording
of her speaking in a formalised interview could not have conjured up the
greater sense of her past which we mutually created with the aid of visual
images' (1994: 50–1). Okely notes that a history related through a series of
'selective images of the past', and captioned by a verbal narrative, is
inevitably subjective, selective and fragmented. Nevertheless, she also

shows how this collaborative research allowed her and her informant to work together to create a particular version of the past that extended beyond the limitations set by the linearity of a verbal or textual narrative:

> Both of us pieced together the memories from whatever was picked up from the box, and created a synthesized whole. In reacting to the visual images, randomly stored, the woman was freed of linear chronology, any set piece for a life history and a purely verbalised description. The images did some of the work for both of us in ways which adjectives and other vocabulary could not supply. (1994: 51)

Okely emphasizes the need for reflection on how researchers experience informants' photographs. She notes how in her own experience she was 'watching, listening and resonating with the emotions and energy of her living through the photographs' (1994: 50). It is important for ethnographers to be aware of their own contributions to collaboratively produced narratives. For example, when I later analysed my personal feelings and field diary notes about photographs I had been shown when I first arrived to do research in Guinea Bissau, I was able to understand how my initial interpretations had been informed. For instance, one evening Miranda, a young Guinea Bissauan woman who later became my friend and informant, began to tell me the story of her affair with a white development worker who was the father of her daughter. My attitude to her 'story' was already shaped by a version of it that my partner had told me. He had represented it as an unequal and exploitative relationship with a man who had now deserted her. I suggested to Miranda that he must be a *bandido* (bastard). 'No!' she had contradicted me, telling me that he cared very much, but it was just difficult to send money. She proposed to return the next evening to show me her photographs of him. On seeing the photograph collection I was struck by a sense of the bizarre. I found myself viewing not what I considered to be Miranda's own photograph collection, but a collection of photographs that *he* had left in Guinea Bissau. It contained European studio portraits of him, his wife and his adult children in Europe, distant people whom Miranda had never met and who had no idea of her existence. Other photographs were taken in Guinea Bissau of Miranda, and her daughter and lover, during carnival and other parties. Through the photographs she recounted events in the life she had shared with this man and her contacts with other white people. Our conversations around the photographs led us on to many topics and stories such as when his wife had visited and Miranda had remained, like any respectful lover, silent, not acknowledging their affair. Through these narratives with which the photographic images were interwoven, I learned how her view of her relationship with this white man differed from my own understanding. Our discussions of the portraits helped me understand how Miranda situated herself in relation to these different characters.

While in the ethnographic literature such examples of people 'talking with photographs' are infrequently described, ethnographic films often include scenes in which informants show and discuss photographs with the filmmaker. Examples of this can be found in *Photo Wallahs* (MacDougall and MacDougall 1991) and *Faces in the Crowd* (Henley 1994).

Displays and exhibitions: viewing photographs with informants

Viewing photographic displays or exhibitions with informants offers further ways of exploring and creating relationships between visual and verbal knowledge. This may involve visiting public exhibitions, viewing sets of photographs displayed publicly (for example, in schools, club houses, or bars), or simply talking around the photographs displayed on the wall or mantlepiece of someone's home. By paying attention to how people interweave such images with verbal narratives, researchers may learn about how these individuals construct their lives and histories. Okely found that her elderly informants drew the photographs they had on display into their conversations with her: 'The selected icons of photos which the aged displayed at institutional bedside or on familiar sideboard in their own home were both cultural and individual presentations' (Okely 1994: 51). In Spain I discussed individual collections and public displays of images to explore my informants' visual representation of their 'bullfighting world' and its history, and to see how individuals used these visual representations to situate themselves within that bullfighting world. In photographic displays individuals and groups often used photographs to establish identities and to imply relationships. Most bullfighting bars and clubs owned permanent exhibitions that mapped out a local version of the history of bullfighting. When informants took me to see 'their own' bullfighting bar or club, I was frequently given a guided tour of the bar's photographic display. As I was led through these photographic wall displays, narratives of history, place and kinship were developed as informants emphasized family relationships between different bullfighters, their historical authenticity and their local links. The histories I was told when viewing the images were, as in the case of the box of images that Okely's informant drew her faded prints from, multilinear. The chronological history of bullfighting that my informants outlined was intersected with family histories as links between fathers, sons, nephews and great uncles formed particular routes across the various different photographic maps of the bullfighting world that I was shown. For a bullfighter, it was especially important to be situated in this world by having his photograph included in the exhibition, since inclusion in a display and the social relations involved in achieving this are crucial for a bullfighter's career. The cultural construction of history and the contemporary configuration of the bullfighting world depends on

the strategic inclusion and exclusion of photographs of certain people
(Pink 1997b: 56). Bullfight *aficionados* used similar strategies in their semi-
public displays at home. These include photographs of themselves in
amateur performances, or photographed with famous bullfighters, and
thus mapped personal versions of the 'bullfighting world' that placed the
owner of the exhibition at their centre.

I was also invited to the openings of many exhibitions of bullfight
photography during my research in Spain. At these events I discussed
photographs with informants as we milled around the exhibition spaces.
Their comments about the content and style of photographs gave me a
better understanding of how different photographic representations
fitted with each person's vision of the contemporary and historical world
of bullfighting and of how they constructed their own place and identity
in that world (see Pink 1997b).

Absent photographs

In Chapter 1 I introduced the idea that sometimes people speak about
absent images. This may mean describing a famous photograph, a
photograph seen in yesterday's newspaper, a photograph of a child or
relative, a photograph that they hated so much that it was torn up and
thrown away, or simply a photograph that is somewhere else. For
example, during my research in Guinea Bissau, one of my informants
often spoke of a photograph that hung on the wall in one of the offices of
one of the NGOs working in the area. It was a group photograph of a
project team in which she was included due to the connections she had
with the development workers. These links formed an important part of
her identity and she used her references to the photograph to endorse
these relationships and her representation of her self. A few months later
when I visited the office I saw the photograph and recognized how it had
been used as a way of representing her identity and social status.

While in many instances ethnographers may never actually see the
photographs informants describe, they provide interesting examples of
how informants may visualize certain emotions, values and experiences.
It is also important to pay attention to how informants speak about
images that they have hidden or thrown away: it is not only the photographs that people keep that are of interest, but those that they reject and
their reasons for doing so may be of equal interest.

Summary: image producers, visual cultures and visualizing conversations

This chapter has emphasized two dimensions of ethnographic research
with photographic images and technologies: an appreciation of both the

local and academic visual cultures in which ethnographers work and
how researchers may employ photography and photographs in the
production of knowledge. Ethnographic image production and discussions of images both respond and refer to local and academic visual
cultures. Ethnographers should recognize that neither local nor academic
visual and written cultures are superior to the other. As the individual
through which the experience of each is mediated, photographers/
ethnographers should attempt to maintain a reflexive awareness of how
the demands of each inform their work.

More often than not the processes of learning about local visual
cultures and the production of one's own images go together. However,
in different projects photographing and interviewing with/talking about
images will inevitably develop in different ways. Therefore the ways of
doing photographic research described above are not intended to be
comprehensive; they are intended to present a series of ideas and
examples of existing work and of the potential for photography in
ethnographic research. Variations in the methods developed in different
projects are not just contingent on 'the culture' in which researchers
work, but also on the personal styles of ethnographers and the social
relationships in which they are involved. Therefore, the key to successful
photographic research is an understanding of the social relations and
subjective agendas through which they are produced and the discourses
through which they are made meaningful.

CHAPTER 4

Video in Ethnographic Research

Many ethnographers and their informants produce and view video in their personal lives and professional work. However video is normally allowed only cursory (if any) mention in ethnographic texts on research methods (with the exception of Ratcliff n.d.) and published discussion of ethnographic video as a method, genre or medium for ethnographic research or representation has been limited. Visual sociologists have largely concentrated on photography, rarely considering the potential of video in the research process (see Lomax and Casey 1998: 2). Visual anthropologists became interested in video in the 1980s, applauding new developments in video technology for the convenience, economy, durability and utility they offered. In comparison with film, which was used extensively in anthropological research in the 1970s (see Morphy and Banks 1997: 5), video was cheap and could record for a considerably longer period of time. During this period the potential of video was often harnessed to serve a scientific-realist approach. For example, Collier and Collier saw the idea that a video camera may be left running continuously for several hours as an advantage compared to the relative selectivity imposed by both the cost of film and the need to reload a camera more frequently (1986: 146).

As video technology advances, film and video continue to offer rather different possibilities in ethnographic research. These developments, combined with shifts away from a scientific approach, imply that the specificity of video needs to be engaged with anew. In the 1990s some researchers have begun to explore reflexive uses of video in ethnography, using video images and technologies not simply to record 'data', but as media through which ethnographic knowledge is created. Simultaneously, technological developments, especially in digital video, invite new practical possibilities for video in research and in electronic representation (see Chapter 8). In Chapter 2 I discussed how particular cameras may be interpreted by video subjects, thus impacting on their strategies of self-representation. It is also worth reflecting on the design of the video technology used and how this affects the researchers' or video makers' strategies. Chris Wright describes how the Sony PC7 digital video camera differs from more conventional cameras. In place of a viewfinder, the PC7 has a fold-out mini-TV screen that creates distance between the camera operator's eye and the camera, allowing the camera operator to see both the camera screen and the scene recorded. Thus the camera no longer follows the operator's eye but allows him or her a split vision and to see and decide what is being recorded in relation to the scene in front of the camera (C. Wright 1998: 18–19). My experiences with a similar model, the Sony PC1E, in 1999 support this. Moreover, such technology changes not only the camera operator's view, but also what the video subjects see. Using the open camera screen of the video, a researcher can maintain better eye contact with video subjects because the camera itself is not hiding his or her face. Video footage can also be viewed 'in the field' on this screen and listened to through the external speaker, with informants or people who have appeared in the video. In comparison with viewing playback though the camera viewfinder with headphones (see Figure 4.1), this viewing context also allows researcher and informants to discuss the images during viewing.

Ethnographers should develop a self-conscious approach not only to their relationships with the video subjects but also to how both relate to the camera, and to their different agendas regarding the video technology and recordings.

Defining ethnographic video

In the existing literature there has been a tendency to distinguish between 'objective' research film or video footage and 'creative' footage produced for ethnographic filmmaking. This distinction is informed by debates in the 1970s and 1980s about the relationship between cinematography and scientific ethnographic film (see Banks 1992). Some (e.g. Heider 1976) argued that ethnographic film should be objective, unedited, not 'manipulated', it should be guided by scientific, ethnographic principles, rather than cinematographic intentions. Such footage was intended to be stored as a film archive and screened to anthropological audiences: it was part of a project of recording an objective reality. During the same period others produced more creative, expressive films intended for public consumption. In particular, Robert Gardner 'distanced himself from realism' (see Loizos 1993: 140), producing films that used cinematographic and symbolic techniques that challenged the criteria set by Heider. Collier and Collier have applied a similar distinction between 'research' film which 'is made to contain relatively *undisturbed* process and behaviour from which to develop information and concepts' and 'ethnographic' film that 'is usually edited to create a narrative selected by the filmmaker-producer' (Collier and Collier 1986: 152). They dismiss the possibility of using 'ethnographic' film for research purposes, claiming that the selectivity involved in its production makes it invalid as an observational record. These categories persist in recent work (e.g. Barbash and Taylor 1997) that regards research footage as objective data, 'raw material' and a scientific document. In this view creativity is not part of research as the ethnographer's intentionality must be scientific to be 'ethnographic'.

Here I propose three main criticisms of this approach. First, it is usually impossible or inappropriate to video record people or culture 'undisturbed'; people in a video are always 'people in a video'. Moreover, like any ethnographic representation, research footage is inevitably 'constructed'. Secondly, ethnographic knowledge does not necessarily exist as observable facts. In Chapter 1 I argued that ethnographic knowledge is better understood as originating from fieldwork experiences. Knowledge is produced in conversation and negotiation between informants and researcher, rather than existing as an objective reality that may be recorded and taken home in a note book, camera film or tape. Thirdly, and parallel to my discussion of defining ethnographic photography (Chapter 3), the question of the 'ethnographicness' of video footage does not depend entirely on its content or on the intentionality of the video maker, but its ethnographicness is contextual. In the broadest sense a video is 'ethnographic' when its viewer(s) judge that it represents information of ethnographic interest. Therefore video footage can never be purely 'ethnographic': a video recording that ethnographers see as representing ethnographic knowledge about an event and how it is experienced might, in their informants' eyes, be a video of a birthday party.

This broad and contextual definition of ethnographic video invites the possibility for a range of different genres of video to be 'ethnographic'. This includes not only ethnographers' video footage, but (for example) home movies, events videoed by informants for ethnographers, or indigenous videos made for self-representation to external bodies. None of these recordings are essentially ethnographic, but may become so when they are implicated in an ethnographic project.

Ethnographic video and local 'video cultures'

Ethnographers' uses of video benefit from awareness of how informants use and understand video technologies and representations. As Lomax and Casey note, 'the camera . . . is socially significant given both its ability to preserve interaction for re-presentation and participants' awareness of that ability' (1998: 6). However, reflexivity entails more than simply an awareness of how participants' interactions are affected by their 'camera-consciousness'. An ethnographer with a video camera is a person with a video camera, the camera becomes part of its user's identity and an aspect of the way he or she communicates with others. Moreover, in each situation the camera will impact differently on the relationships researchers develop with other individuals and the social roles they play. An individual ethnographer does not have one single and fixed identity as a video maker, but this will be negotiated and redefined in different contexts. To be reflexive ethnographic video makers need to be aware of how the camera and video footage become an element of the play between themselves and informants, and how these are interwoven into discourses and practices in the research context.

Braun's video essay, *Passing Girl, Riverside: an Essay on Camera Work* (1998), a reflexive text about video as 'a tool for cross-cultural research' (The Royal Anthropological Institute's Film Festival Catalogue 1998), explores this theme visually. Braun presents footage from three video projects he developed in Ghana, narrated with his reflexive commentary to represent the relationships he formed with the subjects of his research and video making in each project. The first part of the video discusses a short video recording of a young girl who passed by Braun's rooftop vantage point during a street festival. When she noticed that he was filming her, the girl performed to the camera, delighted at his attention, until, realizing that his interest in her had passed, she appears angry and disappointed. In his commentary Braun discusses the intentionality of video maker and subject. Reflecting on the power relationships and related ethical issues that are implied by such uses of the camera, his text provokes questions about the right of the researcher to film under such circumstances.

In his next project Braun developed a collaborative relationship with his video subjects, this time members of a Ghanaian theatre company. He made a deal with the company to produce a series of commercial videos that they would sell in local villages. In return, they allowed him to travel with, and make his own documentary about, the group. This example demonstrates how the subjects of video may appropriate a video maker and his technology for their own ends. This entails a rather different power dynamic from that Braun experienced in his fleeting relationship with the young girl. Finally, Braun presents footage shot in the Ghanaian village in which he had lived as a child when his parents were missionary doctors. Here he negotiated his video making on yet another basis. His existing relationship with the local community enabled him to video freely and he shared his images by screening the footage for his subjects.

An appreciation of local television and video cultures, and people's interpretations of media narratives and how these inform their understandings of video images also support the use of video as a research method. I would not propose that media research *must* become a part of ethnographic work with video; each individual project will have its priorities and media may not be one of them. Nevertheless television is an important dimension of many local cultures and a growing area of ethnographic interest (see, for example, Hughes-Freeland 1997; Hughes-Freeland and Crain 1998; Pink 1997a). The recently developed 'media ethnography' represents an interdisciplinary approach linking the concerns of anthropology, cultural studies and media studies. Departing from 'audience studies' and 'reception studies', media ethnography proposes a reflexive ethnography of media reception that focuses on how 'audience creativity' intersects with 'media power' (see Morley 1996: 14). This promotes an ethnographic approach to media audiences that explores how people give meanings to media representations. In media studies this may entail participant observation with television, video or film audiences, focusing specifically on viewers' individual and cultural understandings of media representations. 'Media ethnography' can support ethnographic research with video by helping researchers to understand how their informants' interpretations of video cameras and 'ethnographic' video recordings are informed by meanings they invest in other media representations.

For example, a project by three visual anthropologists, Cerezo, Martinez and Ranera, demonstrates the importance of sensitivity to media narratives and the meanings that informants invest in visual representations of themselves. The researchers were working with African immigrant workers in Spain. Since they had used photography quite extensively in the project, to the pleasure of their informants, they found their informants' reactions to their introduction of the video camera surprising. Its presence displeased them and created moments of tension that were difficult to deal with (Cerezo et al. 1996: 142). Neither did the informants like the images of themselves in the video; while they admired its landscape scenes, they found themselves 'ugly' and 'poor' (1996: 143). The researchers situate these responses in relation to popular culture, pointing out that the immigrants, who work very long hours and have a low economic level, nevertheless return home every evening to watch television or videos. From the informants' viewpoint the video images of themselves on a television screen were images of poverty, they were permanently recorded images and could be seen by anyone (1996: 143). The informants' own gaze on the video images of themselves thus objected to the researchers' 'innocently' filmed video footage. This raised ethical issues that led Cerezo, Martinez and Ranera to argue that visual products like video should not be produced without their protagonists' permission. Their work emphasizes how important reflexivity can be in video research. The researchers' self-reflexivity and discussions with their informants about the video representations revealed how each of them had gazed differently on the video footage. By exploring this they learned both why the video images were problematic and how their informants interpreted images of themselves with reference to contemporary popular media culture.

To understand local interpretations of video representations is it is also useful to explore how video technology is made meaningful locally. This might involve examining the discourses through which video is discussed. For example, is it discussed in relation to notions of, or exhibitions of, wealth or of scientific innovation, in what categories do local people situate video, such as popular culture, art, domestic activity or leisure?

Ethnographer as video maker: examples from the field

Above I have demonstrated how a consideration of local visual or video cultures can inform the use of video as a research method. In some projects the relationship has been ethnographic video making and local culture has led researchers to abandon the camera. For example, Metzgar found that when he was attempting to make an ethnographic film on the island Lamotrek Atoll, he was faced with the dilemma of either being a filmmaker, and thus 'outside' local culture and spheres of meaning, or 'going native' and participating in local cultural activities. In his experience, there seemed to be no meeting point that the two cultures could negotiate through film:

> I was caught in a vicious cycle – in order to continue filming the culture, I had to maintain separateness; in maintaining separateness, I felt alienated and alone. As long as the film work had direction and meaning, I did not mind being considered a misfit in Lamotrekan society; but without the inner sense that the film was making progress, there was no choice but to give up the fight and join the dance. (Metzgar n.d.)

In other projects researchers have found that it is only sometimes appropriate to use the video camera. For example, Lomax and Casey include extracts from a field diary in their article about the use of video in a project about midwives and their clients. Sometimes they felt it was socially incorrect to video. This is demonstrated in their reflections on a situation in a participant's house where the 'social' element of the occasion led the researcher to decide not to video:

> . . . the apparent social inappropriateness of switching on my camera means that I am missing some really interesting data. For better or worse I decided to go with my 'gut instinct' and leave the camera in its case. My feelings that it was inappropriate to video at this juncture appear to be confirmed by the way in which the initiation of the 'midwifery' activity of the visit was organised . . . (Lomax and Casey 1998: 14)

In other cases it is necessary to prepare for video recording well in advance. From 1997–98 Alberto Martinez and I researched carnival in Canchungo, Guinea Bissau. The first stage of the project involved learning about local understandings and uses of video in everyday life and in carnival. During my first year of fieldwork, carnival fell only two weeks after my arrival. I had already begun to take photographs, but felt that it would be inappropriate to use video immediately. I did not know many people in the town and felt uncomfortable pointing a video camera at them, whereas with my stills camera I would be able to take portraits of the people I had met and photograph the school carnival. I also gained an insight into how video *was* used in carnival where several video cameras were present. One belonged to a Taiwanese development worker who stood on the pavement, video recording the events at a distance. A well-dressed Guinea Bissauan man, undoubtedly a migrant returned for his season 'at home', stood in the centre of the main boulevard with a camcorder on his shoulder. Video technology is not available locally to most Guinea Bissauans. It is not sold in local shops and has to be imported, usually from Europe. It is a commodity associated with the wealth of migrants or development workers and with economic power located outside Guinea Bissau.

Carnival in Canchungo is a time where people represent their 'translational imaginations and aspirations' (see Pink 2001). In this carnival, video technology became a metaphor for wealth. As the migrant stood in the boulevard in his smart European clothing, local people paraded by, many walking the carnival route dressed in local icons of migration and wealth, wearing suits and carrying suitcases, one youth held a cardboard camcorder on his shoulder. Stills photography dominated local image production in carnival. The local studio photographers were at work, both in and out of their studios, photographing people in their carnival disguises for their usual fee. Video and photography clearly fitted differently with the visual culture of carnival. Photography was part of the locally based carnival activity; it was within the financial scope of my informants and being photographed was part of their regular carnival practice. Therefore participating in carnival with a video camera would have entailed a rather different relationship to local visual culture. Moreover, showing informants the results of video recording, and offering them copies of the footage was more complicated.

The following year, Alberto, having then lived in Canchungo for 18 months used the Hi-8 domestic video camera during carnival. He enlisted the help of a Guinea Bissauan friend who stayed with him throughout the whole time he used the camera. He wanted to avoid the role of being a white person with a video camera simply standing at the roadside videoing local people at a distance, as we had witnessed development workers doing at past carnivals. However, he could not help being seen as a white development worker with a piece of expensive technology. His friend helped to reassure and negotiate with local people regarding the video recording. They promised several of those who appeared in the video that they would provide a copy that could be viewed in Canchungo at a later date. The Hi-8 tapes were posted to me in the United Kingdom where I made a VHS copy to post to Alberto in Guinea Bissau. His Guinea Bissauan neighbours had a video player and TV. For several evenings the living room was filled with people viewing the video, delighted to see themselves and their friends in carnival.

The local 'success' of his video helped Alberto and local people to develop further knowledge and ideas about video in local culture. For instance, one informant asked Alberto to video his father's annual funeral party so that he could send a copy to his brother, a migrant in Portugal. Another suggested that they take an interview tour of the neighbourhood. The ideas about the use of the video camera were thus becoming joint initiatives and negotiations that involved local and transnational social networks and transcultural collaboration, rather than being driven by the researcher/video maker's interest. Unfortunately, these projects could not be developed in Canchungo because in June 1998 an attempted military coup, followed by an armed conflict, broke out in Guinea Bissau. The video footage that I received in the United Kingdom also became appropriated for another visual culture. From the 30 minutes Alberto had sent, I edited a shorter 10-minute version of the carnival footage on to VHS to present with a conference paper (Pink 1998e). Here the footage was intended to give viewers a sense of the carnival disguises that people prepared and of the use of visual symbolism that I was discussing in my paper. In the visual culture of academia the footage had a different interest to a new audience.

In contrast, experience of video recording a public event in Northern Ireland was very different. In this case I was carrying a large JVC semi-professional camera and was accompanied by a sound recordist with a professional looking microphone. The video was part of an ethnographic project about migration from Belfast to London. We were to video record the unveiling ceremony of a statue of William of Orange, just outside Belfast, and were developing a commentary on this event through interviews with George, the key informant, a migrant from Belfast to London, and interviews that he was leading. Once we had requested permission to film, with our professional looking equipment we were ushered by the organizers into the enclosure reserved for television and film crews. Our presence with the camera developed various responses from people attending the event. One woman treated us as a source of public information, another interviewee gave well-considered responses to George's questions as if to a TV audience. In this case my collaboration with George involved negotiation over the planning and direction of the video. The other informants were in a sense also *his* informants. The ways we worked at the public event were also framed by our interviewees' and the organizers' interpretations of our activities, this being contingent on their own knowledge about video.

A final example of a reflexive approach to video in the production of ethnographic knowledge is demonstrated in Ferrándiz's video work with Venezuelan spirit cults (1996, 1998). Situating the role of video in his fieldwork in relation to the cult's existing relationship with, and experience of, media representation, Ferrándiz pays particular attention to the way the video recording developed through the intersubjectivity between himself and his informants. In some instances the video became a catalyst that helped create the context in which it was used, as in the case of a ceremony that was organized by his informants as part of the event of videoing it. However, of particular interest is that when Ferrándiz began shooting video, six months into his fieldwork, the informants with whom he was closely collaborating also took the camera to shoot footage themselves, each of them creating 'completely different visual itineraries of the same place' (Ferrándiz 1998: 27). Ferrándiz takes his analysis further than merely the question of how different people created different video narratives of the same context. He forms continuities between the video making and the ritual activities in which his informants were involved; the visual practices of video recording and the ritual practices coincided as people moved in and out of trance and in front of and behind the camera's viewfinder as the ceremony proceeded. In this research the video camera became part of the material culture of the ritual and its recording capacity an aspect of the ritual activity. Therefore Ferrándiz was able to learn about ritual practices through his use of video.

Knowledge that situates video technologies and representations locally can benefit ethnographic work and support collaborations with informants in a number of ways. This may include knowledge of local visual media and video culture, about local people's interpretations of video technology, reflexivity about the researcher's own role and informants' understandings of this.

Collaborative/participatory video

As I have noted above, ethnographic video production may become interwoven with local video cultures. In Chapter 2 I raised Engelbrecht's question: for whom do we make ethnographic films? Engelbrecht refers to documentaries that are edited and screened to anthropological and other audiences. But the question also applies to research footage: for whom do we shoot this footage when we collaborate with individuals and groups who also have an interest in the footage? Such collaboration results in ethnographers working with informants and participating in 'their' video culture, as well referring to other video cultures (for instance, video conventions in ethnographers' personal lives as well as in their academic discipline). Here I discuss two collaborative video projects that have produced research footage that was guided by the intentionalities of both researchers and informants, and also responded to the demands of academic and informants' video cultures. Both projects take a feminist approach to collaborative video.

Barnes, Taylor-Brown and Weiner (1997) describe a project to produce video-tapes in which mothers with HIV recorded messages that would be viewed by their children after the mothers' deaths. The researchers' intention was to use 'the concept of "eternal mothering"' to provide 'a framework to study the interactive aspects of mothering and the significance of impending maternal death from a stigmatising illness' (1997: 7). They collaborated with each mother to produce a video document that she felt would represent her appropriately to her children once she was dead. Barnes, Taylor-Brown and Weiner follow Chaplin (1994) in attempting 'to replace the sociology *of* a topic with a sociology that emphasises less distance between verbal analysis and visual representation as data' (Barnes et al. 1997: 10), thus reducing the distance between the researcher and the subject. Conscious of the positivist tradition that has informed their discipline Barnes, Taylor-Brown and Weiner weigh up the 'experimental' restraints of their project, concluding that it offers limited opportunity for triangulation and noting how the presence of the camera and researcher may have affected the 'reality' recorded. However they argue that these limits are outweighed by the quality of the self-representation and narrative created by the mothers as 'the method offers the spontaneity and vividness of an uninterrupted stream of information from the individual, as the mother is allowed to talk without researcher intrusion in the form of questions' (Barnes et al. 1997: 13). The project departs from a scientific experimental stance by applying the feminist approach advocated by Chaplin (1994), whereby the knowledge is produced not about, but for women and the women themselves are situated 'at the centre of the production of knowledge' (Barnes et al. 1997: 13). They write, 'We acknowledge that there is no one single interpretation of social action that can claim to be definitive', and follow Chaplin's point that such representations do not convey singular meanings, but that '[i]n post-positivist and feminist philosophy the study offers a range of suggestions and an opportunity to construct a constellation of meanings about mothering' (1997: 14). They realize that they are dealing with:

> What mothers, within the contexts of their social worlds, select to represent of themselves to their children in permanent, structured, visual form, is interrelated to their attitudes about how mothers care for and protect their children, how their impending death from AIDS influenced their mothering and how stigmatisation from AIDS may be transferred from them to their children . . . their self-presentation. (1997: 21)

They see this video-tape as an empowering visual medium: it 'offers women, minorities, HIV infected people, and other marginalised groups, an opportunity to reproduce and understand their world as opposed to the dominant representation depicted in the mass media' (1997: 27). Here the collaborative video research was situated in a particular cultural use of video that the mothers found appropriate to develop. Through it the researchers assisted the mothers in producing cultural documents that allowed them to develop simultaneously a sociological understanding of self-representation and experiences of mothering.

In Chapter 1 I noted how, in her work with a youth and community dance group in south-east London, Thomas developed a feminist approach and reflexive research process using video to record rehearsals, performances and a group interview. This example demonstrates how in certain cultural contexts video technology can become an important element in the social relations and intersubjectivity through which knowledge is produced. During the research process Thomas participated with the dancers by video recording the rehearsals and performances and offering the dancers a means of viewing the videos. In the group interview her participatory approach was developed differently by her moving to the other side of the camera:

> The concern to maintain an interactive approach in the research that would enable the dancers' voices to be heard in the discourse . . . led to the proposal that I should take part in a videoed group interview with the dancers at the first viewing of the video, and thus the researcher would also be put into the 'actual' research frame under the gaze of the camera. (Thomas 1997: 146)

In the group interview Thomas used the camera not solely as a recording tool, but as a device that informed how power relations were structured within the group and in particular between her and the group members. She used the camera as a democratizing technology, breaking down one dimension of the research/researched distinction by 'observing' the researcher along with her informants.

The potential of video as a recording method

The approach I have advocated is critical of the realist stance and of methods texts that limit the potential of video to recording focus group discussions and interviews to avoid 'losing' important visual data and cues. Video is undoubtedly good for such visual 'note-taking', but such uses ought to be qualified with a rejection of the naive assumption that video records an untainted reality in favour of a reflexive approach that accounts for how video can become part of a focus group discussion or interview. This, combined with knowledge about the video or media culture of interviewees or focus group participants, should help the researcher to decide if video would be appropriate for that particular group, and how video could successfully be used in that specific research scenario. For example, Lomax and Casey used a video camera to record midwife–client interactions. They rightly acknowledge that 'the research is not marred by the necessary involvement of the researcher, but conversely, she is a contributor to the constitution of the interaction' (Lomax and Casey 1998: 26). While their use of the tape is realist, they also use it as a device for reflexivity, noting that 'the involvement of the researcher in the interaction can be analysed and understood from the video text. The analysis, in turn, is informative about "normal" consultations; i.e. how midwives organise an overall structure of the visit' (1998: 26).

Video can serve as ethnographic diary-keeping, note-taking (including surveys of the physical environment, housing, etc.) or of recording certain processes and activities. However, such video materials should be treated as *representations* rather than visual facts and their analysis should take note of the collaborations and strategies of self-representation that were part of their making.

Getting started

There is never any single 'right moment' to start using a video camera. In some cases video recording may become an element of a researcher's relationship with informants right from the first meeting. For example, in Guinea Bissau, Tomas was contracted to weave traditional cloth and allow me to video record and photograph him at work. This agreement was part of the verbal contract made with Tomas at the beginning of our acquaintance (how my use of video developed in relation to and beyond the terms of this contract is discussed in detail in Pink 1999b). In this case, video images and technology were an integral aspect of the relationship between researcher and informant. In other projects, however, uses of video are negotiated on different terms. It may even be several months before the ethnographer considers it the 'right moment' to introduce video. Ferrándiz did not begin to use video in his research in Venezuela until he was already six months into the fieldwork, and then, as he notes, the 'most complex visual project had to wait a couple of months more' (1998: 26).

Similarly, video work with different informants may start at different times in a project as relationships between ethnographers, technology, images and different individuals develop at different paces and in different ways. For example, when I was shooting my masters degree project (*Home from Home*) in Northern Ireland, the grandmother of George, my key informant, was keen to be video recorded talking with George in a conversational interview. However, initially, his mother did not want to participate. As the project proceeded, we continued to video record interviews with various members of the family – an outing that George made with his nieces and some local public ritual events. Every evening we returned to George's parents' home where we were staying and viewed the SVHS footage through their video recorder and television. Although the SVHS images were not perfectly projected through the VHS recorder, we could see and hear enough to know we had the footage we wanted. George's mother also became interested, keen to see her grandchildren and other family members on video. As her interest and confidence in the video making increased, she volunteered to be interviewed.

Getting started is not solely a matter of finding the right moment but also involves technical procedures. This varies according to the equipment used but includes getting the camera out and setting it up, organizing sound recording and lighting. These procedures become bound up in the research process. For example, in their sociological research on midwife–client interaction, Lomax and Casey found that actually starting the video-taping 'became, in our research, a matter of some complexity and analytic interest' because 'even with specific arrangements, it is not possible to enter a person's home and set up camera without becoming interactionally involved' (Lomax and Casey 1998: 7). Similarly, when I interview people with video in their homes, I often collaborate with my interviewees to arrange that lights are strategically placed and switched on as we move around video recording. Here the technical demands of video recording become a collaborative issue as both the interviewees and interviewer seek extra sources of indoor lighting.

Viewing footage with informants: interviewing with/talking around video

Showing video footage to informants can also become part of a research project. The extent to which this method is formalized varies from project to project. In the examples discussed below this ranges from a formal video-recorded interview, during which the informant viewed and commented on video footage of an event in which he had participated, to much more casual screenings in which informants have become involved out of personal interest rather than by request. Whatever the context, the purpose of this method should not be simply to use video images to elicit responses from informants or to extract information *about* the images. Rather, viewing video with informants should also be seen as something of a 'media ethnography'. This combines ethnographers actively discussing video images with informants while also attempting to understand how informants situate themselves as viewers of the footage, therefore engaging with questions such as: How do informants' commentaries on video footage relate it to other aspects of their video/media culture? And what discourses do they refer to in their comments and discussions of the footage?

While studying at the Granada Centre at the University of Manchester, I collaborated with a fellow MA student to make a video about a Jewish family Passover meal. After shooting footage of the family meal, we asked our key informant to view and comment on this footage in the context of an interview that was also video recorded. This interview was held in his living room, where he sat by the video player, with a purposefully arranged array of family photographs and icons in the background behind his head. On viewing the 'ethnographic video' of the meal, our informant began to reflect on a range of related topics that were of ethnographic interest and served to contextualize the participants and the ceremony in religious, historical and kinship terms.

During my fieldwork in Guinea Bissau a different way of viewing video developed. Alberto and I often spent the evenings with Tomas and his son, Antoine. Once the electricity supply was switched on at around 8 pm we often took it in turns to look through the camera's viewfinder to see the video footage I had shot. Alberto also lent Tomas his headphones so he could hear the video's synchronous sound. Unfortunately we never had a monitor on which we could view the video together, nevertheless these regular viewing sessions played an important part in the research. Tomas, like most people in the town, was used to watching television. Guinea Bissau has its own national state television and those local people who own a television usually make it available to their neighbours by putting it on their veranda facing out into the street, or allowing people into their homes. However, Tomas had never viewed video in this way before. As with some photographs we had shown him previously (see Chapter 3), it took some time before he recognized himself and his son in the viewfinder. In this project it was not so much Tomas's commentaries on the video, for he made few, but his enjoyment and enthusiasm about this aspect of the project that was important. His participation by viewing the footage gave him a new understanding of what I was doing with the camera and encouraged him to collaborate in the video process because he was interested in viewing it later himself.

In other instances interviewing or talking with video can become incidental to the project. When I was shooting the Belfast-based part of *Home from Home*, George and I viewed the footage in his family's living room most evenings. Other family members also became keen to view and comment on these screenings of interviews and activities in which George and relatives were involved. I was able to learn more generally from their comments on the themes we were exploring in the video, part of which was concerned with why George had left to live in the United Kingdom, and their views on this.

Editing, distributing and viewing video footage with his informants was also an aspect of Ferrándiz's project in Venezuela (described above). Ferrándiz produced a tape when his informants asked to see copies of the video. He edited the footage to include expressive imagery by using slow motion to represent some trance sequences. The video was widely viewed and well received in the shanty town where

Figure 4.1 Tomas and his son Antoine viewing the video footage I had recorded of them though the viewfinder of the video camera, and listening to the sound through headphones borrowed from a personal hi-fi.

Ferrándiz was working. The slow motion sections were to the satisfaction of his informants: 'it is important to stress the success of the use of slow motion, which seemed to embody with more accuracy the emotionality and fuzziness of the temporality experienced during the ceremonies, somewhere in the scales of trance, as opposed to the times where real time was used' (Ferrándiz 1998: 30). Viewing the video produced with informants can help researchers to work out what are and are not appropriate representations of individuals, their culture and experiences.

In some cases informants' responses to video can be surprising and may even change the direction of the research (see Chapter 2). Hoskins describes how her research developed in tandem with her use of video in a project originally intended to be a study of ritual communication in the Indonesian island of Sumba. Hoskins screened video footage of past ritual events to the villagers who had participated in these activities. Treating the footage as a 'visual record' of the rituals, she proposed to ask her informants specific questions about their activities. Their answers were to be used as data for her wider project that aimed to resolve 'cognitive problems concerning the sociology of knowledge and this distribution outside an inner circle of specialists' (Hoskins 1993: 81). However, once she began to screen the video footage to her Sumbanese audience, she was struck by 'the feelings of discomfort, shock and sorrow' they expressed. Her research changed direction 'to explore issues relating to the filmic distribution of time' and 'the emotional responses to images of dead persons' (1993: 78). Situating her analysis of the responses to the film in terms of her knowledge of Sumbanese culture, Hoskins began to develop research about 'cultural perceptions of time' (1993: 80). Her video images of people who were now dead had accidentally disrupted the temporal and emotional process of mourning the dead that was so important to her informants.

Ethnographic uses of digital video

Technological innovations usually create or inspire new possibilities. Above I have noted how using digital cameras may change ethnographers' perspectives on what is being filmed. Digital technology may also have implications for how video is used in research and representation and in creating continuities between these stages.

Fischer and Zeitlyn have designed a digital video research project that has a brief similar to Hoskins's (see above) original research aims. Entitled 'Mambila Nggwun – the construction and deployment of multiple meanings in ritual', their research intends to use digitized video recordings of ritual to 'produce specific models of how collective representations of a specific socio-cultural ritual event are structured and distributed between participants and observers, and how these are accessed and used by people to solve problems in the present' (http://www.lucy.ukc.ac.uk/dz/Nggwun/nggwun_1.html). In order 'to capture the many perspectives that contribute to the [ritual] event' the researchers use video in two ways: first, in existing fieldwork they have 'videoed segments of the event from as many points of view as possible, filming under the advisement [sic] of indigenous consultants'; secondly, they propose to 'select segments of this video . . . under the advisement [sic] of indigenous consultants, to prepare computer-based multimedia documents as an elicitation device for a range on participants and observers' (Fischer and Zeitlyn n.d.). Fischer and Zeitlyn's collaborative use of digital technology allows this project to stand out from most existing ethnographic research with video. This opens up new possibilities for the representation, organization and analysis of visual materials with the collaboration of informants in the field, as well as for the post-fieldwork organization and interpretation of materials (see Chapter 5).

Summary

In this chapter I have suggested a reflexive approach to video in ethnographic research. This considers the relationship between the researcher and the subject of ethnographic video, the technologies used, and local and academic visual cultures. Recently, uses of video in ethnographic research have developed in tandem with new technologies, innovations and theoretical perspectives. Shifts from a realist approach to video as 'objective' reality to the idea of video as representation shaped by specific standpoints of its producers and viewers have encouraged the development of collaborative approaches to the production and inter-pretation of video images. The introduction of digital video and computer-based techniques seems particularly appropriate for the application of these methods and is likely to form the basis of future development in video research.

CHAPTER 5

Classifying and Interpreting Photographic and Video Materials

The ambiguity of visual images and the subjectivity of their viewers have been central concerns of Chapters 1–4. In this chapter I take a similar approach to academic interpretation, analysis and categorization of ethnographic photography and video. The academic meanings that ethnographers give to visual images are also arbitrary and are constructed in relation to particular methodological and theoretical agendas. Individual researchers classify and give meanings to ethnographic images in relation to the academic culture or discipline with which they identify their work. Moreover, ethnographers are themselves subjective readers of ethnographic images and their personal experiences and aspirations also inform the meanings they invest in photographs and video. A reflexive approach to classifying, analysing and interpreting visual research materials recognizes both the constructedness of social science categories and the politics of researchers' personal and academic agendas.

There are points in most research projects when ethnographers need either to use an existing method of organizing, categorizing and interpreting the visual materials they have accumulated, or to invent their own. While a good number of visual sociologists and anthropologists have clearly developed ways of ordering and analysing photographs and video from their fieldwork, little has been written on the storage and analysis of qualitative visual research materials. This may be because when photographs and video are used to represent ethnographic knowledge, the 'behind the scenes' stage of analysis through which 'visual data' would be 'translated' into verbal knowledge becomes redundant.

Analysis: a stage or a practice

In some ethnographic research projects the distinction between 'fieldwork' and 'analysis' appears clearly defined. In 'traditional' ethnographic narratives this is usually achieved either spatially or temporally as researchers return from a fieldwork location to the place where analysis will take place, or when project schedules dictate that the fieldwork period is over and analysis and writing up must begin. However, as most texts on research methods emphasize, analysis actually continues throughout the whole process of ethnographic research (see Burgess 1984: 166; Hammersley and Atkinson 1995: 205). As Fetterman writes for word-based ethnography: 'It begins from the moment a fieldworker selects a problem to study and ends with the last word in the report or the ethnography' (Fetterman 1998: 92). Recently, ethnographers have begun to account for the constructedness of distinctions between 'field', 'home' and academic institution, arguing that interdependencies and continuities, as well as differences between these different times and location, be recognized (see Chapter 1). Sometimes ethnographers do research 'at home' or 'write up' their work while still in 'the field' (see Amit-Talai 1999). A strictly conventional fieldwork narrative whereby researchers go to the 'field', get the images and then take them 'home' to analyse them is not always appropriate or available. Research and analysis may be conducted in the same or different locations or time-periods and researchers may develop insights into the relationship between research experiences, theoretical concepts or comparative examples at any point in the process of 'doing ethnography'. Given the multiplicity of forms the relationship between research and analysis may take, researchers should be aware of how these two elements interlink in any single project. For visual research this means scrutinizing the relationship between meanings given to photographs and video during fieldwork, and academic meanings later invested in the same images.

Like other items of material culture, visual images have their own biographies (see Appadurai 1986). When they move from one context to another they are, in a sense, 'transformed'; although their content remains unaltered, in the new context 'the conditions in which they are viewed are different' (Morphy and Banks 1997: 16). This also applies to the biographies of images that travel through the research process. Photographs and video images are interpreted in different ways and by different individuals at different points in ethnographic research, analysis and representation. Images first produced, discussed and made meaningful during fieldwork will be given new significance in academic culture where they are 'separated from the world of action in which they were meaningful and placed in a world in which they will be interrogated and interpreted from a multiplicity of different perspectives' (Morphy and Banks 1997: 16). Analysis is not a simple matter of interpreting the visual content of photographs and video, but involves examining how different producers and viewers of images give subjective meanings to their content and form.

I intend to outline an approach, rather than describe a method for visual analysis, therefore the principles discussed in the first sections of this chapter refer to ethnographic video and photographs. However, the two media do offer different possibilities for ethnographic analysis. These are discussed in the final sections.

Images and words: the end of hierarchies

The modern project of ethnography has largely been 'to translate the visual into words' (C. Wright 1998: 20). This approach, which formed the basis of 'scientific' approaches to visual research, assumes that while ethnographic information may be recorded visually, ethnographic knowledge is produced through the translation and abstraction of this 'data' into written text. For example, Collier and Collier see 'analysis' as a distinct stage of research at which the visual is decoded into the verbal through a process analogous to the translation of art to science or subjectivity to objectivity. This 'involves abstraction of the visual evidence so we can intellectually define what we have recorded and what the visual evidence reveals' (Collier and Collier, 1986: 169–70). Through this procedure, they assert that images may become 'the basis for *systematic knowledge*' (original italics). However images can only ever be 'primary evidence' that has an 'independent authority' and 'authenticity', but that 'may often have no place in the final product of the research, except as occasional illustrations' (1986: 170).

Here I outline a different approach that begins with the premise that the purpose of analysis is not to translate 'visual evidence' into verbal knowledge, but to explore the relationship between visual and other (including verbal) knowledge. This subsequently opens a space for visual images in ethnographic representation (see Chapters 6–8). In practice, this implies an analytical process of making meaningful links between different research experiences and materials such as photography, video, field diaries, more formal ethnographic writing, local written or visual texts, visual and other objects. These different media represent different types of knowledge that may be understood in relation to one another. For example, when I analysed my visual and written materials from fieldwork in Guinea Bissau, I found that different types of written and visual knowledge about particular themes of the research was represented in my field diaries, notes, video recording and photography. During fieldwork I used each of these media to represent the 'story' of the research in different ways and each medium evoked different elements of my fieldwork experience. Therefore the photographs did not simply 'illustrate' the field notes, and the video was not simply 'evidence' of conversation, interviews or actions. Rather, images and words contextualized each other, forming not a 'complete' record of the research but a set of different representations and strands of it. Working with visual and verbal fieldwork materials in this way does not constitute a new method. Some anthropologists have developed reflexive texts that interrogate the process by which the knowledge represented in written or visual work was produced (see Chapters 6–8). For example, in Biella's electronic text *Masaai Interactive* (n.d.) fieldwork and interpretive processes are made explicit through a series of layered notes that show how Biella's work with the fieldwork materials developed (see Chapter 8) (see Biella 1997). However, normally these reflexive texts concentrate on how knowledge was produced intersubjectively during fieldwork, between individuals, images and objects. They pay less attention to questions of analysis and the intersubjectivity of researchers, research materials and academic discourses and texts.

The idea that subjective experience can be translated into objective knowledge is itself problematic for reflexive ethnography. Therefore an 'analysis' through which visual data becomes written academic knowledge has little relevance. Instead, ethnographers need to articulate the experiences and contexts from which their field notes, video recordings, photographs and other materials were produced, their sociological or anthropological understanding of these ethnographic contexts, and their relevance to wider academic debates.

Analysing images: content and context

The relationship between the context in which images are produced and their visual content is important for any analysis of ethnographic photography or video. However, different theoretical and methodological approaches view this relationship quite differently. Here I briefly contrast two approaches. The scientific-realist approach seeks to regulate the context in which images are produced in order that their content should comprise 'reliable' visual evidence of 'complete' contexts and processes. In contrast, a reflexive approach argues that it is impossible to record 'complete' processes, activities or sets of relationships visually, and demands that attention be paid to the contexts in which images are produced.

Realist approaches to images in ethnography assumed the object of analysis would be the image itself or its content. The context of image production was thought to be important in two ways. First, contextualizing information provided knowledge about the activities, individuals and objects represented in the images' content. Secondly, by regulating contexts in which images were produced, the 'representativeness' of their content could be ensured. These procedures were thought to create the conditions for a reliable analysis because, as Collier and Collier insist, '[t]he significance of what we find in analysis is shaped by the context established by systematic recording during fieldwork'. This approach demands that, in order to be 'responsibly' analysed, 'visual evidence' must be 'contextually complete and sequentially organised' (Collier and Collier 1986: 163). This approach has two fundamental problems. First, its assumption that the context may be completed (and closed). Secondly, the idea that the sequence determined by series of photographs or video produced by the ethnographer represents *the* relevant narrative of events or *the* key set of actors.

An examination of how the realist approach has been applied to visually recording technology demonstrates its strengths and limitations. Collier and Collier's approach to visual documentation of technology was based on the idea that 'when we record all the relationships of a technology we have, in many circumstances, recorded one whole view of a culture' (1986: 65). Their case study discusses an Andean Otavalo weaver. Through photographing the weaver and discussing the quality and content of the photographs with him, they were able to record the Otavalo weaving process. He became their guide, helping them to document photographically the work and technology of other weavers. They describe the work as 'an acted out interview stimulated by the feedback of photographs' arguing that 'if the subjects of a study have the initiative of organising and informally directing the fieldworker's observation, the result can be a very complete and authentic record' (1986: 73–4). This method clearly allowed the researchers to develop a close collaboration with their informant and thorough ethnographic knowledge about Otavalo culture and weaving. They produced a series of images that were informed by and represented local knowledge about weaving. The case study presents a good example of collaboration in action. My criticism is of their claim that this technique allows ethno-graphers to 'record one whole view of a culture'. In Chapter 1 I introduced Clifford's (1986) argument that ethnographic 'truths' are only ever 'partial' and incomplete. Collier and Collier's method actually consists in isolating the key elements of a process; they suggest that '[a] process must be photographed so exact steps can be isolated. It is by this systematic observation that a technology can be conceived functionally' (Collier and Collier's 1986: 69). One could argue that a series of photo-graphs that record a process represent only one standpoint on weaving technology and, moreover, in isolating this technological process, decontextualize it from other important elements of weaving. In short, rather than being 'complete' the visual record is inevitably 'partial'.

In Chapters 3 and 4 I described a video and photographic project about a Guinea Bissauan weaver, Tomas. Here it became clear that rather than simply being a standard process, weaving was bound up with diverse social relationships and plural visions of reality. In our case the relationships with which weaving was intertwined were characterized by relations of colour and race, kinship, ethnicity and other aspects of status in our neighbourhood. Through these relationships certain elements of the technology were modified and the actual sequence of the weaving process developed in relation to a set of negotiations between individuals. For example, because of disputes over the design of the cloth, there was some 'back-tracking' and new stages that would not otherwise have been included were introduced. While weaving may be referred to as a technological process, it also entails other elements and to single out the visible observable reality of a technological narrative would explain very little about how the cloth was woven. In fact the narratives of technological processes may be redefined in each context in which they are played out. Tomas applied a known order to a process by which he wove the cloth. However, there was scope for reorganization and modification of the actual sequence and techniques he used. In fact the process he used was only ever defined and completed in practice. To isolate the stages of a generalized version of a technological process can provide an abstract or ideal model of that process. However, this cannot be a 'complete' or 'authentic' record. Rather, it is a representation of weaving, and is inevitably 'partial'. Even if the context of visually recording such a process is regulated, the content and chronology of the images will not necessarily represent a reliable, 'complete' and truthful account. Therefore analysis of their visual content would not be an objective analysis of a truthful visual record, but one (academic) gaze interpreting a subjective (even if collaborative) visual narrative.

'Scientific' approaches to social research, informed (like 'realist' approaches to documentary photography) by a notion of visual truth, tend to categorize and interpret images in terms of their content and chronology. The contrasting approach I outline below assumes, first, that as it is impossible to photograph or video an objective and 'true' visual record of any process, event or activity; analysis will never be of a complete authentic record. Secondly, rather than being a place for *controlling* visual content, the context of image production should be analysed reflexively to examine how visual content is informed by the subjectivities and intentions of the individuals involved (see Chapters 3 and 4). Thirdly, analysis should focus not only on the content of images, but on the meanings that different individuals give to those images in different contexts.

Between the 'field' and 'home': local and ethnographic meanings

Ethnographers usually re-think the meanings of photographic and video materials discussed and/or produced during fieldwork in terms of academic discourses. They therefore give them new significance that diverges from the meanings invested in them by informants, and from meanings assumed by ethnographers themselves at other stages of the project.

For example, in 1994 I returned to the United Kingdom after two years fieldwork in Spain, and in 1997 after eight months in West Africa. Each time I brought with me photographs I had taken, printed and discussed with informants, and video footage I was yet to view on a colour monitor. These visual representations were as important as my field diaries and other bits and pieces of local material culture that I had packed in

my suitcases. Yet they also bore their own specific relationship to the
fieldwork context. Unlike the field diaries, their visual content had been
(or was yet to be) shared and discussed with my informants in Guinea
Bissau. Now extracted from their Spanish and Guinea Bissauan contexts,
these images, memories, experiences and artifacts had already become
re-situated within my personal narrative, as well as having moved to a
new physical location where they would inevitably be made meaningful
in relation to new objects, gazes and commentaries. They had been
extracted from the cultural context where they were produced, to be
viewed and discussed in the context of my personal life and the
academic world in the United Kingdom. Meanwhile, in Spain and
Guinea Bissau copies of some of these very photographs and video-tapes
remained in the collections of my informants and friends. In Guinea
Bissau I left photographic portraits and edited video clips of carnival and
weaving, and in Spain I distributed many copies of photographic prints
among my informants (see Chapters 3 and 4). In these contexts these still
and moving images no doubt continue to be invested with different
meanings, taking on a life that departs from the context in which I was
present. Maybe they were used to talk about me and how I had
photographed or video recorded them, to discuss the event during which
the image had been taken, or as realist representations of their subjects.

However, while the images I had taken home were given new
academic and other meanings in new UK contexts, these meanings did
not replace the others previously invested in them during fieldwork.
Rather, the images can be thought of as icons in which a range of
different meanings may be invested. As such they are used to represent
or refer to diverse persons, activities and emotions that may not
obviously or directly form part of the visible content of the image.
Indeed, social scientists often complain that photographs alone do not
represent, for example, emotions, social relations, relations of power and
exploitation, but need to be contextualized with verbal discourse or other
knowledge in order to invoke such experiences. To analyse images, then,
it is more useful to examine how people's uses and definitions of the
visible content and form of photographs or video sequences attach them
to particular ideologies, worldviews, histories and identities.

In Chapters 3 and 4 I discussed how informants may talk with or
around photographs and video. For example, in her Waucoma photographic interviews (see Chapter 3), Schwartz sought to make her
photographs sociologically meaningful by exploring the meanings local
people invested in them. Here the sociological significance of the
photographs was not that they documented a particular social 'fact', or
that their content comprised 'ethnographic information'. Rather, the
differences in Schwartz's informants' responses 'offered evidence of the
negotiability of photographic meanings, undermining the pictures'
authority as "truth"' (Schwartz 1992: 15). This led her to interpret the
photographs as images that were used to say a variety of different things

and as keys to understanding diversity within local culture. Through this collaborative process Schwartz's informants taught her 'how to interpret images of their lives' (1992: 15). Schwartz's sociological interpretation was thus rooted in the research process – it regarded the images as subjectively and plurally defined, rather than having one single 'ethnographic' meaning or status.

Similarly, in Spain the 'anthropological' meanings I gave my photographs were informed by meanings that informants gave to these images. For example, one photograph, 'The Bullfighter's Braid', became a focus of attention during the research. The photograph was published in a local newspaper and won a regional photography prize. Several informants and bullfighting clubs asked for copies. This gave me the opportunity to discuss the photograph and its content with a range of different people who I found fitted it into different narratives. Some discussed it in terms of art and its artistic value. One informant commented on its 'natural', unconstructed and 'authentic' appearance. Others used it to publicize a forthcoming event. Through my exploration of the different local meanings the photograph was given, I began to invest my own anthropological meanings in it. When I interpreted the photograph in relation to the conventions of the photographic culture of bullfighting I saw it as an ambiguous image that both imitated and challenged the gendered iconography of 'traditional' bullfight photography. While it copied a standard composition in bullfight photography, the conventional symbolism was broken as the bullfighter's hair braid was long, blonde and feminine, rather than the short thin coiled braid of the male performer (see Pink 1997b). When I analysed this ambiguous symbolism together with people's comments on the photography, I linked this to gender theory. Building on different 'local' meanings given to the photograph I added meanings derived, first, from my understanding of local oral and visual discourses on 'tradition' and, secondly, from anthropological theories of gender. For me, 'The Bullfighter's Braid' is laden with local and academic meanings; the photograph itself represents the point at which these different meanings intersect, thus linking the contexts of research and analysis.

Images we can't 'take home'

Analysing ethnographic images does not only imply images ethnographers take themselves and then take home. In Chapter 3 I described Okely's research with elderly people (see Okely 1994). During these interviews Okely's informants showed her their photographs and these images formed part of Okely's experience of their memories and histories. The photographs Okely describes comprise part of her ethnographic knowledge and are indispensable to her discussion and analysis. However, Okely does not mention having the photographs copied or

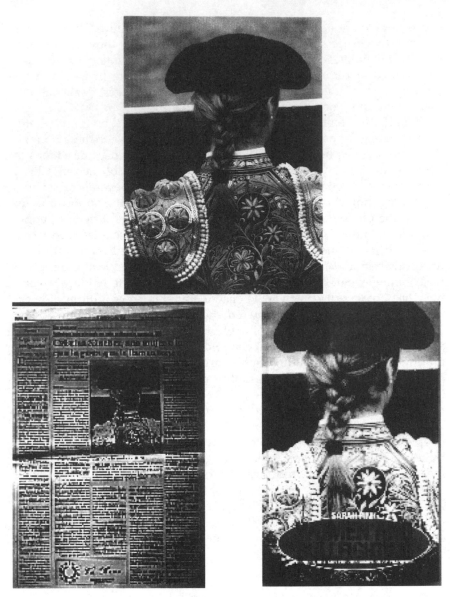

Figure 5.1 This photograph of Cristina Sanchez, entitled 'The Bullfighter's Braid',
became central to my research. During the research it was exhibited on local
television, formed part of the collections of local bars, as well as of local people who
had asked for copies. It was also published in a local newspaper (Pink 1993). Once
I returned to the United Kingdom it was exhibited in an ethnographic photography
exhibition, published in book chapters and journal articles and was used for the front
cover of my book (Pink 1997a). Not only was the image published in different places,
but also it was defined in different ways and given new meanings as it travelled
between these different contexts.

taking them away for analysis. Similarly, Riches and Dawson (1998) could not copy the images of dead children that the bereaved parents showed them. Nevertheless, these absent images were the topic of their article and informed their understanding of the how bereaved parents represented their identities and experiences. Such images, materially absent from our field notes, still form an important part of the analysis of ethnographic knowledge.

For example, when I researched carnival in Guinea Bissau informants frequently showed me their photograph collections. I did not ask for copies of their carnival photographs, but was careful to note their composition and content, how they had been presented to me and the conversations in which they were embedded. In Spain I researched the career of Antoñita, a woman ex-bullfighter (see Pink 1997a). Similarly, Antoñita showed me her collection of snapshots that documented moments of development and success in her short career and she lent me a video of her performances that I viewed with a group of her friends. It did not feel appropriate to ask for copies of the prints and tapes. However, these images and her uses of them to criticize her perform-ances and reminisce about old acquaintances and events were central to my analysis of her career and how she represented herself in relation to other individuals, institutions and activities in the local 'bullfighting world'. I also took notes on the event of viewing the video and how Antoñita's friends had used it to discuss her performance, skills and career. My analysis was not only of the visual content of video text, but also of how my informants used it to speak about the woman bullfighter.

In these projects the visual content of Guinea Bissauans' carnival photographs and Spanish bullfighting video were relevant to my analysis. However, it was less important to copy these images to 'take home' and subject them to a systematic analysis than it was to analyse how they were used to represent and discuss the themes of my research. It is not only images that cannot be removed from some research locales. The field notes, diaries and images that do accompany researchers 'home' should always be understood in connection with those represen-tations and experiences that it is impossible to transfer spatially or temporally in any tangible form.

Organizing images: the issue of the archive

Just as research methods are usually shaped by the project they serve and are frequently developed 'in the field', categorizing research materials is often a task that researchers develop for themselves in connection with their particular research materials. While there is no set method for organizing ethnographic images, the systems researchers develop for categorizing images should be informed by appropriate theoretical and ethical principles. Here I outline the implications of ethnographic archives and classification systems and argue for a reflexive approach to this aspect of ethnographic work.

Archives and visual classification systems have been characterized as objectifying systems, imposed on the weak by the powerful. The political agendas that informed the classificatory work of visual anthropologists and sociologists in the 1970s and 1980s doubtlessly differed from those of colonialism and state order (see also Chapter 3). Nevertheless, both modern social science and the institutions of modern states have participated in a 'project' that has used photography to 'map humankind', 'to define humankind, as individuals, as types or genres of humankind, and as a species' (Lury 1998: 41). This realist approach to photography catalogued and defined visual records according to their content. A critique of this practice and the power relations that it entailed highlights some problems associated with the concept of the archive. Sekula's (1989) critique of Victorian photographic archives highlights the repressive potential of portrait photography. Sekula discusses how photographs were used to record systematically the characteristics of criminals' faces, arguing that 'photography came to establish and delimit the terrain of the *other*, to define both the *generalized look* – the typology – and the *contingent instance* of deviance and social pathology' (Sekula 1989: 345, original italics). Anthropologists have similarly taken issue with repressive uses of photography during the colonial period. Edwards (1992) discusses the importance of situating colonial photographs of people from 'other' cultures in relation to the ideologies and intentions of their producers. She points out that '[t]he power relations of the colonial situation were not only those of overt oppression, but also of insidious, unequal relationships which permeated all aspects of cultural confrontation' (Edwards 1992: 4). Thus regarding colonial photography as symbolic of this power relationship that was 'sustained through a controlling knowledge which appropriated the "reality" of other cultures into ordered structure' (1992: 6).

This realist approach to cataloguing and ordering images of individuals from 'other cultures' was a means of objectifying and categorizing 'the other', an exercise that implied hierarchy and the oppression that was part and parcel of colonialism. The critique of colonial photography illustrates not only the repressive potential of image archives, but also the difference between scientific-realist and reflexive approaches to photography. The colonial system categorized images according to their content and validated their authenticity in terms of the context in which they were produced (for example, this sometimes involved using a grid-type background against which physical characteristics could be measured). The critical analysis of colonial photographs lends them new meaning by reconstructing the social relations and intentions through which they were produced and therefore transforming their symbolic potential. Previously, colonial photographs were seen as scientific evidence of cultural difference and hierarchy; a critical analysis re-situates them as symbols of a 'controlling knowledge', domination and inequality (see Edwards 1992).

By revealing this agenda, the critical approach disempowers the archive as a controlling mechanism. Moreover, by redefining its contents as individual images with situated meanings (rather than a body of scientific evidence) it challenges the idea of the archive as a coherent 'whole' and suggests that the connections between images are constructed rather than 'given' or 'natural'. As I argue below, connections constructed between and among photographs and other visual and verbal materials are key to the production of academic meanings. Archives are important in the disciplines that use ethnography and should continue to have a role. Not all archives are 'oppressive', for example, appropriate ethnographic photography and film archives exist in European and US institutions (such as, the ethnographic film archive at the Institut für den Wissenschaftlichen Film (IWF), Goettingen, and the Royal Anthropological Institute's photographic archive), forming valuable resources for researchers. However, ethnographers should take a responsible and ethical approach to the potential of archives to create knowledge. As curators, they should not underestimate the power of archives to 'play an important function in the creation of knowledge' (Price and Wells 1997: 36). This is just as important in the organization of images from individual ethnographic research projects as it is for large collections, since when their power to create knowledge is used to validate one particular vision of social order and reality archives can become repressive and hierarchical.

There is always some tension between different ways of ordering reality through visual images. For example, when ethnographers organize fieldwork photographs they have to contemplate differences between their own personal and academic ways of ordering reality and the orders by which local people construct their worlds and histories visually. Below I suggest some ways this may be resolved, arguing that this tension should be represented in the way images are organized; it may in fact be a creative tension.

Sequential organization and the 'authentic narrative': whose order is it?

Collier and Collier have insisted that to be analysed correctly the spatial and temporal order in which images were recorded must be maintained. If not, they warn that 'reconstructive ordering of the photographs can inadvertently confuse the actual sequence of occurrence' (1986: 180). This approach argues that there is only one authentic visual narrative, and that the chronological linear sequence by which images are produced forms the narrative that represents their true meaning, to which all other sequences or meanings must be subordinate. While recordings of temporal chronologies of events and activities are important research materials, they do not necessarily represent either an undisturbed or 'complete reality'. Moreover, a linear visual chronology may not consistently represent the way in which reality was experienced or conceptualized by all the individuals involved. Narratives and sequences are not necessarily fixed. The order in which events and activities are experienced may change, and the orders in which they are remembered and spoken about may differ from the chronological order in which they happened. For instance, certain aspects of an event or specific individuals may be prioritized in certain cultural discourses and individual memories and representations. Therefore a visual representation of an event inflexibly ordered by its temporal chronology may represent the participants' experience of the event less than it stands for the ethnographer's view of the event's structure.

For example, in Spain I showed three women informants my photographs of a bullfight we had attended together. I had kept (and numbered) the photographs in the order in which the printers returned them. However, they soon became reorganized as my informants prioritized and selected images that represented the event for them. For example, they categorized the images into those of their favourite bullfighter, of themselves and photographs they found aesthetically pleasing but not of documentary significance. Their reorganization of my photographs represented aspects of their experience of the bullfight, centring on their own participation and their favourite bullfighter's performance. Key images showed him waving to the part of the arena where we sat and highlights of his performance. For my analysis, the temporal sequence in which I took the photographs was less important than my informants' comments on, and arrangement of, them, for this was the moment where their knowledge intersected with my photographs. In my analysis these photographs became visual representations of local and personal knowledge and understandings of a specific bullfight and of particular individuals. Ordered temporally and photographed as a systematic record of the procedure of the event on *my* terms rather than on my informants' terms, the set of images would have been little more than a representation of particular performers working to the usual format of the bullfight.

While I have suggested the original shooting order should not be the dominant narrative of any visual representation, it should not be abandoned as it will help situate the images temporally and spatially within the research process. It is useful to keep note of the shooting order to describe the formal structure of events and activities and reflect on how ethnographers structure visual narratives. However, this is not the only or the most authentic version or narrative. Other edited or reorganized versions of my visual narrative of the bullfight also represented knowledge and experience of the performance and were equally ethnographically rich. This applies not only to visual recordings of events and performances, but also to other activities and procedures. While it is useful to record visually the process and sequence of activities, the ways people structure and experience the reality of those activities may not be encapsulated in the temporal sequence photographed.

Thematic organization and multiple categories: dealing with diverse photographic meanings

The meanings of visual images may be determined exclusively by neither the temporal sequences in which they were shot nor by categories based solely on their content. The same image may simultaneously be given different meanings in different (but often interconnected) situations, each of which has ethnographic significance. Any system of ordering and storing images should account for their ambiguity of meaning and fickle adherence to categories. This means developing ways of categorizing images that acknowledge the arbitrary nature of their interconnected meanings and are not dominated by content-based typologies or temporally determined sequences. Below, by interrogating just one photograph, I demonstrate that to place an image in a single category denies the richness of its potential for facilitating and communicating ethnographic understandings.

This example discusses how a single photograph taken during fieldwork in Spain was invested with ethnographic meanings that drew together other resources of knowledge about the photograph's subject and her culture. While the image alone reveals nothing, it is given ethnographic meaning when linked to other types of knowledge through my analysis.

The photograph in Figure 5.2 was taken in 1992 in the afternoon during *feria* in Córdoba. Encarni, my friend and informant, had dressed up in her *traje corto* especially to meet me for the afternoon, show me around the *feria*, and have a drink. She also wanted to show me her outfit because she thought seeing it would be interesting for me and useful for my research. We were engaged in two different leisure activities. Mine was vacation and tourist leisure, and in part my photography was structured by this. Her leisure was *feria* and time with a friend. Simultaneously our professional agendas were intertwined: one theme of the outing was my anthropological research; another was her chance to practise the spoken English that she needed to do well in her exams. When we planned to meet she mentioned that I should take my camera to photograph her *traje corto*. This portrait was one of three photographs that we took. It was taken in the *casetta* (temporary open-air bar) of the *Finito de Córdoba* bullfighting club.

When I analysed the photograph and considered how it could represent 'ethnographic knowledge', I reflected on the context of its production. The afternoon was a special occasion, or at least not a normal occasion, for various reasons. First, we were in *feria* – a context some anthropologists would say is distinct from 'everyday' time. In this sense

Figure 5.2 This photograph of Encarni became the subject of my other informants'
discussions about the image of a 'traditional woman'; it became part of her family
and personal photograph collection and it also became a reference point in my own
academic work, at a conference and in my book (Pink 1997a).

it was a 'classic' context for an anthropological photograph. Secondly we
were in a bullfighting club's *casetta*. Encarni does not usually spend her
afternoons drinking in bullfight club *casettas* or in the clubs themselves.
She took me to the *casetta* because she thought it was the kind of place I
should be researching. Thirdly, the occasion was a photographic
moment: it was worth taking a photo because Encarni was wearing her
traje corto. When someone dresses up in a *traje corto* or gipsy dress it is
quite normal that a friend or relative should photograph them. In this
sense the photograph simply documents a conventional photographic
moment.

These aspects of the context helped me to think through how mine and
Encarni's intentions had intersected to represent themes of anthropological visual interest, local visual conventions and personal objectives. This enabled me to associate certain anthropological and local
meanings to the photographs. However once the photograph was
printed, it was invested with new meanings in Córdoba. These interpretations helped me to link the photograph to other aspects of my
research, each time making it more heavily laden with meanings.

The photographs were originally taken as slides. I had two copies of
this one printed and gave one to Encarni. A couple of days later she
asked me if she could also have a copy for her mother; the photograph

had already begun to travel. Leisure is a key theme in family photo-graphy (see Chalfen 1987; Slater 1995), thus the photograph fitted into the family collection. While the 'photographic moment' was not a family event, dressing up at home in the *traje corto* was. The photograph was also in my 'research' slide collection (ready for a seminar presentation at the university the following year). A print was in my 'personal' collection of photos of friends and parties I had enjoyed in Spain. During my fieldwork this photograph album also became part of my research. Some Spanish friends who flicked through this album of friends, parties and trips said Encarni looked very traditional, very *Cordobesa*. Wearing her *traje corto*, she represented the beautiful 'traditional' Córdoban woman. My mother, who met Encarni when she visited England with me and stayed with my parents, recognized her friend. Later in England the photograph had further adventures. In my PhD thesis I used the photograph to visualize one of the paradoxes of the notion of 'tradition' in Córdoban identity. Encarni had dressed as a traditional woman for *feria* and other informants had used the photograph to identify her as representing local traditional femininity. However, Encarni did not describe herself as 'traditional'. She has two university degrees and is an English teacher. She said she had learnt a lot about local traditions by helping with my research.

This analysis of the photograph was informed by my understandings of a number of other visual and verbal, individual and cultural, narra-tives, discourses and practices. The focus of the analysis was not so much the content of the photograph, but how the content was given meanings relevant to my project. For example, the photograph of Encarni could be fitted into a temporal sequence of a series of photographs that I took of the *feria* that day, or a series of photographic portraits of 'traditional' costumes. In my book I used it to represent knowledge about changing gender roles and identities in contemporary Andalusia (see Chapter 6). In the future the same photograph may take on further ethnographic meanings.

The multiple ways that just one image may be significant implies that classifying sets of hundreds of photographs or hours of video footage would develop as a complex web of cross-referenced themes and images. For some projects it will be worthwhile to develop systems of codifying images. However this can be time-consuming and the extent to which images can and need to be formally managed in this way may depend on the sheer quantity of images, commentaries and themes involved. In some projects images can be managed more intuitively. In my own experience, I have found that during fieldwork particular images and sequences of images become the focus of informants' attention and these have tended also to become the main images in my analysis.

Rather than proposing a formula for organizing ethnographic images, my intention is to offer a series of suggestions from which to begin working. Any system of organizing and storing ethnographic images should situate them in relation to the multiple meanings and themes of the research. Therefore, for example, the photograph of Encarni would be linked to themes of discourses on family photography, traditional iconography and festivals, and this would connect with a range of other visual and printed materials and notes from field notes, photography, video and local documents. It would entail a way of attempting to map the interconnecting elements of discourse and experience to which each image may refer when used in a specific context. A codifying system would also need to account for how any one image may later be invested with new meanings as the project develops and researchers make new interpretations and connections between visual, verbal and written materials.

Organizing video footage

Above I suggested how ethnographic photographs may be organized and connected to other elements of ethnographic and theoretical enquiry during 'analysis'. Some of these general principles also apply to video. First, in Chapter 4 I described some video production scenarios, emphasizing the collaborative element of video making and the intersubjectivity between the video makers and informants. These social and wider contexts of video production should be accounted for. Secondly, the different meanings informants and ethnographers invested in the video footage at different times and the discourses to which these meanings are linked should be considered. In Chapter 4 I discussed 'talking with video' and a 'media ethnography' approach to informants' viewing practices. Different people interpret the same footage differently, giving their own meanings to its content. As my discussions of 'The Bull-fighter's Braid' and the portrait of Encarni suggest, local interpretations of images are of equal interest to ethnographers as the visual and verbal content of video. Thirdly, relationships between video footage and other research materials and experiences (including memories, diaries, photographs, notes and artifacts) provide important insights as each medium may represent interrelated but different types of knowledge about the same theme.

Video also differs from photography in that it communicates different types of knowledge and information and has different potentials for representation. Video communicates through moving rather than still images, includes sound, and the information represented on video is usually accessible only lineally (unless it is organized and stored electronically, see below and Chapter 8). Categorizing and analysing video materials can be more costly, cumbersome and time-consuming than it is with photographs. It involves more technology (including recorders and players), possibly tape transfer to different formats for viewing and transcriptions of verbal dialogue.

The specific research methods and visual technologies appropriate to each project vary (see Chapters 1 and 2). Video therefore plays diverse roles in different projects (see Chapter 4). Correspondingly, there is not *one* process or method for categorizing or analysing ethnographic video that every researcher may follow. Rather, this varies according to researchers' objectives, the content of the tapes and the meanings attached to them. In some cases video recordings are treated as realist representations of specific interactions or activities; in others they are used as symbolic representations, evocative of (for instance) emotions, experiences, power relations or inequalities. In some projects they fulfil both roles simultaneously. First, I briefly describe conventional treatments of video-tape, logging visual data and transcribing verbal data, suggesting their implications and proposing appropriate uses.

Above I criticized analytical processes that translate visual images into printed words. Logging and transcribing certainly involve representing visual and verbal representations in printed form. As such they could also be said to define video footage. I am not recommending that printed transcripts and verbal descriptions replace video footage, but that logging and transcription are used to map visual and verbal knowledge otherwise only accessible lineally, to make it more accessible. This should identify and categorize different parts of the tape according to their content and/or the diverse meanings that can be invested in them, and in relation to the contexts and relationships of their production.

Different projects require that video is logged to different degrees of formality. Especially when there is a limited amount of footage, it may be possible simply to work with these materials visually, without documenting their contents verbally. However, in many cases detailed documentation of visual and verbal knowledge represented on the tapes may facilitate easier access. For close scrutiny of video-tapes this could include producing time-coded log tables with information on camera angles and distances, spoken narrative and visual content. If footage includes significant verbal dialogue or interviews, then these may be transcribed. Ethnographers who are interested in the subtleties of conversation and communication among the subjects of the video (and between the subjects of the video and the video maker) may find that a log of the visual and verbal narratives of such interactions is useful for analysis. Visual logs and written transcripts provide easily accessible versions of the content of tapes, if they are also time coded, so that images can be easily located for reviewing.

Closely scrutiny of video-tapes should also account for links between the content of the video and other aspects of the ethnography (such as photographs, field diaries and notes). When I analysed the transcripts of video 'conversations' between Alberto and Tomas recorded in Guinea Bissau, I realized that their dialogue was more meaningful when I linked it to other strands of our experiences and relationships. Therefore my analysis of the transcripts also referred to a set of photographs they were discussing, ongoing conversations (about money and education) that the two men continued having in other contexts, the 'history' of their friendship and 'landmarks' in their relationship (such as disputes, moments of realization and of understanding). The video conversation was just one part of a wider set of narratives and experiences and while its content implied discourses and themes from the research, it did not itself provide 'visual evidence' of these themes. Nevertheless, I also saw the video as a realist recording of an event that I had experienced and participated in, because it was a representation of my experience of reality. Another piece of video footage of Tomas and his son Antoine played a different role in my analysis. I originally recorded the footage during Tomas and Antoine's first days of work, measuring out threads in our garden. I intended the footage to be a realist representation of a stage of the process of weaving in which they were engaged. However it also came to mean something else as I interpreted it later in terms of the development of my collaboration with Tomas and Antoine. Elsewhere I have represented this experience of analysis as follows:

> The morning that Tomas and Antoine began the tedious task of re-measuring the base threads Alberto was teaching an early class at school. I loaded the video camera. *Why not video?* I resolved my dilemma: *Tomas was angry, he was playing with us, but we had a deal. This was an important stage in the* pano *making process.* On this single occasion I proposed a distanced recording of technique similar to the positivist strategy I have critiqued above. In my diary the video work became embedded in what reads back as an uncomfortable narrative:

> Canchungo, Monday 17th March
> Alberto went to Bissau yesterday to change the thread. Tomas arrived this morning and got started with the blue and white thread. They [Tomas and Antoine] went to a funeral yesterday and came back early this morning. I did some video work with the process and with some general shots of Jacqueline [one of the neighbours] who was wearing a *pano*. Tomas got really angry with his son, who evidently had wound the threads incorrectly again, he shouted at him in Manjaco and hit him. When Alberto got up he continued explaining to Tomas what *panos* we want now and he now seems settled with the idea that we want five of each type.

> The video footage represented Tomas hesitant and short with my questions, Tomas and Antoine silently walking up and down the garden unwinding threads onto sticks. They wound the tension into the base threads of the blue and white *pano*; the second *pano*. I videoed Tomas shouting at, but not beating Antoine . . . I invested the tension in the video footage, the distance was fundamental to the sensation of shooting it. When, months later, I viewed the footage in Derby, I saw not an objective visual record of technological process but a subjective representation of distance. (Pink 1999b)

It is often by making connections between different sets of visual and written research materials that a deeper understanding of the materials is possible. Visual methods are rarely used in isolation from other methods (see Chapter 1). Correspondingly, visual materials should be analysed in relation to other research texts.

The specific categories used to organize video footage in any one project also depend on how researchers intend to use video to represent their work. If footage is to be edited into a documentary video or a series of short clips, scenes may be categorized because of their ability to communicate on the terms of video editing conventions, their aesthetic appeal, and the quality of sound recording. A different basis for selection and categorization might be established if the footage is to be organized thematically for a hypermedia representation or screened unedited as part of a conference presentation (see Chapters 7 and 8).

Electronic archives

In the late 1990s social scientists began to use electronic media increasingly to store and analyse visual research materials. Digitally stored photographs or video can be coded and rapidly accessed through electronic databases as individual files or thematically-grouped sets.

Electronic storage has several advantages over conventional video-tapes. Tapes only allow visual data to be accessed lineally by moving backwards and forwards, making analysis, cross-checking and comparison time-consuming and clumsy. In contrast, digitized and stored electronically, footage can be accessed directly at any selected point. Rapid movement between different footage and simultaneous display of multiple recordings on the same monitor facilitates more efficient access to and comparison of visual data. Conventional video-tapes are usually logged on separate printed sheets. Using appropriate software, extracts from digital video sequences or stills can be selected, labelled, logged, annotated, book-marked and rapidly accessed.

Electronic storage also allows visual and written text to be stored in the same medium, such as CD ROM or DVD. Video sequences can be hyperlinked to other footage of comparative interest, still photographs or written transcripts, translations, research notes and conclusions, all of which can be readily printed out. In this way an accessible visual and written archive with easy access to all the research materials can be constructed, and may also be shared with co-researchers or informants. This can be achieved using quite standard technology. For example, I have had digital video-tapes transferred into mov files and stored on CD ROM, making hours of video accessible on my lap top for viewing and analysis alongside interview transcripts stored in Microsoft Word files. I logged video clips according to time codes shown on the Windows Media Player or QuickTime Player. Using slightly more sophisticated software, such as QuickTime Pro, sets of video clips for comparison or thematic categorization can be edited and archived.

As yet few social scientists engage fully with the potential of 'electronic archives', but some have taken important steps. Fischer and Zeitlyn are using electronic technologies for the analysis and storage of their Mambila ritual project (see Chapter 4), for 'indexation and digitization of field material' and '[c]rosslinking (layering) of these to relevant interview material and fieldnotes' (Fischer and Zeitlyn n.d.). For archiving they propose to use a Cogent Coding System (see http:// lucy.ukc.ac.uk/Accs1) called Accs that 'facilities context-sensitive retrieval of texts, images and video sequences in response to formal queries' (Fischer and Zeitlyn n.d.: 10). Another computer programme named HyperRESEARCH, reviewed by Hesse-Biber, Dupus and Kinder (1997), has been developed for the analysis of qualitative multi-media data. This programme allows the researchers to code, categorize and retrieve visual, audio and written text. It will also perform hypothesis tests on the data as well as statistical analyses or the frequency of codes. It is likely that in the future a greater number of archiving and database programmes that are appropriate for archiving visual research materials will become available.

Summary

I have suggested a departure from the idea that 'analysis' of ethnographic video and photographs entails translating systematically recorded and contextualized visual evidence into written words. Instead, a reflexive approach to analysis should concentrate on how the content of visual images is the result of the specific context of their production and on the diversity of ways that video and photographs are interpreted. Photographs and video may be treated as both realist representations of the reality of fieldwork contexts as ethnographers understand them (as in the 'realist' tradition in documentary photography). But they are always representations of the subjective standpoints of the image producer and other viewers, including informants. This has implications for how visual archives and categories are conceived and demands researchers pay attention to the interlinkages between visual and other (verbal, written) knowledge. This approach to visual meanings has implications for how photography and video are used in ethnographic representation (see Chapters 6–8).

PART 3

VISUAL IMAGES AND TECHNOLOGIES IN ETHNOGRAPHIC REPRESENTATION

The production of ethnographic text, whether an undergraduate dissertation, MPhil or PhD thesis, or an ethnographic monograph or article, is usually referred to as 'writing up'. In Chapter 5 I criticized the related analytical practice of converting fieldwork experience, notes and images into written words. In Chapters 6–8 I question this dominance of written words in ethnographic representation. I suggest that representation of ethnographic knowledge is not just a matter of producing words, but one of situating images, sometimes in relation to written words, but also in relation to other images, spoken words and other sounds. Part 3 therefore discusses the potential of photography and video for ethnographic representation in printed, video and hypermedia text. In Part 2 I focused on the social relations, personal standpoints, cultural discourses and social science theories through which images are produced and given meaning in ethnographic research. Part 3 builds on this by exploring how these elements of ethnographic image production can inform their subsequent uses for ethnographic representation.

In Chapter 5 I criticized approaches that treat ethnographic photographs as a mere 'supplement to the notes' (Hastrup 1992: 13) and analysis as the translation of images into words. Such approaches have a correspondingly problematic perspective on the potential of images for ethnographic representation (see Taylor 1996: 67). Hastrup has argued that 'writing may encompass the images produced by films, but not the other way round' (1992: 21), thus seeing written text and images as hierarchically related. She claims written text is capable of invoking a degree of reflexivity and self-conscious knowledge that the iconographic visual communication of ethnographic film, which must be 'taken at face-value', cannot achieve (1992: 20–1). While Hastrup is right that the written word can communicate in ways images cannot, the idea that this implies a hierarchical relationship unduly privileges written words over images. I suggest an approach to the visual in ethnographic representation that acknowledges the interrelationship between the visual, the verbal and the written in ethnographic experience, social relations and cultural practices and sees this as a basis for its potential for reflexive ethnographic representation. The idea that written text inspires reflexive reading, while visual text does not, also underestimates the potential of photography and video for ethnographic representation and is challenged by the practical and theoretical work of 'visual' ethnographers (e.g. Biella 1994; MacDougall 1997).

While different media certainly communicate in different ways, the medium of representation used does not alone determine its reception. Viewers and audiences of ethnographic images are also interpreters of text and by acknowledging their agency we can understand better how ethnographic knowledge is received. This understanding may in turn inform how ethnographers construct their texts. For example, for film this implies regarding 'film as *experience* – and as such never completely controlled by film makers, subjects or viewers' (Mermin 1997: 49, original italics). Mermin suggests that film narrative should be understood 'as a means by which film makers begin to supervise and direct their viewers' experiences of reading and creating meaning from their films' (1997: 49) (see Chapter 7). Similarly, as I argue in Chapter 6, photography is not necessarily taken at 'face value' but is 'experienced' by viewers. Therefore, an ethnographer's role would be to inspire viewers to question self-consciously the content and meanings of their photographic representations. In constructing written and visual texts ethnographers are concerned not simply with producing different forms of representation and knowledge, but also with what their readers, viewers and audiences will do with these representations. As James, Hockey and Dawson remind us, 'representations, once made, are open to re-representation, misrepresentation and appropriation' (1997: 13). One concern for contemporary authors of ethnographic representations should be how to create texts that will be engaged with self-consciously and reflexively and not taken 'at face value' as written ethnographic facts and visual illustrations or evidence. This issue is addressed for each medium discussed in Chapters 6–8.

The agency of readers/viewers to make ethnographic representations meaningful on their own terms also raises ethical issues. As James, Hockey and Dawson warn, 'once we have committed to words on paper, or to visual representation through film, we may at one and the same time lose control yet be haunted by our representations of others' (1997: 13). Similarly, from their ethnographic filmmaking experience, Barbash and Taylor predict that '[e]thical problems will arise despite your best intentions. They may even emerge after your film is finished and in distribution' (Barbash and Taylor 1997: 49). New textual strategies give rise to new ethical concerns and in Chapters 6–8 I discuss ethical issues specific to the use of each media.

Montage, multivocality and democratic texts

In Chapters 1 and 2 I argued that academic and local epistemologies and knowledge are equally 'truthful' and the former should not be regarded superior to the latter. Correspondingly, in Chapters 3 and 4 I proposed an approach to photography and video in ethnographic research that accounts for the different ways researchers, informants and others experience and understand the realities in which they live. This diversity of worldviews, narratives and understandings of reality that ethnographers encounter during fieldwork therefore forms the basis of ethnographic knowledge, and some would argue that it should also be represented without 'translating' these 'local voices' into the 'authoritative voice' of social science. During the 1990s several scholars began to consider how the 'many voices', or 'multivocality', of ethnographic experience can be integrated into the design of ethnographic representations.

Some (e.g. Kulick 1995) have challenged the usefulness of seeing ethnography in terms of a linear narrative that represents the ethnographic experience as one in which ethnographers go to 'the field', get the 'data' and then go 'home' to analyse and 'write it up' (see Chapters 1 and 5). Similar criticisms have been made of ethnographic representation for failing to recognize the multiple and simultaneous realities in which people live and participate, the intersubjectivity between ethnographers and the 'subjects' of their research and the different voices, perspectives and temporal and spatial locations that ethnography involves. Marcus proposes that to resolve this, ethnographic text should be constructed according to a principle of montage to create ethnographic representations that incoprorate the multilinearity of ethnographic research and everyday lives (see Marcus 1995: 41). In contrast to the linear narratives of a conventional ethnographic text, a 'montage' text would recognize that sets of diverse worldviews exist simultaneously and would represent these without necessarily 'translating' them into the academic terms of a social science. In Marcus's words, '[s]imultaneity in ethnographic description' replaces 'discovery of unknown subjects or cultural worlds' (1995: 44). Marcus is calling for a type of written text that does not confer hierarchical superiority on academic discourses and knowledge above the discourses and knowledge of local individuals and cultures (I make a parallel argument for a non-hierarchical relationship between written and visual text here). Marcus argues that while it is important to maintain an academic 'objectifying discourse about processes and structure' (1995: 48), this should not be privileged above representations of other discourses. Instead, he insists that a simultaneous and non-hierarchical representation of different local, personal academic and other epistemologies, each coherent in themselves, should be developed within the same text.

Therefore ethnographic text becomes a context where ethnographers/authors can create or represent continuities between these 'diverse worlds, voices or experiences', and describe or imply points in the research at which they met or collided.

Stoller's book, *Sensuous Scholarship* (1997), demonstrates how representations of diverse realities might coherently intersect in the same text. Stoller proposes a 'sensuous scholarship' that accounts for how ethnographic knowledge is created not just through the observation of visible phenomena, but through other sensory experiences, such as physical pain and taste. For Stoller, the 'flexible agency' of the sensuous scholar is key. This combines the 'sensible and intelligible, denotative and evocative' and the 'ability to make intellectual leaps to bridge gaps forged by the illusion of disparateness' (1997: xviii), in his terms 'to tack between the analytical and the sensible (1997: xv). A flexible representation 'underscores the linkages of experience and reality, imagination and reason, difference and commonality' (1997: 92). To achieve this, he combines a range of different textual styles, including a mystical Sufi story, poetry, autobiographical accounts, academic writing, photographs and a discussion of both performance and ethnographic film.

Text that allows academic, local and individual narratives to co-exist, implying no hierarchical relationship between either the discourses that are represented or their medium of representation offers a temptingly 'democratic' model. However, it should not be used naively or without caution. As James, Hockey and Dawson have warned, the question of how to represent multivocality should not be approached in isolation from a consideration of its political and ethical implications. While the ideals and intentions of multivocality are important, the question of 'whether such democratic representations are in the end possible, or even desirable, remains' (James et al. 1997: 12). Moreover, Josephides has questioned the possibility of a democratic multivocality as 'letting the people speak for themselves, or allowing them agency as actors with their own theoretical perspectives still may not escape the suspicion that the ethnographer is using them for her own ends' (Josephides 1997: 29). She questions whether ethnographers' strategies, apparently intended to bring the reader closer to the informants' subjectivity, really only constitute ethnographers' uses of informants' words to make their own points. Textual practices that are designed to give the subjects of the research a voice (such as printing, recording, or keying in *their* stories, perspectives, words, narratives or photographs) may constitute only a new textual construction in which the narrative of the ethnographer is just as dominant and those of the subjects subordinate. Issues surrounding multivocality and democratic representations raise many questions that are equally important for printed text, photography, video and multimedia. These questions will be raised in the discussions of the implications of different media for the construction and interpretation of ethnographic text.

The following three chapters cover visual representations of ethnography using printed text, video and hypermedia. These have not been selected because they are superior to other media, but because in my experience they are the media with which students of ethnography have most opportunity to work. Photographic exhibitions, poster presentations, slide shows and other visual representations are also valuable ways to communicate ethnographic knowledge. Each of the media discussed here has had a different historical relationship to ethnographic research and representation. The structure of each chapter therefore differs slightly to situate uses of the medium in relation to particular discourses and practices.

CHAPTER 6

Ethnographic Photography and Printed Text

Printed text as a medium for ethnographic representation

This chapter explores uses of photography in printed ethnographic publications. Photographs usually form part of texts that are also made up of written words and possibly other visual depictions. In many existing publications photography has been incorporated into a structure already established for written ethnography. Therefore, first, I briefly discuss ethnographic writing before focusing on the potential of photography for the printed text medium.

In the Introduction I discussed the implications of Clifford's (1986) comparison of ethnographic writing to fiction. Contemporary ethnographers have largely incorporated an understanding of ethnographic text as a subjective, but hopefully 'loyal', representation of culture and experience into their work. Subsequently, comment on the constructedness of ethnographic text has become an almost mandatory passage in ethnographic methods textbooks published since the last decade of the twentieth century. This has involved an insistence that careful attention is paid to the literary nature of ethnographic writing, and how ethnographers convince their readers of the 'authenticity' and authority of their accounts. Modern ethnographic writing has been criticized for its tendency to describe the people studied in abstract and generalizing terms, and in the ethnographer's dominant and objectifying voice. Instead, it has been suggested that informants' voices should also be allowed a place in ethnographic text, and that ethnographers should write reflexively in order to acknowledge the subjectivity and experiences on which their writing is based. It is usually now taken for granted that ethnographic texts cannot communicate the 'truth' about any one culture or society, but are inevitably, like any other visual or verbal narrative or image, representations.

This attention to the qualities of written text as a medium has led to a large literature that has discussed these issues in detail from theoretical perspectives (e.g. Clifford and Marcus 1986; James et al. 1997; Nencel and Pels 1991; Stoller 1997) and in methodology texts (e.g. Ellen 1984; Hammersley and Atkinson 1995; Walsh 1998). In some of these the importance of reflexivity for both reading and writing ethnographic text is rightly stressed (e.g. Back 1998). In response, some ethnographic writers have developed 'experimental texts' that explore the possibilities of alternative uses of narrative, structure and textual strategy (e.g. Stoller 1997; Tyler 1991), and attempt to produce representations that take readers closer to the perspectives and experiences of the subjects of their research (see Josephides 1997). The uses of photography and written text, I suggest here, also seek to respond to the demands of this critical approach.

Deconstructionism turns to photography

The introduction to *Writing Culture* (probably the best-known critical text on ethnographic representation) begins with a passage in which Clifford describes the photograph featured on the book's cover. In this photograph, he tells us, 'the ethnographer hovers at the edge of the frame – faceless, almost extraterrestrial, a hand that writes' (1986: 1). Clifford does not discuss the reality of the specific ethnographic experience represented in the photograph, but uses his written words to invest meanings, relevant to the theme of the book, in the photograph. However, after this brief demonstration of the ambiguity and arbitrariness of photographic meaning, and the potential of photographs for producing 'fictional' accounts, the contributors to *Writing Culture* do not return to the role of images in creating the 'ethnographic fictions' and partial truths of ethnographic writing (see Clifford 1986: 19). Some have made connections between this 'literary turn' in ethnographic writing and developments in ethnographic film (e.g. Henley 1996; Marcus 1995) (see Chapter 7). However, until recently (with the exception of Edwards 1997a) there has been little comment on the implications of these debates for the inclusion of photographs in (or as) contemporary ethnographic text.

In the 1990s anthropologists began to examine how photography has been used to create particular types of ethnographic knowledge in existing texts. Much of this work focused on historical texts. For example, Edwards's two edited collections (1992, 1997b) interrogate (mainly) colonial uses of photographic representation (see Chapter 3). Below I discuss how others have analysed how photographs are situated in twentieth-century ethnographies to comment on the implications of this for the production of ethnographic meanings and understanding other cultures (e.g. Brandes 1997; Chaplin 1994; Davis 1992).

Photography and claims to ethnographic authority

Deconstruction of how ethnographers/authors go about convincing their readers of the authenticity of their representations has been central to discussions of ethnographic writing. This has included a critical perspective on how grammatical tenses have been used to situate the subjects of research temporally within ethnographic texts (e.g. Fabian 1983; Pratt 1986). Conventionally, ethnography is written largely in the present tense, the 'ethnographic present', and some research methods texts (e.g. Fetterman 1998: 124) recommend this to students. However, Pratt (drawing on Fabian 1983: 33) has critically deconstructed the use of the 'ethnographic present', arguing that 'the famous "ethnographic present" locates the other in a time order different from that of the speaking subject', thus abstracting and objectifying the 'other' (Pratt 1986: 33). In contrast, descriptions of the research experience locate 'both self and other in the same temporal order', usually represented in the form of personal subjective narrative and written in the past tense. This inserts 'into the ethnographic text the authority of the personal experience out of which the ethnography was made' (1986: 33). Thus writing in the present tense has abstracted and objectified the subjects of research, while writing in the past tense has constituted the ethnographer's claim to authority and authenticity.

Davis has interrogated ethnographic uses of photography in a similar way. Drawing on Barthes's comment that the claim of the photographer is that he or she 'had to be there', Davis points out that in ethnographic texts photographs are often used in the past tense, as the ethnographer's proof that 'I was there' (Davis 1992: 209). As such, photographs have been used to support ethnographers' strategic claims of authenticity and authority to speak as a person with first-hand experience of the ethnographic situation, and as a source of privileged knowledge. Brandes has noted a similar use of photographic portraits in his analysis of photography in existing ethnographies of Spain. Here, in Pitt-Rivers's (1954) and Press's (1979) ethnographies, photographic portraits have been used to represent 'evidence' of 'considerable trust between subject and photographer' and to contribute 'to the authenticity of the anthropological study' (Brandes 1997: 10). In this way photographs were part of a strategy to convince the reader and to position the ethnographer as an authoritative voice within the text.

Davis points out that, as part of another textual strategy, ethnographers often situate photographs and maps in the present tense to indicate that 'these kinds of artefact . . . are permanent and continuous. Anyone can see them and comment appropriately in the present tense' (Davis 1992: 208). In this way photographs are incorporated in what has been called the 'literary illusion' of the 'ethnographic present' that represents 'a slice of life – a motionless image' (see Fetterman 1998: 124–5), thus becoming part of an objectifying practice. Often it may be appropriate that students follow the convention that Fetterman suggests, of using the 'ethnographic present' for the sake of 'linguistic convenience'. However, as Pratt (1986: 33) and Davis (1992: 214) have shown, in fact, ethnographers tend to mix past and present tenses in their writings to particular effect.

When a photograph is situated in the present tense and is treated as a realist representation, a particular relationship between the text, the image and the ethnographic context is constructed. The specificity of the photographic moment, set in the past, is lost and instead the photograph is situated in a continuous present. It becomes a photograph that could be taken any time, a generalized representation of an activity or type of person. Such uses tend to present images as evidence of an objective reality that exists independently of the text, yet can be brought into it through the image.

Audience shot of the "woman only" bullfight. Photo © Sarah Pink

Figure 6.1 This image is treated as a realist representation of the audience of a particular bullfight. The caption is designed to refer to the incongruity between the verbal label of the bullfight as 'women only' and the actual composition of the audience represented in the image (Sanders and Pink 1996: 51).

In contrast, by situating a photograph in the past, the content of the image may be interpreted as the product of a specific 'photographic moment'. The approach allows ethnographers to locate photographs within the research reflexively (Figure 6.2) (see Chapter 3).

Images and written text: captions, narratives

Historical and contemporary uses of photographs in sociological and anthropological texts have tended to use captions or references in a

Figure 14: This photograph of me with Cristina Sánchez was taken when an informant requested my camera to provide me with an appropriate visual image.
Photograph by an unidentified informant.

Figure 6.2 Situated as such, with the caption, this image is intended to function differently from the 'I was there claim' of an ethnographer photographed in 'the field' with his or her informants. Instead, it is intended to represent the process by which my knowledge about local photographic collections and aspirations is linked to representations of self-identity in the bullfighting world, see Chapter 3, p. 62 (Pink 1997a: 102).

'main body' of written text to situate photographs (for a detailed review, see Chaplin 1994: 197–274). Below I discuss how the relationship between word and image contributes to the production of ethnographic meanings.

In existing ethnographies photographic captions have tended to make photographic meaning contingent on written text. In Chaplin's interpretation this subordinates photography to the written word since when a photograph is captioned by text, 'it loses its autonomy as a photograph and thus any claim to make a contribution in its own right' (Chaplin 1994: 207). As Chaplin concedes, captioning is not always inappropriate: used correctly photographs and words can work together to produce the desired ethnographic meanings. However, in other contexts photographs need more autonomy. Chaplin proposes that to achieve this, photographs should be separated from written text (1994: 207). As an example of this, Chaplin cites Bateson and Mead's *Balinese Character* (1942), in which a

series of images are printed on one side of a page and opposite the
extended captions are printed. This arrangement creates a subtle separa-
tion of image and text, thus allowing some autonomy to the images and
permitting the viewer to interpret them in relation to one another rather
than connecting each image primarily with its written caption.

Different ways of combining written words and photographs in
ethnographic texts are informed by particular theories of photographic
meaning. For example, a realist approach to photography would be
associated with a text that uses photographs as evidence, to support and
illustrate written points. For example, as Chaplin (1994: 232) shows,
while making innovative uses of word and image in Bateson and Mead's
Balinese Character (1942) and in Goffman's *Gender Advertisements* (1979),
photographs are treated as ethnographic evidence and displayed in
terms of 'scientific categories'. Brandes's (1997) survey of photography in
the ethnographies of Spain during the period 1954 to 1988 shows how
photographs were used to illustrate abstract versions of social and
cultural life of towns and villages that were often given false names and
of informants whose identities were 'hidden'. For example, Brandes
claims that the photographs in Pitt-Rivers's *The People of the Sierra* (1954)
both distance the village from 'reader's direct experience' (1997: 7) and
'impart an image of the Other' living in a 'rural, poor, religious, super-
stitious, technologically-backward Spain' (1997: 8). Brandes argues that
Pitt-Rivers's use of photography created a problematically primitivizing
representation of rural Spain. More recently, as publishing technology
develops, uses of captioned images as 'evidence' and 'illustration' have
become increasingly frequent. However, as I argue below, these realist
uses are not always inappropriate. For example, the contributors to
Cohen, Wilk and Stoeltje's (1996) ethnographic collection on beauty
pageants illustrate their chapters with photographs of women participating in these and related events, and the written text of Harvey's
(1996) study of EXPO 1992 in Spain contains 13 captioned images of
EXPO architecture taken mainly by the author. While these realist uses of
photography as illustration are not out of place, they should not be taken
'at face value'; they are in fact representations of representations.

Nonetheless most social scientific uses of ethnographic photography to
represent generalized cultural characteristics and specific categories of
activity, or artifacts, have tended to overlook the wider potential of the
visual for ethnographic representation. This is due, first, to a lack of
engagement with photography as a medium and, secondly, to neglect of
the role of readers/viewers in the construction of ethnographic meanings.

Images words and readers

Above I discussed the strategies authors use to make images meaningful
within texts. This discussion would be incomplete without a considera-

tion of how photographs might be interpreted by readers/viewers. If contemporary ethnographers are to create texts that readers/viewers will engage with and experience reflexively and self-consciously, they need to present images in ways that encourage or inspire readers to reflect on the meanings they give to texts themselves. As Barndt suggests, '[a]s viewers, too, we are invited to acknowledge our own locations and subjective responses to these images as generative tools' (Barndt 1997: 31). New forms of representation imply new practices of reading ethnography and innovative uses of photography in printed text will also make new demands on readers/viewers.

Texts that explicitly challenge conventional 'scientific' formats because they are constructed in novel ways or contain 'subjective' prose or images invite new ways of viewing/reading. Some of the best examples of this are found in the work of Berger and Mohr (see Chaplin 1994). Their series of uncaptioned images show how photographic narratives can emphasize the ambiguity of visual meanings, giving viewers/readers greater scope self-consciously to develop their own interpretations of photographs (see especially *Another Way of Telling* (Berger and Mohr 1982)). For instance, in *A Fortunate Man* (Berger and Mohr 1967), visual and written narratives are interwoven in the text but do not explicitly cross-reference one another. The photographs form a visual narrative or story that may be interpreted in relation to the written text, but are not illustrations of it nor explicitly captioned by it. Berger and Mohr's work is not 'ethnographic', in the sense that they do not intentionally and explicitly work to the academic agenda of ethnographic research or representation. Nevertheless, their texts demonstrate the potential of photography for ethnographic representation. In *Another Way of Telling*, they address the question of viewers' participation in the creation of knowledge and meaning from text, seeing photographs as 'a meeting place where the interests of the photographer, the photographed, the viewer and those who are using the photograph are often contradictory' (1982: 7). The photo-essay 'If each time' (in *Another Way of Telling*) is both an exploration in photographic theory and an exercise in offering agency to the viewer. The authors' introduction emphasizes the ambiguity of the images as well as the viewers' role in interpreting them:

> *We are far from wanting to mystify. Yet it is impossible for us to give a verbal key or storyline to this sequence of photographs. To do so would be to impose a single verbal meaning upon appearances and thus to inhibit or deny their own language.*
> (1982: 133, original italics)

As they note, 'There is no single "correct" interpretation of this sequence of images'. Here Berger and Mohr beg that readers take a self-conscious and reflexive approach to inventing their own storylines or interpretations of the photographic narrative, and are aware that theirs is one 'single' understanding, among many possible others. Berger and Mohr emphasize that their photographs are 'ambiguous', and ought not to be taken at 'face-value'. If this approach is applied to photographs published in ethnographic texts, it invites readers/viewers of photographic representations to participate in producing ethnographic meanings. Berger and Mohr's photographic texts present a strong contrast to conventional social scientific texts in their uses of words and images. However, some social scientists have recognized the value of learning from such examples.

Edwards has also suggested that ethnographers respond to the possibilities and challenges of photography by looking 'across the boundaries' of the disciplines that 'traditionally' use ethnography to engage with photographic theory (Edwards 1997a: 53). This, Edwards proposes, would be similar to 'literary awareness' in ethnographic writing where 'creative texts expressive of culture, such as novels, diaries, short stories and autobiography', have been incorporated alongside more conventional 'objective' texts. She argues that, similarly, two categories of photography may be used in ethnographic text: on the one hand, 'creative' or 'expressive' photography (which parallels the use of novels, diaries, short stories and autobiography) and on the other, 'realist' images that treat photography as 'the documenting tool' (which parallels 'objective' written text). Used within the same text, these categories of photography 'might be complementary rather than mutually exclusive' (1997a: 57). These uses of photography in ethnographic representation would challenge the approach 'in which photographic contribution to scientific knowledge depended on the accumulation of visual facts' (1997a: 57) and 'the photograph is intended to function as a *record* rather than an *interpretation* (Wright 1999: 41, original italics). Edwards's ideas suggest new potential for photography in ethnographic representation.

Edwards's approach implies a non-hierarchical use of different types of image and knowledge within the same text, in this case the two categories of 'realist' and 'expressive' photography. As opposed to realist photography, expressive photography (like Berger and Mohr's photographs) exploits the potential of the medium 'to question, arouse curiosity, tell in different voices or see through different eyes' (Edwards 1997a: 54). It breaks the conventions of realist ethnographic photography by, for example, ambiguously representing fragments and details, and acknowledging the constructedness of images. Like expressionism in documentary photography, it 'aims to present a subjective reality' and 'the symbolic value of the image may be more important than straightforward denotation' (T. Wright 1999: 44). Edwards argues that such photography has a place in ethnographic representation because, 'there are components of culture which require a more evocative, multidimensional, even ambiguous expression than the realist documentary paradigm permits' (Edwards 1997a: 54).

Edwards indicates how expressive and realist photographs may work together, as metaphors for different types of knowledge. She suggests expressive photographs are hard to comprehend since '[t]hey do not slip easily into preconceived notions of reading culture' (1997a: 69) and because 'expressive' imagery belies 'the *inevitability* of not comprehending everything' – it challenges the claim to authority and 'truth' that is embedded in the 'realist' approach (Edwards 1997a: 75, original italics). Therefore, by begging that readers/viewers do not take photographs 'at face value', expressive photography would encourage a self-conscious and reflexive approach to viewing and producing meaning from photographs. If expressive photographs are published alongside realist photographs in ethnographic text, they may question readers'/viewers' assumptions about the 'truthfulness' and 'completeness' of the realist photographs, and in doing so challenge conventional ways of reading/ viewing realist images. Edwards's approach demonstrates how different types of photograph, situated in relation to written text and other images, can represent different types of ethnographic knowledge, invoke diverse aspects of experience and address particular issues and questions.

As yet few ethnographers have developed such publication projects and readers'/viewers' responses to such text have not been researched. Indeed, it is impossible to 'know' how such an individual and personal activity as reading is experienced by others. Nevertheless, it is useful to attempt to anticipate (and test with examples) how readers may construct meaning from texts. This includes considering the type of readers/ viewers texts aim to address and the discourses (academic and otherwise) and other texts to which their interpretations of it are likely to refer.

Experimenting with photographs and words

At the beginning of the twenty-first century it is not unusual to find an ethnographic monograph or edited collection that contains no photographs at all. Moreover, those ethnographic texts that include photographs tend to have a dominant written narrative at their core and to use photographs mainly as evidence or illustration. While some ethnographers have experimented with novel arrangements of images and text, most contemporary ethnography does not confer equal importance or space to photographic and written text. In this section I discuss uses of photographs in ethnographic texts where written words form the dominant narrative. There are a multiplicity of ways that ethnographic texts could be constructed with different arrangements of photographs and words, and it would be impossible to cover all of these possibilities here. Below I discuss just a selection. It will be in the practice of researchers and students of ethnography who build on existing work to produce their own visual and written representations that further uses are developed.

In the Introduction to Part 3 I introduced the principle of montage as a model for ethnographic representation. Marcus's vision of a non-hierarchical text (1995) implies a tempting model for creating printed ethnographic representations that do not privilege the 'truth' of written academic text over other representations of knowledge. Such text would imply no hierarchy of ethnographic value between photographs and words, nor hierarchies within these categories. Therefore, just as local written and spoken narratives would be given equal (but different) authority to those of the ethnographer, photographic representations of knowledge produced by both ethnographers or informants, and 'expressive' and 'realist' uses of photography, would all be treated as having equal, although different, authority. Montage is still seen as 'experimental' ethnographic text. However it does offer a model that is an alternative to conventional ethnographic text. Most existing 'experimental' texts tend to fall somewhere between the two extremes of montage and conventional ethnography, drawing from both, but making a commitment to neither. In this way they maintain sufficient continuity with existing forms of representation to allow their authors to participate in existing academic debates, while also departing from and criticizing conventional narratives.

Visual Sociology (the journal of the International Visual Sociology Association) regularly publishes articles with a high content of photographs. These take a variety of forms, such as photo-essays with various different contents and arrangements of photographs and text, captioned photographs, and use photography in a variety of ways. Many articles that have been published in *Visual Sociology* are informed by scientific and realist approaches to ethnography and photography (e.g. Pauwels 1996; Reiger 1996). However (especially more recently), others develop visual and textual narratives that combine realist approaches to photography with an acknowledgement of the arbitrariness of photographic meanings. For example, Barndt's (1997) essay combines her own documentary photography with commercial images, interview transcripts, academic discussions of globalization, and descriptive and reflexive passages. In one section of her text she interlinks photographs and an interview transcript produced on the same day of her research to form a photo-essay in which interview transcripts caption corresponding photographs. In doing so Barndt uses the words of a Mexican tomato worker, Teresa, and the photographs to construct a story related to themes of women's labour and globalization. While Teresa's voice is represented in the text, it becomes one narrative interlinked with others that is used for the purposes of the researcher's wider project. However, this photo-essay itself becomes a sub-narrative in the author's wider, layered story as she later describes how her other informant, Susan, a Canadian cashier who sells the tomatoes, made the representations of Teresa meaningful in terms of her own reality. Barndt's essay takes a step towards multivocality.

In a recent article, '*Panos* for the *brancus*' (Pink 1999b), I attempted a semi-montage style. Rather than captioning photographs with conventional defining statements, the photographs are embedded in the transcript of a conversation in which Alberto and Tomas, who had different understandings of their content, discussed the images (see Chapter 3). In a reflexive, written commentary, I discuss how knowledge was produced through an ethnographic research process that involved woven cloth, photography and video. The article includes diary entries, ethnographic description, theoretical passages, video transcripts and photographs. By leaving the photographs uncaptioned but referenced in the written text, I have attempted to show how the images do not have one meaning, but are made meaningful through a range of emotions, experiences and other discourses that are relevant to their viewers. Moreover, since these images were produced during my own fieldwork, for me each image bears a specific relationship to the different elements of the text. Temporally, they were produced alongside the diary entries and video footage, located with my reflexive commentary, in the past. However, the images and the commentary were also incorporated into another layer of the text in which I use anthropological theory and ethnographic description to develop the academic meanings of the images further and assess their implications for another culture – that of anthropology. My aim in 'Panos for the *brancus*' was not to depart entirely from a realist reading of the photographs. I also interpreted them as representations of the 'real' people I had known and the actual activities in which they had participated. However, my priority was to stress that these images became meaningful on the terms of individuals' understandings of reality. As I explain in the article, my own understanding of the reality of some of the events that occurred during fieldwork actually changed as time went on, thus causing my readings of the photographs also to change.

Realist uses of photographs can provide an important layer of knowledge in ethnographic texts. For example, *Sensuous Scholarship* (Stoller 1997) is presented to the reader as an experimental and reflexive ethnographic text. However, here Stoller uses photographs in a realist stance, as documentary evidence and illustration of his written descriptions, simply captioned as, for example, 'Hauka Spirit Possession, Tillaberi, Niger, 1977' (1997: 50) or 'A medium possessed by the Hauka, Istambula, Tilaberi, Niger 1984' (1997: 54).

Given the context Stoller creates in his text, his realist use of images does not necessarily have a problematically 'objectifying' effect. Embedded in a reflexive written text, these images, overtly realist, provide yet another 'register'. The photographs indeed objectify individuals' performances into generalized roles and actions. Nevertheless, as Marcus (1995) has pointed out, an objectifying discourse is not necessarily out of place in a montage-style text. The reflexive narratives that co-exist in Stoller's written text challenge the reduction of individual subjective experience to objectifying captions and imply to the reader who is really engaging with the text that the captions represent just one interpretation.

In this sense the 'expressive' text serves to fracture (Edwards 1997a: 75) the objectifying potential of the photographs, thus positioning them as just one visual perspective, and not a universal 'truth'.

There are of course many different ways in which photographs may be set within written texts, and vice versa. In the current context of social scientific thesis presentation and academic publishing it is still likely to be the former combination that dominates. However, even when cost limits the number of images that may be included in a written text, photographs may still be used in novel and provoking ways. In *Women and Bullfighting* (Pink, 1997a), wherever possible I tried to use photographs to represent more than simply their content. For example, I captioned images of a bullfighter performing with written details of the technical equipment I had used to take the photograph in order to present my photographs as representations of what amateur photographers may achieve under those circumstances (1997a: 97–8). Other images were captioned in a realist stance (see 1997a: 102) and sometimes I made explicit references between images and the main written text. In one case (1997a: 74), I treat the photograph of Encarni (see Chapter 5) as a realist representation, but its extended caption reflects on the subjectivity of both the context of its production and of the gazes of other informants who spoke about it. The caption aims to provoke readers to question their interpretations of the photograph and recognize the different ways in which the photograph, and the 'traditional' symbols it represents, may be interpreted.

Later in the book (1997a: 173–5) I created a short visual narrative with three captioned photographs. These represented different aspects of the relationship between bullfighting and the media that were not explicitly addressed in the written text, leaving readers/viewers to reflect on the relationship between these and the written narrative.

Figure 21: Media attention is not solely directed at performances. Both *aficionado* and anti-bullfighting meetings (see Figure 22) become 'media events'. In this image a *Canal Sur* television cameraman prepares for a reception in the *Museo Taurino* 1992) whilst the speakers stand by a painting of the deceased bullfighter *Manolete*.
© Sarah Pink

The Commodification of Ritual   173

174   Women   Performers

Figure 22: An interview was carried out by *Antena 3* television during an anti-bullfighting demonstration in Madrid (1992). © Sarah Pink

The Commodification of Ritual   175

Figure 23: This flyer advertises an event to be held in a Madrid bullfighting bar. The speakers include television critics. Such events make explicit the extent to which media discourses are interwoven with aficionado social life and cultural practice

Figure 6.3 These three photographs are set along side the text of a chapter in *Women and Bullfighting* (Pink 1997a: 173–5). They are not treated as illustrations of events, activities or objects described in the text, but are intended to make separate but related comments on the role of the media in the 'world of bullfighting'.

The photo-essay in ethnography

The 'photo-essay', although a relatively well-known genre, is infrequently used for ethnographic representation. The main exceptions include articles published in journals such as *Visual Sociology* (e.g. Bergamaschi and Francesconi 1996; Gold 1995; Harper 1994; Nuemann 1992; Suchar 1993; Van Mierlo 1994). Some have objected to the inability of photographic essays to represent 'data' in a sufficiently objective way. In response, visual sociologists have argued that visual essays can be adapted to the need for objective ethnographic representation. For example, Grady defines the visual essay as 'a statement about human affairs that purports to represent reality', while attempting to avoid subjectivity and ensure validity (Grady 1991: 27, quoted in Simoni 1996: 75). While Grady's approach provides a solution for scientific sociology, as I emphasize throughout this book, subjectivity cannot really be avoided.

Photographs and written text cannot be expected to represent the same information in the same way. If photographs are thought of as a substitute for written words, and expected to achieve the same ends, then a comparison of the two is bound to conclude that written words do the job better. Rather, photo-essays are appropriate for representing certain types of ethnographic knowledge. Therefore, the definition of a photo-essay I use here is not one of solely photographs, but an essay (book, article or other text) that is composed predominantly of photographs. Sometimes the photographs are captioned or will be accompanied by other short texts. Some books or articles are divided into two sections – one photographic, one written – each representing ethnographic knowledge in ways the two media best lend themselves.

This interpretation of the photographic essay invokes the question of what written words can express that photographs cannot, and vice versa. Some have argued that ethnographic photo-essays (and film) cannot offer structural, theoretical or critical analysis. Certainly, photographs cannot represent social structures, words spoken in interpersonal interactions or conventional theoretical and critical responses to existing academic discourses in the *same* way that written texts can. Nevertheless photographs can be used in realist or expressive modes to represent, for example, the corporeal experience and facial expressions of people interacting with one another, or people who stand for institutions and occupy particular places in power structures. Photographs may also be used as critical representations, either with or without written text. Chaplin cites Pollock's (1988) photo-essay of portraits of women, to suggest that 'image-text presentations can make an important contribution to critique' (Chaplin 1994: 97). Schwartz's (1993) Minneapolis Superbowl project is another example of a critical visual essay. In this project Schwartz and other ethnographic photographers worked as 'participant observers' with a team of press photographers. Their project was to produce critical photographic representations that would 'examine the manufacture of the appearance of reality' presented through the iconography of the Superbowl – itself a 'repackaged visual event' (1993: 23). By using novel camera angles they produced photographs whose content represented 'conventional' aspects of Superbowl iconography arranged in 'unconventional' ways. By 'representing representation itself' (Schwartz 1993: 33) in this way, the photographs represent the Superbowl iconography from alternative, and critical, perspectives, making explicit power relations that were not implied in conventional Superbowl photography. Their photographs are supported by provoking captions and a reflexive text about the context in which they were taken. Thus the photographs form the dominant part of the critique of the way the Superbowl spectacle was manufactured.

Photographs can be used to create critical representations that express experiences and ideas in ways written words cannot. This is not to say that one medium is superior to the other, but to seek the most appropriate way to represent different aspects of ethnographic experience and theoretical and critical ideas, and, perhaps most importantly, being prepared to explore how photography can make a significant contribution to this.

Ethics

In Chapter 2 I outlined some standard conventions for respecting informants' rights to anonymity and for demonstrating a commitment to 'protect' their identities and interests. I suggested that the idea of 'protecting' one's informants is sometimes overly paternalistic and that by adopting a collaborative approach, whereby the subjects of the photography participate in producing and selecting the photographs that represent them, some of these issues may be avoided. Nevertheless, whatever the role of informants in the photographic production and representation, ethnographers/authors, in negotiation with publishers, are usually responsible for final editorial decisions relating to those photographs. These decisions should be informed not solely by the willingness of informants/subjects for their photographs to be published, but also by ethnographers' knowledge of the social, cultural and political contexts in which the published photographs will be viewed and interpreted. As James, Hockey and Dawson stress, ethnographers should not only take an academic approach to ethnographic texts that acknowledges they are constructed 'fictions' or 'partial truths', but should also recognize that their representations can have political implications, and may be appropriated and used by policy makers or other powerful bodies (James et al. 1997: 12). When ethnographers use photographs to make academic points they should also consider the personal, social and political implications of the publication of these images for their subjects.

When ethical considerations rule out using some photographs, specific visual representations of ethnographic knowledge or theoretical ideas have to be sacrificed or expressed in other ways. For example, in a recent essay (Pink 1998a) I described how in Guinea Bissau I became involved in the story of a local woman, whom I have called 'Miranda', who had a child with a European development worker. Photography was part of my relationship and communications with Miranda. Visual aspects of physical appearance, especially blackness, whiteness and mixed race colour, were also key to our conversations and my analysis. I do not usually change informants' names, but here I felt that to represent Miranda's story I should conceal the identities of those concerned. Therefore I could not include the photographs that had informed our discussions, and that would have helped me to represent how people discussed sameness and difference in terms of visual references to skin colour. Another strategy for 'protecting' photographic subjects is the practice of blurring or covering their faces. Lomax and Casey (1998) successfully used this technique to publish video stills that guarantee a certain amount of anonymity. However, this practice is uncommon in ethnographic work and is difficult to reconcile with the idea of using photography *because of* its specificity.

This book focuses mainly on publishing ethnographers' own photographs, but other people's photographs may also help support academic points. In the United Kingdom, ethnographers (like artists) usually own copyright to photographs they have produced themselves. However, if a photograph's copyright is owned by someone else, their permission and possibly a fee is required for its publication. As regards publishing photographs of other people, the situation is less clear. Fetterman states that '[a]n individual's verbal permission is usually sufficient to take a picture. Written permission, however, is necessary to publish or display that picture in a public forum' (1998: 67). In my experience, including when photographs of me have been published, written consent was not required. While for Fetterman this might be a moral requirement, it is not always required by publishers, therefore the ultimate decision often lies in the hands of the ethnographer who possesses the photograph. Copyright law can also vary in different countries. While publishers can normally advise on this, ethnographers may wish to inform themselves on both copyright of their own photographs and that of other people. Good starting points for this are the Design and Artists Copyright Society (DACS) (http://www.dacs.co.uk) and the UK Copyright Service (http://www.copyrightservice.co.uk). These websites also provide links to other national copyright sites.

Summary

In this chapter I have proposed a reflexive approach to constructing texts that combine photographs and words. Authors of ethnography should pay careful attention to the theoretical issues, experiential knowledge and textual strategies that inform their practices of representation. This demands attention to captioning and use of tense, and awareness of how different textual strategies imply particular meanings within texts. Meanings do not, however, reside solely in texts, but ethnographic texts are interpreted and given meanings by readers on *their own* terms. Ethnographers should therefore consider how their texts will be situated and made meaningful in terms of other discourses and other texts. Novel textual strategies that combine photographs and written words to use reflexive subjective or 'expressive' texts or images alongside objectifying, realist texts may challenge conventional approaches. To read or create such texts reflexively ethnographers should account for how photographs interact with, cross-reference and produce meaning in relation to other elements in the text, and how these connections are given meaning by discourses and gazes that exist outside the text.

CHAPTER 7

Video in Ethnographic Representation

Video and representation

In Chapter 4 I argued that video is not simply a 'data collecting tool' but a technology that participates in the negotiation of social relationships and a medium through which ethnographic knowledge is produced. Here I discuss how video may subsequently be used to represent ethnographic knowledge.

Anthropological filmmakers have led the way in using moving images for ethnographic representation, conventionally producing edited ethnographic documentary films or videos. Successful ethnographic documentaries are screened at ethnographic film festivals, are used for teaching or are broadcast on television. This remains the practice of most visual anthropologists and the aspiration of many postgraduates. However, this chapter is not a hands-on guide to ethnographic video production; Masters degree programmes in the United Kingdom (e.g. at the University of Manchester's Granada Centre for Visual Anthropology) and elsewhere provide practical training in camera, sound and editing skills, as well as ethnographic film theory. Ethnographic documentary production is a vast and detailed topic and is covered in depth in other texts (e.g. Barbash and Taylor 1997), written by practitioners with years of ethnographic filmmaking experience. These books are excellent sources of reference and rather than repeating their work I take a different focus. Not all students and researchers who use video in their research aspire to produce ethnographic videos, or have video footage of the appropriate technical or visual format or quality to do so. Here I explore other possible uses of video in ethnographic representation, including using video footage and stills in conference presentations and/ or printed text.

Defining 'ethnographic video'

Crawford (1992: 74) lists 'Ethnographic *footage*' as the first of seven categories of ethnographic film, the others being: research films (for

academic audiences); ethnographic documentaries; ethnographic television documentaries; education and information films; other non-fiction
films; and fiction films. Here I use the term 'ethnographic video', similarly
in its broadest sense, to refer to any video footage that is of ethnographic
interest or is used to represent ethnographic knowledge. From this
perspective 'ethnographic video' does not need to conform to specific film
styles or conventions. Rather, it becomes 'ethnographic' when it is used as
such. Therefore video representations of any length or style that are used
to represent ethnographic knowledge may be referred to as 'ethnographic
video'. While video (or film), such as fiction, home movies, or television
documentaries may be used ethnographically and might be 'ethnographic' in that they are of interest to ethnographers (see Crawford 1992:
74), they are not discussed here. This chapter is about how video footage
shot as part of ethnographic research might be used to represent
knowledge about that research to mainly academic audiences.

Debates about the definition of ethnographic film/video have concentrated on documentary film production. However, knowledge of the
historical and contemporary theoretical perspectives that have informed
these discourses is also relevant to other uses of video in ethnographic
representation. Early ethnographic film theory and practice suggested
ethnographic film should represent 'whole' cultures and, to ensure its
scientific value, ethnographic film styles should (among other things)
avoid close-ups and attempt to film 'whole' contexts, activities and
action, as well as be minimally edited and use only original synchronous
sound (e.g. Heider 1976). These approaches intended to avoid subjectivity and specificity and insisted that 'ethnographic' concerns should
be prioritized above 'cinematic' strategies. In the 1980s, responses to
these initial approaches suggested new theoretical perspectives that put
new demands on film styles. For example, Rollwagen argued that
anthropological film should be informed by existing anthropological
theory and structured according to anthropological demands (1988).
Ruby, one of the first visual anthropologists to engage with notions of
reflexivity in the early 1980s, argued for a reflexive approach to
ethnographic filmmaking that would break down the art/science
dichotomy that had dominated social science (1982). More recently,
MacDougall (1997) proposed that ethnographic documentary film
should be used to challenge objectifying approaches in anthropology
to emphasize the experiential and individual nature of social life and
develop its potential to represent individuals and specific aspects of
experience. This approach informs a style of filmmaking in which
individuals rather than 'whole cultures' dominate and the subjectivities
of both filmmakers and subjects are appreciated.

The debates over ethnographic film have been well rehearsed (e.g.
Crawford and Turton 1992; Devereaux and Hillman 1995; Heider 1976;
Loizos 1993; Morphy and Banks 1997; Rollwagen 1988). A detailed
analysis of them here is not my concern, but *is* a necessary background for

any aspiring ethnographic documentary maker. Not only is it important to understand how theories inform ethnographic documentary styles but, as Loizos has pointed out, 'there are several contexts in which the question of classification becomes practically important' (Loizos 1993: 8). These include seeking funding for film production, eligibility of films to compete in ethnographic film festivals (and how they are classified by film prize judges) and acquisition and use of films by educational institutions and libraries. Not only film/video makers' own definitions, but also other people's classifications of ethnographic films determine how they are eventually used and interpreted. If an ethnographic documentary video is produced for dissemination in academic or popular circles (at film festivals, as a teaching resource, or television documentary) the video's style, technical specifications and image quality must conform to the demands of those audiences and institutions.

The relationship between video research and video representation

In Chapter 4 I discussed how researchers may combine video with still photography, tape recording, note taking and other methods in projects in which video making was not the main objective. Then, in Chapter 5, I suggested how video materials might be analysed alongside other research materials. Here the focus is on how such video recordings which are already interlinked with other ethnographic media may be integrated into ethnographic representation.

In Chapter 4 I described how a distinction between research footage and 'cinematic' footage has associated the former with science and the latter with art, thus arguing that the former should have no role in representation. Here I suggest that these categories of ethnographic film and 'research footage', and corresponding roles proposed for them, should be re-thought. Some have rightly argued that the same footage may participate in more than one category. For instance, Crawford defines 'Ethnographic *footage* . . . [as] . . . unedited film material, which may be used in its unedited form for research purposes or eventually be edited into a film' (1992: 74). However, subsequent approaches have treated research and documentary footage as two distinct types shot with different intentions. Barbash and Taylor argue that while documentary footage, shot with an intentionally creative narrative, would be edited into ethnographic film, 'the essential point of research footage is that it be as unselective and unstructured as possible – in other words that it provide less *discourse about* social life than an *objective record* of it (Barbash and Taylor 1997: 78). In research, '[t]he camera is deployed as an impartial instrument in the service of science, fixing all that is fleeting for infinite future analysis' (1997: 78). In this scenario research footage has no place in ethnographic representation; it would be 'translated into words' in the way I criticized in Chapter 5. According to Barbash and Taylor, it would be unsuitable for finished films since good observational documentary differs from research footage as 'in its pursuit of objectivity, research filming tends to lack that engagement with human affairs that makes them, to their participants, real. The desire to be impartial tends to make the filming unselective, and so the footage may seem unstructured to anyone not already in the know' (1997: 78). Barbash and Taylor are right to insist that ethnographic documentary footage is selectively and carefully shot to correspond with structural and stylistic demands of documentary making. However, by using an art/science dichotomy to associate artistic, subjective and selective creativity with representation and scientific, objective and systematic recording with research, they not only ignore the inevitable subjectivity research involves but by defining research footage so narrowly rule out its potential for ethnographic representation. They delimit video research and video representation as two essentially different projects and in doing so restrict the potential of video rep-resentations for reflexive engagement with the research context. The relationship between video research and video representation needs to be explored in terms that go beyond existing discussions which focus almost solely on the production of ethnographic videos or the translation of video recordings into verbal knowledge. This argument follows on from many of the points I made for photography in Chapter 6. Just as different styles of 'expressive' or 'realist' photography may co-exist within the same text, different types of video footage may similarly be combined.

The methods I suggested in Chapter 4 aim to produce research video that is not objective recording, but subjective text, often produced colla-boratively with informants. It is never impartial and not necessarily unstructured and usually *does* engage with human experience and individual concerns. A reflexive approach to using research video in representation involves situating video footage in the research process to understand how knowledge was produced through video recording, exploring, for instance, the relationship between video recording and other verbal, written or photographic knowledge produced during the research. By examining how different visual and written materials give meaning to one another, researchers may find some video footage is best used as realist recording, while other sequences communicate expressively.

Researchers develop different sets of methods for different projects. For example, my research in Spain privileged photography and writing. This research was represented in a small photographic exhibition, a book with photographs (Pink 1997a), journal articles and a CD ROM. In Guinea Bissau I simultaneously used video, photography and written notes. My ethnographic knowledge was produced through and between these different media and I represented it in a combination of written text, photographs and video clips and hypermedia. In contrast, the brief for my MA final project in Visual Anthropology was to produce an ethnographic video and dissertation. Since the ethnographic video was a requirement, the video making process dominated the project and the dissertation was

based on the video making process as well as participant observation and
in-depth interviews.

The ways ethnographers intend to represent their research inevitably
inform how they approach their projects, the technologies used, their
relationships with informants, and the experiences and knowledge they
produce. These relationships, technologies and experiences might also be
reflected in their representations. When video plays a key role in the
research it seems appropriate to incorporate video in its representation.
This does not necessarily mean editing a documentary ethnographic
video, but, for example, using video clips, stills or transcripts in conference
presentations or hypermedia texts, or with written descriptions in printed
publications. Below I suggest some ways in which researchers may
experiment with ethnographic video representations. First, however,
I discuss video as a medium for ethnographic representation, its difference
from and similarities to other media and the theories attached to its use.

Video, other media and reflexive text

As Edwards has argued for photography (see Chapter 6), use of video for
ethnographic representation should be informed by an understanding of
the nature of video as a medium, and the type of knowledge it best
represents. In the existing literature there is virtually no discussion of
video in ethnographic representation. However, visual anthropologists
have engaged with related issues in an extensive debate about the
relationship between written text and ethnographic film which form a
relevant background for discussing ethnographic uses of video.

There has been no absolute agreement over the purpose and nature of
ethnographic uses of moving images. Historically, approaches to this
have shifted with new theoretical ideas. In the 1970s and 1980s filmmakers like Heider and Rollwagen (although in different ways) argued
that ethnographic films should respond to the same scientific criteria
applied to ethnographic writing (see above). Working in the scientific and
realist paradigm of the time, they selected corresponding bases upon
which to compare film and text. However, during the 1980s and 1990s the
art/science distinction that had made ethnographic film so problematic
was increasingly dissolved. During this period the demand for reflexivity
in ethnographic writing increased (see Chapters 1 and 6) and some
ethnographers began to characterize their representations as inevitably
selective constructions, 'partial truths' and ultimately literary works –
'fictions'. It was argued that the scientific objectivity that had been
assumed for written text, and that 'artistic' film could not achieve, was in
fact unattainable. Written text was therefore potentially equally as subjective and artistic as film. Ruby suggested that reflexivity also had a place
in film, arguing that anthropological filmmakers should ensure their
audiences were made aware of the differences between reality and film as

a constructed representation. He proposed that more artistic, expressive forms had a space in anthropology Ruby (1982: 130) and that 'since film allows us to tell stories with pictures, its potential becomes enhanced within a reflexive and narrative anthropology' (1982: 131). By this time reflexivity had begun to develop in Australian ethnographic filmmaking (especially in David and Judith MacDougall's films), during a period of technical and epistemological innovation in which 'the ability of the film-makers to be increasingly explicit about how the films were made, and the whys and for-whoms of their making' (Loizos 1993: 171).

New bases for comparing film and text developed as the art/science dichotomy was challenged and they were seen as equally selective, constructed representations rather than objective realist texts. However, new differences between film and written text were also emphasized, maybe most importantly because they have different potentials for rep-resenting human experience and a different relationship to the 'reality' of ethnographic situations. However, anthropologists have differed in their conclusions about where these differences lie. For instance, Hastrup argues that the reflexivity that helps contextualize meanings and differ-ences in ethnographic writing cannot be achieved in ethnographic film because the iconographic visual communication of film is 'taken at face-value' and cannot invoke the degree of reflexivity and self-conscious knowledge that written text does (Hastrup 1992: 21). In contrast, the ethnographic films and theoretical written work of MacDougall demon-strate that reflexivity is not a unique characteristic of written text, but may also be represented visually.

Other visual anthropologists have compared anthropological film and text on a different basis. For Barbash and Taylor, ethnographic writing is not concerned so much with reflexivity. Instead,

anthropological texts tend to be . . . (although of course by no means exclu-sively) concerned with non-intuitive abstractions like social structure or population statistics

while

[f]ilm is a quintessentially phenonemological medium, and it may have a different orientation to social life than anthropological monographs. It has a unique capacity to evoke human experience, what it feels like to actually be-in-the world. (Barbash and Taylor 1997: 74–5)

Devereaux similarly argues that 'the camera's special virtue . . . is its direct relation to the personal and the particular', pointing out that whether or not ethnographic film can represent 'reality', its 'ties to the specific' cannot be denied. In contrast

Writing, especially academic writing, flees the particular and takes hold of the abstract, that enemy of experience. The expository project, extrapolating from the particular, sticking close explaining, is not impossible in documentary film. But sticking with the particular, sticking close to experience, is, if anything, more possible in anthropological film than in writing. (Devereaux and Hillman 1995: 71–2)

Moving images and written text certainly bear different relationships to 'experience' and 'the particular' and represent these differently. However Barbash and Taylor and Devereaux's almost binary distinctions seem to ignore how many ethnographers write texts that go beyond structures and statistics to contend with subjectivity and the evocation of experience (see Chapter 6).

MacDougall's comparison of ethnographic film and writing focuses on how anthropologists have struggled with the 'problem of the individual'. This has been the 'raw unit of anthropological study' but ironically has not conventionally been an acceptable element of ethnographic representation. MacDougall suggests that while, 'ethnographic writing can more easily elide' this contradiction, in ethnographic film the individual 'is sometimes felt to claim altogether too much of their [ethnographic filmmakers'] attention' (1995: 220–1). Therefore written text can subdue the individual, whereas film cannot. While conventionally ethnographic text tended to the abstract, ethnographers are now writing an increasing number of 'reflexive' texts that aim (although may not always achieve) to come closer to individual experience and the specific in social life (see Chapter 6). Therefore the 'problem of the individual' is a current concern for ethnographic writers and filmmakers. Nevertheless, moving images and written words have the potential to specialize in different elements of the general and specific and thus represent different types of ethnographic experience and theory. They should not therefore be expected to represent these themes in the same way, as their differences in fact allow ethnographers to broach key issues in different ways. In common, moving-image and written representations form part of ethnographers' projects to represent relationships between different elements (individual, specific, abstract, general, between theory and experience). In some projects the best strategy may be to combine these media.

Below I suggest a reflexive approach that takes advantage of the different ways video, photography, and written text can represent ethnographic experience, theory and critique. By combining different media for ethnographic representation researchers can juxtapose different types of knowledge, subjectivity, epistemology and voice in ways that compliment one another. However, reflexivity does not exist just within the text. In Chapter 6 I noted how new types of text demand new forms of readership. Therefore, first, I discuss video and reflexive viewing.

Ethnographic video audiences

While there is an existing literature on ethnographic film audiences, to my knowledge audience responses to ethnographic video footage have not been analysed (with the exception of screening video for informants, see Chapter 4). Until recently, little was known about the viewing practices of ethnographic film audiences. However, since the 1990s ethnographic research into how audiences interpret ethnographic film (e.g. Martinez 1992) has developed in tandem with new approaches to studying audiences in media studies (e.g. Morley 1996). These disciplines have also converged in what has been called 'media ethnography' (see Crawford and Hafsteinnson 1996) which takes an ethnographic approach to studying audiences. It has been argued that audience research is a moral issue and is part of the ethnographers' duty to protect their informants. Even if informants agree to footage of them being presented publicly, they may not understand the full implications of such public exposure. As Braun points out in his video *Passing Girl, Riverside: An Essay on Camera Work* (1998), when a Ghanaian village chief agreed to Braun showing video images of his village in North America, did he really understand the implications of this? Consent is one thing, the extent to which it is really informed, or by what it is informed is another.

Ethnographic texts, be they books, videos or photographs, are not usually released for public consumption without some consideration of how they communicate. It is advisable to research audience responses to video representation before disseminating it in the public domain. Documentary video makers normally show rough-cuts of their work to various viewers. This may offer professional guidance on the content, stylistic and technical matters before a final edit as well as examples of viewers' responses. As I suggested in Chapter 4, when possible, rough-cuts may also be shown to ethnographic video subjects for their comments and approval before the final version is cut. Sometimes informants can anticipate how certain other viewers may interpret the video and can comment on this. However, it is difficult to predict precisely how video texts will be made meaningful as once they are available in a public domain they are subject to diverse (mis)understandings.

Visual anthropologists now pay serious attention to the politics of ethnographic film representation and spectatorship. In a series of essays (1990, 1992, 1996), based on his research with ethnographic film audiences, Wilton Martinez has shown how individuals' readings of ethnographic films are embedded in complex sets of existing power relations and cultural narratives that 'conventional' ethnographic film narratives and pedagogical strategies do not challenge. Martinez has followed Baudry's (1996) suggestion that ethnographic film viewers are presented with at least two subject positions – 'those constructed by the film(maker) on the one hand, and by the represented subjects on the other' (1996: 74) – therefore demonstrating that individuals' actual viewing practices depend on how the relationship between these different subject positions is constructed *in* the film text, and in viewers' *own* interactions with these subject positions. However, Martinez criticizes conventional ethnographic filmmakers for assuming a subject position for their viewers that is part of an objectifying and disempowering approach to ethnographic representation. Martinez's research indicates that even when filmmakers intend to situate the viewer in a position that challenges ethnocentric and racist ideas, these aims are often not achieved as 'mostly conventional ethnographic films help reinforce students' ethnocentric beliefs' (1996: 77–8). Martinez's critique has alarming implications for ethnographic filmmakers and has been widely referenced.

MacDougall has also highlighted the complexity of viewers' relationships to film. Drawing from the ideas of film critics, he points out the multiplicity of ways that film may act on viewers: 'the conventions of filming and editing do not simply direct us to different visual points of view in a film but orchestrate a set of overlapping codes of position, narrative, metaphor and moral attitude' (1995: 223). MacDougall also emphasizes the specificity of the relationships individuals develop with texts:

> Our reading of a film, and our feelings about it, are at every moment the result of how we experience the complex fields this orchestration creates – partly dependent again upon who we are and what we bring to the film. This complexity extends to our relationship to different modes of cinematic address. (1995: 223)

MacDougall's points can be applied not only to documentary ethnographic film, but also to other types of video representation. Differently constructed videos will both act on and be acted on by different viewers in their own individual ways.

Viewers' interpretations of films depend not only on the subjective relationships individuals develop with film texts, but also on the circumstances of viewing, including the interactions between audience members and the intersubjectivity among viewers. For example, when I screened part of *The Women Who Smile* (Lydall and Head 1990) to a group of second-year sociology students, their interpretations of the film were framed by their individual readings as well as the viewing context and how they negotiated these meanings with fellow students. I introduced *The Women Who Smile* as an 'ethnographic' documentary and asked them to view the film thinking about what made it of ethnographic, rather than purely documentary, interest, and what specific information of sociological interest it contained. I told them that after the film they would discuss these themes in groups and then present their ideas to the class. Therefore the viewing context itself was constructed: the group was to view a film that I had defined as ethnographic, consider its elements of ethnographic interest as individuals, and then share that information with a group of three or four others with whom they had previously worked. Predictably, the students gave the film sociological meanings; they identified the film as being about kinship, ritual, economic activity, gender roles. We also discussed how members of a popular television audience with no access to the academic categories the students had used might have seen the film as 'documentary' rather than 'ethnographic'. The group suggested that a TV audience may have empathized with themes such as motherhood by creating continuities and differences between their own personal experiences and those of women represented in the film.

Once people begin to discuss their different interpretations and experiences of film it becomes clear that it would be impossible to produce a text that has the same effect on, or pleases, everyone. In 1992 I attended an ethnographic film festival in Granada (Spain). One of the films screened was *The Condor and the Bull* (Getzels and Gordon 1990) a film about an Andean village festival. During the festival the locals become drunk and a live condor, captured for the event by local men, is tied to the back of a bull. Discussions began during the session after the screening and continued later that night after dinner when the festival participants (mainly anthropologists and filmmakers from Europe and Latin America) sat around a large table in the open air. Some viewers found this film, made by a British woman and a North American man, problematic. They felt it represented Latin American villagers as drunken and their festivals as primitive and chaotic. Filming people when they are drunk always raises ethical issues, but whether these create ethical problems also depends on how the film is interpreted. Other viewers had a different impression of the film. Some felt the villagers' drunkenness was only to be expected as people in many places get drunk at festivals. They did not feel it was a negative representation of the villagers or their festival.

I noted above that reflexivity has already been incorporated in ethnographic filmmaking practice in films that recognize filmmakers' roles and intentions and the constructedness of the reality they represent. Some have also begun to consider how a self-conscious approach to viewing ethnographic documentary may be developed or guided through novel narrative forms (see Mermin 1997) and this is important reading for aspiring ethnographic filmmakers. Here, however, I am not concerned with ethnographic film narrative, but to suggest uses of video in reflexive ethnographic representations that may themselves be read reflexively.

Video representations of ethnography

There are various options for using video in ethnographic representation. For example, ethnographic documentary, showing clips in conference presentations, exhibitions or electronic representations (see Chapter 8), combining moving and still images, voiceover and text in edited documentaries, or printing video stills and transcripts alongside descriptive passages in books or journals. Some of these are discussed below.

Producing an ethnographic documentary about a piece of research

While good ethnographic documentaries can sometimes be edited from footage not intended for documentary making, successful documentaries are usually carefully planned and shot with a documentary narrative in mind. In such projects video making becomes part of the research narrative itself. However, while there are some parallels between ethnographic research and ethnographic video making, some ethnographic filmmakers would argue that ethnographic documentary making requires specialist study and training in practice and theory. Moreover, whereas ethnographic documentary making is often likened to participant observation in that it involves a long-term association with the film's subjects, ethnographic films are not always shot during long-term fieldwork. Television documentaries like Granada Television's *Disappearing World* and the BBC's *Under the Sun* series were based on an ethnographer's existing work and shot as a collaboration between ethnographers, filmmakers and the film subjects. Thus documentary designs may be informed by existing knowledge of people and cultures. Sometimes existing research can support funding applications or encourage the collaboration of trained filmmakers (if this is needed). Video footage shot during original fieldwork can help potential collaborators or sponsors assess a project's potential and provide examples of visual work for the film's potential participants to view. Ethnographers who work with commercial filmmakers may find that academic, practical and ethical conflicts arise when different agendas of filmmakers and social scientists clash (see Barbash and Taylor 1997; Loizos 1993; Lydall 1990; Woodhead 1987). Another option is for ethnographers to collaborate with specialist ethnographic filmmakers (for example the ethnographic documentary, *Faces in the Crowd* (Henley 1994) represents the sociologist Ann Rowbottom's research but was shot by ethnographic filmmaker Paul Henley).

(Edited) clips

Footage of activities, actions, events, interviews, landscapes, artifacts, or other visual aspects of culture can be carefully edited or simply selected as unedited footage. While a set of clips may not fit together coherently as a full-length documentary narrative, they may be combined with written or spoken words, sound or stills to tell another story. Each clip may itself represent a short story, demonstrate an activity, or represent an informant's spoken narrative or visual self-representation. Some clips may be realist references to actions and events that respect the order these occurred in. Others might be edited to represent 'real' sequences of events, that divert from the original chronology of the footage. There are multiple options, depending on what researchers intend video clips to represent and how clips are situated in relation to other texts that represent aspects of the same ethnographic project.

Each such set of video clips that tells its own ethnographic story may also be part of a larger representation. This wider narrative might include still images, sound and different styles of written text. Rather than photographs and videos serving as illustrations to the written or spoken text, it may be led by any of these media. The same set of video clips may also be used to represent the work in different ways. For example, on my return from Guinea Bissau in 1997 I edited a series of short clips from my weaving project. These sequences represented some key themes from the research and the relationship between the researchers and informants. These clips could be used in a variety of ways to represent different approaches and visual themes. For instance, as a realist recording they represent stages in the technological process of weaving. At the same time they represent the changing nature of the video footage as the friendship between researchers and informants developed and thus become a set of reflexive commentaries about the negotiations between them. Simultaneously, they represent a series of interconnected comments on individual experience and cultural prac- tices and beliefs about animist ritual, attitudes to money and alcohol. Here they could be used to generalize about aspects of local experience through the example of our informant Tomas's subjectivity and his personal enactment of local cultural practices.

Another piece of video footage shot during the carnival in Guinea Bissau was edited down from 30 to eight minutes and used in a con- ference presentation along with a written conference paper (Pink 1998e). In this context the video was intended to work in two ways. It was presented as a realist representation of the town I worked in and its carnival. It documented carnival performances and at the conference this provoked useful discussion and comments. It also represented local people's interactions with the camera and video makers, showing that this was part of the context that produced the video.

In both projects my video clips were selectively shot and edited to represent my own interpretation of the events I experienced in Guinea Bissau. They have some documentary video qualities and would not conform to Barbash and Taylor's definition of research footage. Yet neither are they ethnographic documentary; they tell only very short stories that need to be situated in a wider more informative ethnographic context to be meaningful. These video clips sit between realist and expressive representations since they are short visual documents that form part of constructed ethnographic narratives where they are situated by words and photographs. Clips from unedited video footage may be used similarly.

Video clips, like quotations from field notes or interview transcripts may also be used in conference and seminar presentations. Clips from video interviews can allow informants to 'speak for themselves' and introduce interviewees' voices and visual self-representations into a presentation. Interviewees speak through actions, and by showing researchers images and artifacts as well as in words. By using video clips researchers can avoid having to use spoken words to describe visual knowledge.

Ethnographic representation is not just 'books and films'. Whereas these are more permanent ways of making statements about ethnographic experiences and theoretical concerns, conference and seminar presentations are also an important part of academic work and offer opportunities to present ideas to wider audiences. Conferences and seminars are also ideal situations for presenting short video clips in combination with other images and texts. Moving images (and sound) can distinguish a dry paper, read to an audience that has already listened to other speakers for hours, from a lively evocative presentation that engages its audience visually, as well as in words, inviting them to participate in interpreting visual knowledge and view images that were part of the research experience described in the paper. Video clips can also be used in ethnographic exhibitions where they may be set alongside written texts, photographs or other artistic installations. When planning video presentations it is important to ensure that appropriate video screening or projection facilities are available.

Video that mixes ethnographic footage with other media

Video clips that are combined with other visual, spoken and written text for conference presentations and ethnographic exhibitions may also be edited with these other materials into a more 'complete' video for dissemination. Video offers an option that, like conventional written text, follows a linear narrative constructed by the video editor. Such 'ethnographic videos' differ from 'conventional' ethnographic documentaries as they consist of not only observational documentary footage but also other visual sources and spoken narratives that might include voice over, written text inserts, photographic stills, the researcher's 'talking head', or acted-out reconstructed scenes. They may include novel uses of video footage that challenge conventional ethnographic documentary formats, but explore the potential of the medium further. For example, *Passing Girl, Riverside* (Braun 1998) uses the same video clip of a girl passing his camera repeatedly to the voice over of the video maker reflecting on the power relations involved in producing that image. The composition of such documentary videos emphasizes their constructedness and their authors' selectivity.

Description, transcripts and video stills

Some would predict that in the near future print publishing will be superseded by the ever-increasing on-line publishing. Nevertheless, at the beginning of the twenty-first century book and journal publishing is still the dominant medium for disseminating ethnography as well as for advancing academic careers, thus obliging researchers to represent their work in written words. In this section I discuss how video may form part of printed ethnography as written description, transcripts of video conversations, and captured video stills. In contrast to the idea that visual knowledge should be interpreted and translated into written words, this approach emphasizes the presence of video in research and representation. While written description, transcription and stills do not act on the reader of written text in the same way that screening ethnographic video can, they allow the visual and spoken knowledge of video to become part of ethnographic representation. Existing printed texts that use video stills or transcripts tend to reflect on the role of video in the research and make the process of analysis and the relationship between research and representation explicit (e.g. Ferrándiz 1998; Lomax and Casey 1998; Pink 1999b).

In Chapter 4 I described Lomax and Casey's use of video in research about midwives' home visits. This work is published in an on-line article that embeds video transcripts, digitized sound tracks and video stills in the written text. Lomax and Casey take a realist approach, arguing that '[v]ideo generated data is an ideal resource . . . as it can provide a faithful record of the process as an aspect of the naturally occurring interaction that comprises the research topic' (1998: 1). Their sociological approach incorporates a response to anticipated criticisms from 'traditional' sociology (as do Prosser and other visual sociologists discussed in Chapter 1), that suggests that greater reflexivity can be achieved by including video in the text. Justifying their use of video against 'scientific' sociological opposition they argue that: 'Far from being a distraction or unimportant a reflexive analysis of the research process can contribute to an understanding of the phenomenon under investigation' (1998: 6). In addition to video materials, Lomax and Casey also provide lengthy quotations from field notes where the use of video was discussed, thus situating video within the wider research process. Each line of their transcribed conversations is numbered and submitted to a 'conversation analysis' by which the transcripts and digitized sound presented in the text are analysed. By presenting field notes, video transcripts and stills in the same text, the processes of research and analysis are evoked in the text. Lomax and Casey also make good use of video stills to discuss how midwives and their clients 'managed' the camera during examinations of genitalia and other personal body parts by either switching it off or using their bodies to obstruct its view. The authors also participate in this strategy of concealment by blurring their informants' faces to guard their privacy. Lomax and Casey succeed in representing the visual and verbal qualities of video without including moving video images themselves in the text.

In Chapter 4 I also discussed Ferrándiz's use of video in his research with a Venezuelan spirit cult. In his (1998) essay about using video in this research, Ferrándiz includes descriptive passages about the video footage, sometimes quoting words spoken by the video's subjects and including still images captured from the video. In contrast to Lomax and Casey's descriptions of using video in research, Ferrándiz attempts to evoke the *experience* of video research in his text. The article begins with the following text alongside a video still of a fingerprint and the handwritten name 'ELOY':

'What is this fellow doing?'
'He is filming, *compadre*'
'Filming what, a paper or something?'
'Yes'
'Find me a feather, and ink, and all that stuff, so I can also film. Let me show
    you how I film, *carajito*'
(Ferrándiz 1998: 19)

Having attended a presentation of this project, accompanied by a screening of some 20 minutes of the footage that Ferrándiz describes (at a conference organized by the *Taller de Antropologia Visual* in Madrid, in 1996), my own reading of the article was inevitably influenced by my experience of seeing the footage. However, even without an accompanying screening, the text succeeds in interlinking a narrative that represents the experiential elements of video production and viewing with theoretical and ethnographic narratives about the visual and spirit possession. Ferrándiz includes twelve still images from the video-tapes. In one section of the article, where he describes how his informants used and interacted with the technology when being filmed by him and when filming one another, he includes a series of video stills from footage shot by himself and different informants. These are either captioned with quotes from tapes in which video subjects addressed the camera verbally, or with Ferrándiz's descriptions. For example, an image of a woman videoed by 'Ruben' is captioned: 'Ruben as cinematographer, interacting with Carmencita la Canelita (possessing Teresa) through the camera' (1998: 28). In this project video images and technology became a medium of communication and representation between and among researcher and informants. As video was so important to Ferrándiz's research narrative his written text would be incomplete without it: the video images could not be translated into words. The video stills are not merely 'I was there' images or realist recordings, but fragments of the video images through which meanings were created and communicated in the research. These video stills play at the edge of realism and fiction. They challenge the idea of visual truth as, in the case of the caption I have quoted above, some of the stills are of people who are not there, but whose bodies are possessed by spirits and are therefore someone else.

Further uses of video stills may include constructing visual narratives, as in a photo-essay (see Chapter 6), montage images, or poster presentations. Photographic narratives or montage might be composed, for example, of video stills that represent a series of points or themes from the research. Arranged together in the same montage image or as a series of captioned images, stills can create expressive representations that interlink different moments and themes in the research. Presented in this way, stills can also allow people to view a visual research narrative differently, without demanding that it is viewed in a linear video narrative. Expressive montage images and poster presentations offer possibilities for further creativity – montage or posters may combine video stills, photographs and other depictions, interview quotations and academic commentaries.

Video stills and transcripts may be used in printed text as both realist and expressive representations. As the examples I have discussed demonstrate, ethnographers have used stills as evidential data, claims of the ethnographer's authority, as well as symbolic or evocative images of the context in which they were produced, the social relationships this involved and the knowledge associated with it.

Collaboration

As Barbash and Taylor point out, 'Documentary filmmaking is by nature collaborative. Quite simply, it's impossible to make a film about other people completely on your own' (1997: 74). Video research is equally collaborative. However, making finished ethnographic representations tends to involve less collaboration and, as Barbash and Taylor note for film, there is a danger 'the film maker will remain the real author, with the participants simply being brought in to legitimate a collaborative rubber stamp' (1997: 89). In Chapter 4 I discussed collaborative uses of video in research. In some documentary projects the film's subjects have participated in editing or commented on how they and their cultures are represented. For example, the film *Zulay Frente al Siglo XXI* (Prelorain, Prelorain and Saravino 1992) represents the experiences of Zulay, who travels from Ecuador to Los Angeles in the USA to participate in editing an ethnographic film from footage shot of her. When documentaries cover sensitive topics this may help ensure that a film's political implications are not problematic for its subjects. Nevertheless, ethnographers usually edit their video clips or documentary and write up their texts alone or with the support of technical specialists. Particularly for students and unfunded researchers, it could be costly to return to a distant research site, or host informants 'at home', making it difficult to show people how they are represented and receive their impressions of rough-cuts. Researchers who work in areas close to their own homes might have more opportunities to collaborate with informants, whose participation may not solely let them influence how they are represented in the public domain, but may also increase the researcher's understanding of them.

Ethics

General ethical concerns were discussed in Chapter 2, the examples discussed above have highlighted some ethical issues specific to using video in ethnographic representation and demonstrate how these were dealt with in existing projects. For example, Lomax and Casey (1998) have blurred their informants' faces to conceal their identities and Braun's (1998) video raised the question of whether, when people consent to be filmed, they are really 'informed' about how they will be represented and how others will interpret this. Some ethnographers have tried to resolve this by showing their video footage to the people represented in it, inviting them to participate in the process of editing and representation. Finally, as I noted in Chapter 2, an ethical approach also involves attempting to anticipate how one's representations will be interpreted by a range of other individual, institutional, political and moral subjectivities.

Summary

In this chapter I explored some of the issues and potentials of video for ethnographic representation. As I have demonstrated, there are many more possibilities for video representation than simply ethnographic documentary production. Nevertheless, while I have departed from the emphasis on 'finished' ethnographic documentary videos or films, the debates surrounding ethnographic documentary provide a background for understanding video in ethnographic representation. These existing debates will inevitably inform how other academics receive video representations of ethnography. Moreover, the theory that informs discussions. of contemporary ethnographic documentary is well developed and can inform other video representations. Producers of video representations can also learn from the attention ethnographic filmmakers and critics have recently begun to pay to the audiences of their representations.

CHAPTER 8

Electronic Texts

Electronic technologies and ethnographic representation

The internet and other electronic technologies are part of the everyday personal and professional lives of many researchers and students of ethnography. Electronic media are also used increasingly to produce, store, represent and view ethnographic materials. In Chapters 3, 4 and 5 I discussed uses of digital media in research and for archiving, interpreting and analysing images. Electronic hypermedia is also rapidly becoming established for publishing ethnographic work, signified by the growing number of on-line journals, individual academics who independently publish their work on-line, university departmental websites, specialist organizations and internet groups, and CD ROM and DVD publications.

Electronic hypermedia offers exciting possibilities for ethnographic representation, some of which are demonstrated in existing publications. Others will be created along with changing theoretical and practical innovations. New technologies also invite new fields of research and debate for social scientists, including the study of electronic text as a medium of representation, ethnographic study of how new technologies are experienced, and theories of electronic communication. Some of these themes have been broached in anthropology (e.g. Pinney 1994) but studies of cyber-space and cyber-identities have become more established in sociology and cultural studies (e.g. Mitchell 1995; Poster 1995). The questions these authors raise have implications for electronic representations of ethnography especially concerning the relationship between the author, user and the medium.

In this chapter, I explore three areas of electronic text's potential for ethnographic representation by examining the nature of electronic text as a medium, how ethnographic hypermedia representations are constructed, and how they are experienced and interpreted by their users. I suggest that a reflexive approach to knowledge may be applied to hypermedia. First, by embedding reflexivity in the text itself as an element of hypermedia *representation* and, secondly, by encouraging hypermedia users to take a reflexive approach to how they create knowledge through their own interactions with hypermedia, thus developing reflexivity as *practice*.

What is ethnographic electronic hypermedia text?

In contrast to the lengthy debates that have raged over ethnographic film (see Chapter 7), the idea of using electronic hypermedia for ethnographic representation has been quite readily accepted by social scientists. While electronic representations can differ radically from printed text, they can also be made to imitate and reproduce the conventions and objectives of printed words and images. Therefore, electronic media do not necessarily dramatically challenge existing styles of representation, but can embody many continuities with established forms. Indeed, as I demonstrate below, most existing hypermedia representations tend simultaneously to imitate and transgress written text, photography and film.

Interactive hypermedia publications usually consist of sets of interlinked files that might contain written words, still or moving images, sound, or a combination of these. The interlinkages between files, or points (e.g. words and images, theoretical sections and ethnographic description) within files support the interactivity of hypermedia; 'the links themselves have meaning' (Biella 1996: 595). Users can normally move between files through hyperlinks embedded in their text as well as using other navigation tools. Links are usually represented with words or visual symbols. Generally, by clicking on the right spot users can follow a hyperlink from one text to another. The ways users can interact with different texts depends on how their authors have used specific software packages to develop and construct links between different text files.

In this chapter I shall usually use 'hypermedia' and 'electronic text' to refer to internet and CD ROM representations. However, these media do have different potentials. CD ROM can have better capacity for storage and fast retrieval of higher-quality photographic and video images, while internet publications are more widely accessible and, because they are published on-line, are usually less bounded than CD ROM texts. In some cases they can be combined, by writing a CD ROM that links to a website to provide enhanced-quality images. Nevertheless these technologies are rapidly developing or being replaced. At present DVD is becoming increasingly popular, and new higher capacity technologies will shortly be available.

The 'ethnographicness' of hypermedia texts should be judged in ways similar to those recommended for ethnographic photography or film. No hypermedia text is essentially ethnographic. Indeed, different approaches might label the same text (or parts of it) ethnographic, or not. Hypermedia texts may contain different texts and narratives, some of which may conform to conventional styles of ethnographic writing or visual representation, whereas other parts of the text represent 'experimental' forms created by the author, informants' texts, or other research documents of various origins. Some texts may be composed completely of ethnographic research materials and reports; in others only certain strands will represent the ethnographic element of a project. The 'ethnographicness' of hypermedia texts is determined partially by the intentions of its authors and users and the routes that they choose to imply and take through it.

Ethnographic hypermedia, the written word and conventional forms

Despite the enormous potential of hypermedia for visual representation, many ethnographic hypermedia representations imitate word-processed printed styles (see especially on-line journals such as *Sociological Research On-line*). Even electronic journals' use of the 'multimedia' potential of hypermedia to include visual and sound files tends to follow conventions set by printed text and is dominated by written words (e.g. *The Journal of Music and Anthropology*). In on-line journals hyperlinks facilitate some strategies that readers may already practise, such as inserting hyperlinks that take readers directly from a reference in the text to a full citation in the bibliography (e.g. *Sociological Research On-line*). Hypermedia responds well to readers' established expectations. Biella has pointed out that one of the 'conventional' requirements of scholarly work is that it 'must be inscribed in a medium which allows rapid, non-linear access to all its components' (Biella 1993: 144) and that authors should assume that their texts will be read non-lineally (1993: 145). Comparing electronic text to printed and film representations, Biella notes that '[r]andom-access navigation is often attributed exclusively to electronic media, but it is clearly a property which facilitated scholarship in books [but not in film] long before the computer revolution' (1993: 144). Nevertheless, as Howard has noted, the linearity of printed text imposes constraints because 'writers are forced into linear sequential mode and are compelled to choose which aspects of a total experience are to be placed first, second, third, etc. The only way to vitalize interconnections that are nonsequential, or multisequential, is to refer back to previous pages' (Howard 1988: 305).

Clearly, hypermedia supports and even encourages non-linear approaches to reading ethnographic representations. In doing so, Howard would argue that '[h]ypertext thus articulates with actual modes of thinking far better than linearly written materials' (1988: 306). This suggests the linear narrative of printed text is not conversant with how we produce or use ethnographic knowledge. Some would take this further to argue that the very construction and content of ethnographic texts should challenge the notion of linearity (e.g. Marcus 1995). Later in this chapter I discuss the potential of hypermedia for such 'experimental texts'.

Articles published in on-line, refereed journals also imitate printed versions as they are presented as 'complete'. This limits how their authors can respond to the possibilities of on-line publishing. Once published, articles tend not to be updated or altered. Moreover, subscription-based on-line journals are usually discrete entities, isolated from other internet resources or websites, and can only be accessed through routes created by their publisher. While this is necessary to restrict access to subscribers, it also limits the potential of internet publications to be interconnected with, and accessed from, other websites. Some journals, like *iNtergraph* (http://www.intergraphjournal.com) are freely accessible and provide open spaces for dialogue with users. Independently published electronic essays (e.g. Banks 1994; Biella 1994) similarly imitate printed text, but are freely accessible and can link or be linked directly to other articles or websites and are more 'open-ended'.

Below I discuss continuities and differences between ethnographic hypermedia representations and the uses of photography and video discussed in chapters 6 and 7. The written word is an able and important means of communicating ethnographic knowledge that certainly has a place in hypermedia representations. However, ethnographic hypermedia need not be dominated by written words; it can be led by images, or even sound. It is up to authors to decide how their texts reference existing forms of representation and combine visual, written and other narratives.

Ethnographic photography and hypermedia

Electronic publications of digitized or digital ethnographic photography are increasingly common in on-line journals (e.g. *Music and Anthropology* and *Sociological Research On-line*), 'virtual galleries' and ethnographic resources (e.g. Stirling's *Turkish Village*; Michael Fischer's *Greentown Pakistan Fieldnote Summary* both accessible at http://www.lucy.ukc.ac.uk). Hypermedia offers interesting opportunities for both conventional and experimental uses of digitized photographs. While there are continuities between uses of photographs in printed and hypermedia ethnographies, hypermedia representations simultaneously transgress and imitate print conventions.

Attempts to theorize the relationship between 'conventional' and digital photography have largely been concerned with the implications of digital imagery for practices and assumptions of conventional photography. It has been suggested that the 'manipulated' digital image destabilizes the assumptions of visual truth associated with the printed still image, and therefore the introduction of digital photographs threatens the very essence of realist photography (see McQuire 1998: 42; Chapter 1). However, this proposal is limited because it neglects to consider the implications of existing assumptions (including the realist paradigm) for digital photography. Any consideration of changes that the introduction of digital photography is likely to invoke should also refer to how it has been appropriated in practice. Digital image manipulation has made it *possible* for ethnographers digitally to 'reinvent', reconstruct and dramatically alter photographs. However, there is little evidence to suggest that new technologies have inspired dramatic shifts in approaches to uses of photography for ethnographic representation. Techniques of manipulation have been available to ethnographers since long before digital photography. As Wright points out, 'the introduction of digital manipulation to photography' has not brought about the 'rupture from existing practices in visual representation' (1998: 207) that Robins has claimed signifies the 'death of photography' (1995: 29). But in practice there has been 'a gradual incorporation, rather than the heralded revolution, in image-making' (T. Wright 1998: 207).

A review of existing ethnographic hypermedia publishing indicates that uses of digital photographs often follow the conventional realist approaches I described in Chapter 6 (e.g. Banks n.d.; Lomax and Casey 1998). Other digitized photographs are treated as products of 'photographic moments' rooted in fieldwork experience (e.g. Biella's *Masaai Interactive* and my own *The Bullfighter's Braid*). In much existing work these are prints that have been scanned and digitized. While they are accessed differently, existing examples also tend to follow the conventions of captioning, illustration and written references to photographs I discussed in Chapter 6 (see, for example, Gledhill and Harris's *Peasant Social Worlds and their Transformation (Mexico and Brazil)* at http://res1.man.ac.uk/multimedia/). My hypermedia text, *Carnival and Cameras* (in progress), is led by a photo-essay that forms its main structuring narrative, through which users may enter other sections of text via hyperlinks embedded in the images themselves and written text. Chalfen's *Traditional Views* (http://nimbus.ocis.temple.edu/~rchalfen/) (n.d.) uses a different strategy by exhibiting a series of 13 photographs, introduced by a page of written text and captioned by explanatory paragraphs. Chalfen's own website is a multistranded text. However *Traditional Views* is a photo-essay that could equally be published in a printed journal.

While digital manipulation certainly offers ethnographers opportunities to use photography in new ways rather than simply rupturing existing approaches, it also allows researchers to enhance how their photographs represent ethnographic information in conventional ways. I have used digital manipulation to enhance my photographs aesthetically and to improve their ability to communicate details of interaction and artifacts. For example, by lightening and altering the contrast of a photograph of a group of women plaiting hair on a veranda I could see the tools they stored under their roof, that had been obscured in my darkly printed photograph.

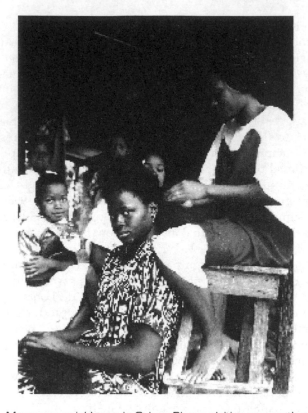

Figure 8.1 My women neighbours in Guinea Bissau plaiting one another's hair in preparation for carnival in 1997. Once this image had been digitized I was able to start working on it with a photo-editing programme. In the United Kingdom the photograph had originally been printed darker than I had intended. When I took it in Guinea Bissau I was originally intending to have it developed locally, where I knew that the print would be over-exposed by UK standards. When I increased the brightness I was able to see details that were previously not visible in the photograph – such as the tools that were stored under the roof over the veranda.

Digital manipulation gives ethnographers more autonomy over how their photographs are presented. These techniques of manipulation (such as cropping, or changing the colour mix, hue or brightness) do not necessarily go beyond the results an experienced colour printer could achieve. While theoretically it can be argued that the very manipulability of digital images implies doubt that they are realist representations, many ethnographic digital photographs do not break with realist conventions and are treated (and often interpreted) as realist representations. As Wright points out, '[r]ather than limiting photography's ability to record a "truthful" image, computer manipulation has the potential to broaden the repertoire of the photographic system and to enrich photography's scope and ability to describe the visual world' (T. Wright 1998: 217).

Figure 8.2 Girls dressed up in 'ethnic' costumes for the carnival celebrations organized by the Catholic Mission School in Canchungo, Guinea Bissau. Once this image had been scanned I manipulated it by adding small white dots to the eyes of the two girls to help the photograph conform to aesthetic conventions and to indicate that their gaze was directed towards the camera (as it was when I took the photograph). Some may feel that such manipulation is unjustified. However, it could be argued that it simply uses visual conventions to represent a specific aspect of the 'photographic moment' (that the subjects were looking towards the camera).

Above I highlighted some continuities and differences between ethnographic uses of photography in printed and electronic representations, concentrating until now on photographs themselves. However, as I argued in Chapter 6, the way photographs are situated in relation to other texts or images determines the ethnographic meanings they represent. Hypermedia presents opportunities to depart from the layouts,

captions and referencing systems of printed text described in Chapter 6
and offers new ways of interconnecting visual and written knowledge.
Embedded in hypermedia text, digitized images can be presented and
situated in new ways. For example, they may be enlarged, linked to
other images and theoretical texts, connected to visual and written
information about the research context, or shown in sequence to
correspond with oral narratives. In my CD ROM *The Bullfighter's Braid*,
for instance, I linked video clips of myself taking group photographs
with the actual photographs and a written discussion. These sequences
show how groups united and dispersed for their 'photographic
moments', and represent the social and material context of those
'moments'. The fixity of visual meanings may be questioned by
presenting the same images in different narratives, in each of which
they may take on a new significance. While in printed text photographs
occupy one single position and the same photograph is rarely printed
more than once, hypermedia allows the same photograph to appear in
any number of different narratives so that the multiple contexts in
which the photograph becomes meaningful and the arbitrary nature of
these meanings can be made explicit. For example, in the 'Photographic
narrative' of my CD ROM *Interweaving Lives* (1998d), I take a selection of
around 40 photographs shot when Tomas and his son Antoine were
weaving in my garden in Guinea Bissau. In this section of the CD ROM
I created two narratives using the same photographs, but sometimes
grouping them differently and using different captions. One narrative
focuses on friendship and how the relationships between the main
characters in the project developed. The other attempts to describe the
technological process of weaving. By using the same photographs in
different narratives the photographs themselves can also be used as
symbols of and meeting points between the different narratives and
experiences they refer to.

Hypermedia representations and ethnographic video/film

With the increasing availability of digital cameras and edit facilities,
digital video is becoming a popular medium among ethnographic filmmakers (see Chapters 4 and 7). As I described in Chapter 4, digital video
implies new relationships between video makers and subjects as well as
new viewing possibilities during fieldwork, and in Chapter 7 I suggested
how video clips and stills produced during fieldwork might be used in
conventional presentation and printed texts. Hypermedia presents a
further opportunity for linking moving and still images, sound and
written words in the same text.

Like ethnographers' uses of digital photography, ethnographic video
and filmmakers have largely appropriated digital technology for their
existing practice. High-quality digital video images and the convenience

of computerized digital editing make digital technologies an attractive option. In contrast, ethnographic hypermedia uses of digitized video introduce new practices that shift the ways linear film can be viewed by connecting digitized documentary video to written texts, stills and other footage. Electronic representations of film can also invite new forms of ethnographic film scrutiny and critique, while '[i]n the past no simple techniques existed to question and explore ethnographic film *inch by inch*. Interactive media has begun to make critiques, reviews and follow-up studies precise and feasible' (Biella 1996: 599). Biella's review of Fruzzetti and Östör's laser disc version of their ethnographic film *Seed and Earth* describes how his close analysis found problematic subtitling and explanatory information given in an alternative soundtrack that gave misplaced significance to conversations, scenes and activities represented in the film (see Biella 1996). However, it would be inappropriate to suggest that digitized hypermedia representations of ethnographic film should replace ethnographic film screenings. While digital video records high-quality images, footage digitized for internet or CD ROM representations tends to be of a lower image quality and there are important differences between an auditorium and a computer monitor as viewing contexts. At present documentary and hypermedia support and complement one another, and have different qualities.

While internet or CD ROM representations can imitate documentaries, there are some important differences between ethnographic film and hypermedia narratives. Biella has proposed that hypermedia has two key quantitative advantages over linear film: it has greater storage capacity and that it allows more rapid access to information (1994: 241–2). Film, and by implication video, has been characterized as having a linear narrative: 'there is the capacity of film, noted by Pinney, to lead the viewer, merely by the (not necessarily chronological) succession of images, along one particular narrative and explanatory path' (Crawford and Turton 1992: 5). The ability of film and video to represent particular narratives and specific aspects of human experience is one of its advantages. However, as Biella points out, this linearity also has the disadvantage in that the elements that are selected for inclusion in them must be divorced from their own contextual surroundings' (Biella 1994: 241). In contrast, electronically, whole edited ethnographic films may be stored and viewed in their linear form, but as hypermedia is 'less restricted quantitatively' it 'has room to include materials that video-makers would reject as outtakes' (Biella 1994: 241). Hypermedia ethnographies may combine clips, unedited footage and full-length documentaries, offer users quicker access to different sections of these texts (see Biella 1994: 242), enable them to play multiple clips on the same monitor and could even be designed to allow users to blow up video stills and re-edit original digitized footage. Video may be connected by hyperlinks to written texts, photographs, transcripts and footnotes about the video recording process (see Biella 1993, 1994).

Examples of hypermedia texts that use video can be found in Gledhill and Harris's *Peasant Social Worlds and their Transformation*, my own *Carnival and Cameras* (in progress) and several other projects published on-line as part of the ERA project at http://lucy.ukc.ac.uk/ERA/. Video has also been used in electronic journal articles where clips are either embedded in written narratives or accessed through a hyperlink to video files.

Reflexive text: hypermedia and the relationship between research and representation

As I argued in Chapters 6 and 7, reflexivity about how ethnographic knowledge is created can be achieved in printed text or film (see Chapters 6 and 7). Hypermedia's capacity for multilinearity and layering information allows reflexivity to be developed differently and can represent the historical development of ethnographic research and interpretation in ways that written text and film cannot. This is often done by creating hyperlinks between academic or report-style texts and files that represent the research documents and experiences these 'final' reports are based on, and aims to make the relationship between research and representation explicit. As Fischer and Zeitlyn have pointed out, the 'fieldwork experience' is important for the development of an 'anthropological understanding' but is rarely reproduced in printed articles. Their *Experience Rich Anthropology* Project at the University of Kent provides excellent examples of hypermedia texts that represent the results of research and the fieldwork experiences on which published articles and books were based (see http://era.anthropology.ac.uk/ index.htm/). These include photographs, field diaries, video clips and other written texts. One of the most significant projects is *45 years in the Turkish village 1949–1984*, an internet resource of Professor Paul Stirling's *Ethnographic Data Archives* (see http://lucy.ukc.ac.uk/TVillage) which includes Stirling's book *Turkish Village* (1998 [1965]), articles and PhD thesis, as well as his field notes, letters, photographs and data base. This uniquely transparent presentation of Stirling's work allows other researchers to interpret the historical development of his ideas as well as his ethnographic research materials. It also recognizes the importance of photography in Stirling's research that was largely undertaken in a period when ethnographic photography remained 'hidden behind' written text and was rarely discussed in published work.

There are various ways that hypermedia can represent historical development and reflexivity. Stirling did not impose his own reflexive authorial narrative on *45 years in the Turkish village*, yet the relationship between research and representation is implicit in the text. In contrast, other hypermedia authors have developed texts that specifically reflected on how individual ethnographers produced, interpreted and represented their knowledge. Sometimes analysis is explicitly represented in the text, rather than treated as a hidden practice of 'translation'. Biella's CD ROM project, *Masaai Interactive*, was developed from a six-week period of fieldwork among the Masaai people in 1980, during which a series of interviews were filmed and recorded and photographs were taken. Biella shows how interactive hypermedia can represent and annotate the historical development of ethnographic work, thoughts, ideas and inter-pretations, using visual, verbal and written texts. One of Biella's purposes is 'to explore how digital technology can enhance the understanding of anthropological research in which camera and tape recorder play an important role' (Biella 1997: 60). In his experience electronic technologies offered advantages film and printed words could not:

> The new technology permitted audio recordings, photographs and texts to be integrated on one study-screen. Through electronic footnotes, texts could instantly 'call up' for review any moment of the audio, any photograph, and any text. Translations, studio and photographs could themselves non-linearly access additional texts, such as my annotations of the Ilpoarakuyo materials . . . (1997: 61)

The digitized interview scenes in the CD ROM are contextualized with annotations written over several years and dated to show how Biella's analysis progressed and how some of his earlier interpretations were misguided. He sees this as a challenge to the conventional strategies of ethnographic representation:

> I leave traces of the different drafts because I think it is important to affirm that 'meaning has history'. . . . This counterposes a dominant conceit in the discipline that advocates non-contradiction in ethnography by the erasure of history, uncertainty, and change from texts. (Biella 1997: 61)

However, the annotations do not force users to disrupt their enjoy-ment of the ethnographic scenes (scripted like a play) in the text. Rather, they can be clicked on and referred to at will. Thus users of Biella's text would be allowed freedom to take their own personal narratives through it, to access different resources of information when they need to and take responsibility for developing their own routes to understanding.

In *The Bullfighter's Braid* CD ROM (Pink 1998b) I develop a less ambitious strategy, publishing an article about photographic research methods with a set of related texts. An earlier version of the article, published in Spanish (Pink 1996), included only one photograph, how-ever the hypermedia publication has links to over 30 photographs and several video clips produced during my research. My intention was that by following these different routes and hyperlinks users of the CD would not only read an article about research methodology as well as less academic pieces, but also view the photographic materials produced and interpreted in the project. My second CD, *Interweaving Lives* (Pink 1998d), included video, photographs, diary notes, interview transcripts and other texts from research about weaving in Guinea Bissau. I aimed to indicate how different types of knowledge were produced and represented through photography, video recording, talking and listening, writing diary notes and 'writing-up' notes on my lap top computer (see also Chapter 3 and 4). By using hyperlinks to connect different materials from my fieldwork, I indicated the interconnectedness of these different media and types of knowledge.

Hypermedia as experimental text: multilinearity, montage and multivocality

In the Introduction to Part 3 I noted how calls for reflexive and multivocal approaches to ethnographic representation have questioned the authenticity and authority of conventional ethnographic writing. Furthermore, challenges to the dominance of the printed word have urged ethnographers to rethink 'certain categories of anthropological knowledge in the light of understandings that may be accessible only by non-verbal means' (MacDougall 1997: 292). In Chapters 6 and 7 I described how ethnographic writers and video makers have responded to these criticisms. Electronic hypermedia, with its capacity to represent still and moving images, sound and written words (and thus verbal and non-verbal knowledge), in a multiplicity of different but simultaneous narratives, also offers exciting possibilities for multivocality.

Above I noted how hypermedia can represent ethnographic knowledge non-lineally. By creating a series of different strands, hypermedia authors can represent simultaneous but different narratives and knowledge and use hyperlinks to connect these strands. While printed text can also be accessed non-lineally, it has been argued that conventional linear ethnographic texts do not appropriately represent the complexity or diversity of contemporary culture, society and experience. Howard, an early advocate of ethnographic hypermedia, pointed out that 'where connections between phenomena are as interrelated as they are in human communities, the job of orchestrating even a limited degree of interconnectivity in the written medium is a struggle at best' (1988: 305). More recently, Marcus has argued that anthropologists should 'come to terms with multiple agencies in varying locales' and study the relationship between elements of an increasingly deterritoralized 'culture' that is 'the product of parallel diverse and simultaneous worlds operating consciously and blindly with regard to each other' (Marcus 1995: 51). He suggests that the conventional linear narrative of anthropological writing needs to be re-thought and that the cinematic technique of montage offers a better template for representing the multiple locations in which culture and individuals simultaneously exist (1995: 53). While

Marcus proposes this effect should be developed in printed ethnographies, hypermedia can also develop multilinear texts that can simultaneously represent narratives told from different standpoints, by different 'voices' in different media as well as the connections between these narratives.

While multilinearity is common in hypermedia representations and forms of montage are sometimes used, multivocal and co-authored ethnographies are not as yet. An example of how these might develop is Lyon's live website developed at http://anthropology.ac.uk/Bhalot. While doing his PhD fieldwork in Pakistan, Lyon regularly published materials on his fieldwork, including his own notes, local people's contributions, music and local cultural texts and texts from visitors to the website.

Ethnographic resources and open-ended texts

The art of creating a structured, bounded and 'finished' written or visual narrative is one of the skills of conventional ethnographic writing and filmmaking. Of course many ethnographers recognize that the capacity of these bounded, linear texts to represent a reality that is in fact continuous and subjectively experienced is limited; at best ethnographers can only reconstruct fragments of a subjective experience of reality. While hypermedia cannot resolve this, it can be used to develop texts that emphasize and recognize the selectivity and specificity of processes of representation and allow their authors to connect 'complete' ethnographic representations to contextualizing materials and wider resources. For example, finished documentaries might be linked to unselected footage or finished photographs may be contextualized by video clips that represent the research or other photographs that informed the composition of the exhibited or published photograph (such as photographs not selected for exhibition, or informants' own photographs).

The notion of open-endedness can also be taken further to regard hypermedia texts as permanently 'unfinished'. Theoretically, this means neither knowledge itself nor representations of knowledge are ever complete; interpretations are open to re-interpretation and representations may be re-represented. Practically, this means that, unlike printed books and finished films, on-line hypermedia texts may be up-dated, added to, or altered. Video sequences may be re-edited, photographs manipulated in new ways, written words changed, and the hyperlinks between them modified.

Hypermedia representations are also open-ended because their users can slip over their boundaries and explore their relationship to other texts. Whereas book and journal readers can also do this by cross-referencing other texts, the experience and ease of doing so on-line is different. If authors create hyperlinks between their ethnographic web pages and other existing sites, users can follow links to sites of related interest. These may be sites that are not 'ethnographic' but are of ethnographic interest.

On-line resources containing, for example, photographs, field diaries, book and PhD manuscripts (e.g. Paul Stirling's *Turkish Village* and *The Virtual Institute of Mambila Studies*, both at http://lucy.ukc.ac.uk), are also open-ended texts. While resource sites may include texts that are 'complete' or 'finished' (as well as 'texts in progress'), they are not necessarily presented as complete, discrete or finished texts in themselves. Rather, they are open-ended representations whose form and content may be up-dated, added to and altered. Their authors may create or delete hyper-links to other websites, in doing so re-situating the resource in relation to other web resources and sites and therefore creating new meanings. In contrast to the 'finished' electronic essay, open-ended hypermedia representations challenge existing forms of ethnographic representation. Their boundaries and form are arbitrary and changing and they lend users greater freedom to organize and structure knowledge and narratives.

Between design and experience: hypermedia texts and their users

As for written text and film, ethnographic hypermedia users also participate in interpreting ethnographic representations. Below I discuss the relationship between author, user and hypermedia text. This raises issues that should inform how ethnographers design the structure and navigation of hypermedia representations. I discuss practical aspects of this in a following section.

The main concerns about ethnographic hypermedia representation refer to their potential 'incoherence' and threadlessness. For example, Henley criticizes a 'tendency for CD ROMs to be presented as authorless aggregates of objective information which the user can wander over at will, creating his or her own narrative threads' (Henley 1998: 55). Likewise, Biella agrees with Banks (1994) and acknowledges that 'disorientation can affect [hypermedia] users who do not follow a plan, a coherent itinerary' (Biella 1994: 6). Henley's and Banks's criticisms represent genuine concerns that I share to some extent. Nevertheless these criticisms do not refer to a characteristic of hypermedia itself. Rather, they imply issues of authorship, design and navigation, and raise the question of the reader/viewer/user. Indeed, these issues could apply equally to montage styles in printed text, which have also been characterized as chaotic and lacking a structuring narrative; Marcus warns that 'extreme montage' may lose both its coherence and its audience (1995: 46).

Henley and Banks both identify the relationship between hypermedia texts and their users as key to the coherence of ethnographic hypermedia. The question of coherence cannot be resolved by simply interrogating hypermedia representations themselves, but needs to account for the dynamic between user and text. Readers/users/viewers of ethnographic text have frequently been neglected in existing discussions of representation that focus largely on ethnographers, informants, texts and their construction. While Marcus (above) reflected on the possible loss of an audience, unlike commentators on ethnographic film (see especially, Crawford and Hafsteinnson 1996; Martinez 1990, 1992, 1996; Stoller 1997; and Chapter 7 of this book), the creativity of readers, lone students, academics, ex-informants, whoever, who experience ethnographic text, scribble in margins, underline 'key points', draw on photographs and participate in producing ethnographic knowledge has received little attention. While some work has considered interactive hypermedia users (e.g. Orr Vered 1998) ethnographic hypermedia users' experiences are largely unknown (apart from Biella 1994 and Pink 1999b). For at least two reasons it seems important to understand how ethnographic hypermedia is received. First, because as Howard suggested 'hypermedia has the potential for establishing an entirely new kind of relationship between authors and readers' (1988: 311). Secondly, Martinez (1990, 1992, 1996) has shown that students have interpreted ethnographic films to express problematic assumptions about 'other cultures' that were not intended by the filmmakers. It is equally important to pay attention to the strategies and intentionalities of ethnographic hypermedia users.

A focus on ethnographic hypermedia users can also inform questions about how and why hypermedia becomes chaotic or coherent. The coherence of ethnographic hypermedia is created in the relationship between the design of the text and how it is interpreted. It depends on authors' creativity for the former and users' for the latter. Howard suggested that hypermedia would challenge ethnographers to provide readers with theoretically informed multiple pathways constructed with 'a sense of interconnectivity that is based on a theory of multi-stranded relationships' (1988: 311). Nevertheless, as Biella emphasizes, users also play a crucial role in making hypermedia coherent as '[l]inks incline: they do not impel. Disciplined users must resist tantalizing distractions if only to pursue with greater fervour those links that reward their research passions all the more' (Biella 1994: 6). While hypermedia texts, properly designed and constructed, offer coherent narratives (see Biella 1994: 6), it is also up to users to construct coherence. However much ethnographers tailor hypermedia representations, without the creative collaboration of their users, texts are only ever implied and partial because while hypermedia representation might be constructed as multi-linear texts, individuals use them to create linear narratives. As Orr Vered has pointed out, non-linearity refers to a situation where 'access to information is not dependent on serial sequencing or reflection on the order of a mirror'. Nevertheless, 'linearity is the end result of this process, despite the order in which information is acquired' (Orr Vered 1998: 42; see also Biella 1994: 6). Therefore, if the user's task is to create his or her own linear narrative through a multilinear text, the author's role is to facilitate this. By obliging users to participate in this way, hypermedia differs from books and films. 'New' texts demand or inspire 'new' types of audienceship or reading.

Audience/readers/users and the production of ethnographic meaning

As for video and photography, our understanding of how individual users interpret hypermedia representations can be informed by considering how electronic technologies are consumed and appropriated in the practices and discourses of contemporary culture and society (see Banks 1994: 2; Silverstone and Hirsch 1993). In Chapter 7 I discussed intersubjectivity between filmmakers, film texts and audiences, and how viewing contexts may impact on how individuals interpret ethnographic films. To understand how users interpret ethnographic hypermedia representations implies questions of how they experience and appropriate technologies, software and multilinearity as well as a text's actual content.

Above I argued that while arguments that digital photography ruptures existing practices and beliefs about photographic truth might make sense at an abstract level, once one explores how digital imagery is used in practice significant continuities between conventional and digital photographic and video practices are evident. Theories proposing that electronic communications signify a radical departure from existing practices and experiences of communication have similar problems. For example, Poster has argued that we live in the 'second media age' (1995: 4) where electronically mediated communication 'enacts a radical reconfiguration of language, one which constitutes subjects outside the pattern of the rational, autonomous individual. This familiar modern subject is displaced by the mode of information in favour of one that is multiple, disseminated and decentered, continuously interpellated as an unstable identity' (Poster 1995: 57). Poster's theory of the self draws convincingly on a critique of modernity that destabilizes grand narratives, modern truths and objective realities in favour of ambiguity, multiplicity and uncertainty. However, it is problematic because it depends on the abstract and general to explain something that happens at a level of individual experience and practice. The relationship between electronic technologies and individuals can be more usefully understood by focusing on practice, experience and the continuities between how individuals experience their identities when using hypermedia and 'traditional' texts.

In Chapter 1 I argued that ultimately ethnographic knowledge is produced through the concrete personal experience of researchers. Here

I apply the same ethnographic approach to the question of how individuals experience, interpret and produce knowledge with electronic hypermedia. Following Cohen's (1994) ideas, individuals' experiences of everyday life can be seen as a matter of assimilating and making sense out of diverse experiences, constantly adapting themselves to these while maintaining intact a sense of their own selves. Therefore, individuals and their sense of self and identity also hold together the multiple narratives of their experiences of hypermedia. Thus hypermedia users produce knowledge by making sense of different types of information presented in multiple narratives, and making the text coherent by producing their own linear narratives from it. Each individual user may follow a different route through the multiple narratives of a hypermedia representation, creating his or her own narratives and unique, experience-based knowledge.

Since individuals interact with and experience hypermedia differently, hypermedia authors might wish to account for the various strategies in which users engage. Research about users' actual practices and experiences can inform this and projects designed to test existing ethnographic hypermedia projects have shown how some users describe their experiences. My research into users' experiences of *The Bullfighter's Braid* CD ROM indicated that some felt 'empowered' by the freedom it offered them to choose their own routes through the materials. Others, who found this choice disorientating, did not engage with the possibility of selecting a route self-consciously, but followed the path they thought the author had made most obvious (see Pink 1998f, 1999d).

Ethics

The idea of empowering hypermedia users to create their own narratives and stories with other people's images and words also raises ethical issues. While Biella has suggested hypermedia authors may be able to guide the way people use and experience electronic representations (see above), as I noted in the Introduction to Part 3 ultimately authors cannot control how their work is interpreted once it is subjected to other gazes. As for photography and video, this demands that ethnographers be informed about the ethical implications that their hypermedia publications raise.

In Chapter 2 I argued that ethnographers should be committed to representing their informants' images and words appropriately and responsibly. While the internet offers unsurpassed opportunities for global dissemination of ethnography, it also raises some concerns (see Pink 1998c, 1999e). Authors of electronic representations of ethnography cannot necessarily control how other people appropriate their images. Digital photographs and video can be copied from CD ROMs. On the internet, where copyright is difficult to regulate, ethnographic still and moving images can be copied and reproduced in new and possibly inappropriate contexts. Ethnographic film or video footage published on-line might be down-loaded, re-edited, and represented in contexts that might produce negative or harmful meanings or consequences for the people represented in it, which could also be disseminated globally on-line. However, to keep this in perspective, illegal copying and re-editing of ethnographic video, like manipulation of photographs has always been possible and the main difference of on-line publishing is easy accessibility.

Copyright regulations constantly change and there would be little point in setting out guidelines here. Up-to-date information may be best found on the internet itself. For subject-specific information see http:// lucy.ukc.ac.uk/ERA/links.html and links to general internet copyright law and etiquette can be found at http://copyrightservice.co.uk. Some measures can discourage copying, for example techniques to 'finger-print' photographs are demonstrated at http://lucy.ukc.ac.uk/ERA/ suresign_sample.html. This involves giving photographs a 'digital fingerprint' that cannot be seen with the naked eye but, as the ERA example shows, even after significantly changing a photograph's resolution and compression, it can still be identified by a fingerprint detector. While this device cannot actually prevent copying, it can identify images that ethnographers suspect has been copied. These issues should not deter ethnographers who wish publish their work on-line or on CD ROM. However, they should inform the design and content of hypermedia ethnographies.

Practical concerns

This book is not a practical skills manual; step-by-step guides to digit-izing and manipulating video and photographs and using hypermedia software would not only merit a whole book in itself, but would soon be out of date. Hypermedia production skills are best gained from appropriate manuals, on-line resources, training groups or university courses, for example the University of Kent's Centre for Social Anthro-pology and Computing has many years of experience in this area and general hypermedia training is available at undergraduate and graduate levels at many universities. My own experience of making hypermedia representations has shown me that each project is a learning experience. It is important to take a critical approach to one's own and other existing works. Above I noted how hypermedia representations tend to imitate their authors' existing practices. To shift from writing ethnography to creating image-led hypermedia texts that exploit the multilinear potential of hypermedia means thinking about ethnographic representa-tion in new ways.

Above I emphasized that careful attention should be given to both hypermedia design and content as well as to how users experience these.

I emphasized two points that have implications for hypermedia design: first, its potential for multilinearity and multivocality; secondly, the importance of links for producing meanings and knowledge. Below I discuss practical aspects of designing the structure, layering and linkages of hypermedia.

Getting started

Before starting an ethnographic hypermedia project it is useful to pose a set of questions, that should inform how it is designed and produced.

WHAT STYLE OF TEXT IS TO BE DEVELOPED? Above I described some possible models for ethnographic hypermedia representations such as electronic photo-essays, 'open-ended' resources and 'closed' journal articles.

WHO IS THE INTENDED AUDIENCE? Different users have specific needs and demands. Hypermedia representations may not be intended for just one type of user, but need to suit the interests of various groups. For example, a text could simultaneously be designed as a learning text for students, a research text for academics, and a community resource for informants.

WHAT MATERIALS ARE AVAILABLE FOR INCLUSION? Researchers may have written texts, photographs, video clips and other documents and images that could be included in the text. Ethical and copyright issues should be checked for each text, and permission sought when necessary.

WHO WILL CONTRIBUTE TO THE TEXT? Some projects are produced independently by researchers, however others might combine the work of different academic authors, informants and technical authors. In collaborative productions ground rules for working together should be set at the outset of the project. Collaboration will also impact on the design process and work schedule. In my experience, working with technical authors provides access to experienced knowledge of software and techniques which can inspire exciting developments in project design. However, when it is taken over by technical authors, ethnographers can lose autonomy over the project, making changes after technical authoring has begun more difficult. If ethnographers can undertake academic and technical design and authoring themselves the content and design of the project can be developed in closer relation to each other as the hypermedia representation takes its form, thus allowing greater flexibility. Above I also noted hypermedia's potential for 'multivocality'. In some projects informants may also play authorial roles and might be involved in producing materials represented in the text or be consulted about the selection and presentation of materials. If informants are to be co-authors, ethnographers need to plan how this will be facilitated.

WHAT SOFTWARE WILL BE USED?   Software rapidly changes and expert advice should be sought to determine the most suitable software for individual projects. Project design is limited by the software selected, therefore ethnographers should reconcile their design and performance priorities with technical possibilities before committing themselves to a particular package or design. Choice of software will also be influenced by intended audiences and markets. For example, museum exhibitions require different presentations from on-line university courses or hypermedia publishing for specialized academic audiences. Some multimedia authoring software is not compatible with both internet and CD publishing and this is also worth checking.

HOW WILL THE PROJECT BE DISSEMINATED?   The dissemination medium has implications for the quantity and quality of the different images and texts that are included and software used. It is advisable to seek expert advice on this at the early planning stages.

Design and structure: strands, narratives, links and clusters

The questions and issues I have outlined above should inform readers how hypermedia designs are mapped out. The ways of mapping out hypermedia projects that I have been introduced to have used a surprising amount of ink and paper. The first two CD ROMS I produced were the most manual pieces of work I had produced since my MA dissertation, using diagrams, printed-out texts, highlighter pen, arrows and symbols. The design stage usually involves visualizing the strands, narratives, links and clusters of the project in diagrammatic form. The diagram need not necessarily represent the definitive design as the project evolves, but it should represent the basic outline of its structure and content. In collaborative projects structure and content also need to be agreed with co-authors and technical authors.

Ethnography of user experience

Above I emphasized the importance of users' experience of hypermedia representations. Once a first version of the project is ready, users' viewing practices and responses to it can be researched to feed back into the design process. Various methods can be used. If a project is screened to viewers by linking a PC to a projector they may be asked to respond in focus groups or by completing individual questionnaires. While this method produces immediate feedback, its does not allow users to interact with the text. Since interactivity is an important aspect of how hypermedia is experienced, it is useful to research how users navigate and respond to it. Depending on the software, dissemination medium and intended audience, this may be done in different ways. Un-refereed academic papers are often published on the internet for comments, CD ROMs and restricted-access internet addresses can be distributed to a limited group for their responses. In my own research I gave participants CD ROMs with either a questionnaire or instructions on how to structure their comments, asking them to report on the routes they followed through the text and their experience of different aspects of it and then followed these up with short interviews.

Futures

There has been speculation over how ethnographic hypermedia representation will continue to be produced and used. One debate refers to personnel. Some believe that soon academics will produce their own texts independently of specialist technical authors, while others argue that as technology develops there will be greater need for technical expertise. For ethnographic representation I would predict a mix similar to that which developed in ethnographic filmmaking. Many academics may independently author hypermedia representations. A good number have already produced hypermedia texts for pedagogical uses or to represent their research to other academics. Other projects might be developed professionally, with larger budgets and commercial markets. These are likely to be representations that are prepared for a broader public, such as interactive museum texts that are used within the exhibition halls, commercial websites, or subscribers to on-line publications.

There is also speculation about future hypermedia technologies. Some argue that CD ROM will become redundant, overtaken by DVD and an increasingly efficient and faster internet. However, at present, CD ROM still has some advantages. Access to the internet is not universal. Moreover, internet connections can often be slow and loading images can not only be frustratingly time-consuming, but also costly, and image quality may be of a lower standard than on CD ROM. However, internet publishing is becoming increasingly popular. Book publishers are making it part of their business by taking on on-line journals and other on-line resources (see, for example, Thompson Learning Anthropology publishing on-line http://www.anthro-online.com). The possibilities for internet publishing are also changing rapidly and no doubt new technological possibilities will soon develop.

After-word

It might seem ironic, or even contradictory, that a text about visual research and representation should primarily be published in the form of a book that makes a fairly conventional use of written words and photographic images. However, there have been some reasons for choosing this form of dissemination. First, because printed books are still the dominant medium of academic representation. While universities are beginning to engage with on-line learning and to develop electronic resources for students, this is still far less developed than existing uses of printed books. But it is not simply for these reasons that I have written a book about visual research and representation. Written and spoken words are good to communicate with, we know how to use and interpret them, and I would certainly not suggest they are abandoned in favour of visual images.

References

Alasuutari P. (1995) *Researching Culture*. London: Sage.

Amit-Talai, V. (ed.) (1999) *Constructing the Field*. London: Routledge.

Appadurai, A. (1986) 'Introduction: commodities and the politics of value', in A. Appadurai (ed.), *The Social Life of Things: Commodities in Cultural Perspective*. Cambridge: Cambridge University Press.

Back, L. (1998) 'Reading and writing research', in C. Seale (ed.), *Researching Culture and Society*. London: Sage.

Banks, M. (1992) 'Which films are the ethnographic films?', in P.I. Crawford and D. Turton (eds), *Film as Ethnography*. Manchester: University of Manchester Press.

Banks, M. (n.d) 'Visual research methods', in *Social Research Update*, http://www.soc.surrey.ac.uk/sru/SRU11/SRU11.html

Banks, M. (1994) 'Interactive multimedia and anthropology – a sceptical view', http://www.rsl.ox.ac.uk/isca/marcus.banks.01.html

Banks, M. (1998) 'Visual anthropology: image, object and interpretation', in J. Prosser (ed.), *Image-based Research: A Sourcebook for Qualitative Researchers*. London: Falmer Press.

Banks, M. and Morphy, H. (1997) *Rethinking Visual Anthropology*. London: Yale University Press.

Barbash, I. and Taylor, L. (1997) *Cross Cultural Filmmaking: A Handbook for Making Documentary and Ethnographic Films and Video*. London: University of California Press.

Barndt D. (1997) 'Zooming out/zooming in: visualizing globalisation', *Visual Sociology*, 12(2): 5–32.

Barnes, D.B., Taylor-Brown, S. and Weiner, L. (1997) ' "I didn't leave y'all on purpose": HIV-infected mothers' videotaped legacies for their children', in S.J. Gold (ed.), *Visual Methods in Sociological Analysis*, special issue of *Qualitative Sociology*, 20(1).

Bateson, G. and Mead, M. (1942) *Balinese Character: A Photographic Analysis*. New York: New York Academy of the Sciences.

Baudry, P. (1996) 'Happy tapes', in P.I. Crawford and S.B. Hafsteinsson (eds), *The Construction of the Viewer*. Aarhaus: Intervention Press.

Becker, H. (1986) 'Photography and sociology' in *Doing Things Together*. Evanston, IL: North Western Press.

Becker, H. (1995) 'Visual sociology, documentary photography or photo-journalism (almost) all a matter of context', *Visual Sociology*, 10 (1–2): 5–14.

Bell, D., Caplan, P. and Jahan Karim, W. (1993) *Gendered Fields: Women, Men and Ethnography.* London: Routledge.

Bergamaschi, M. and Francesconi, C. (1996) 'Urban homelessness: the negotiation of public spaces', *Visual Sociology*, 11(2): 35–44.

Berger, J. and Mohr, J. (1967) *A Fortunate Man.* Cambridge: Granta Books.

Berger, J. and Mohr, J. (1982) *Another Way of Telling.* Cambridge: Granta Books.

Biella, P. (1993) 'Beyond ethnographic film', in J.R. Rollwagen (ed.), *Anthropological Film and Video in the 1990s.* Brockport, NY: The Institute Inc.

Biella, P. (1994) 'Codifications of ethnography: linear and nonlinear', http://www.usc.edu/dept/elab/welcome/codifications.html

Biella, P. (1996) 'Interactive media in anthropology: *Seed and Earth* – promise of rain', *American Anthropologist*, 98(3): 595–616.

Biella, P. (1997) 'Mama Kone's possession: scene from an interactive ethnography', *Visual Anthropology Review*, 12(2): 59–95.

Bourdieu, P. (1990 [1965]) *Photography: A Middle-Brow Art.* Oxford: Polity Press.

Brandes, S. (1997) 'Photographic imagery in Spanish ethnography', *Visual Anthropology Review*, 13(1): 1–13.

Burgess, R.G. (1984) *In the Field.* London: Routledge.

Cavin, E. (1994) 'In search of the viewfinder: a study of a child's perspective', *Visual Sociology*, 9(1): 27–42.

Cerezo, M., Martinez, A. and Ranera, P. (1996) 'Tres antropólogos inocentes y un ojo si parpado', in M. Garcia Alonso, A. Martinez, P. Pitarch, P. Ranera and J. Fores (eds), *Antropologia de los Sentidos: La Vista.* Celeste: Ediciones: Madrid.

Chalfen, R. (1987) *Snapshot Versions of Life.* Bowling Green, OH: Popular Press.

Chalfen, R. (n.d) *Traditional Views,* http://nimbus.ocis.temple.edu/~rchalfen/

Chaney, D. (1993) *Fictions of Collective Life.* London: Routledge.

Chaplin, E. (1994) *Sociology and Visual Representations.* London: Routledge.

Clifford, J. (1986) 'Introduction: partial truths', in J. Clifford and G. Marcus (eds), *Writing Culture: the Poetics and Politics of Ethnography.* Berkeley: University of California Press.

Clifford, J. and Marcus, G. (1986) *Writing Culture: the Poetics and Politics of Ethnography.* Berkeley: University of California Press.

Cohen, A. (1992) 'Self-conscious anthropology', in J. Okely and H. Callaway (eds), *Anthropology and Autobiography.* London: Routledge.

Cohen, A. (1994) *Self Consciousness: an Alternative Anthropology of Identity.* London: Routledge.

Cohen, A. and Rapport, N. (1995) *Questions of Consciousness.* Routledge: London.

Cohen, C.B., Wilk, R. and Stoeltje, B. (1996) *Beauty Queens on the Global Stage.* London: Routledge.

Colclough, N., Bagg, J., Hosking, J. and Coluccelli, R. (n.d.). *The Ascoli Project,* http://lucy.ukc.ac.uk/jb6/archives/

Collier, J. (1967) *Visual Anthropology: Photography as Research Method.* Albuquerque: University of New Mexico Press.

Collier, J. (1995 [1975]) 'Photography and visual anthropology', in P. Hockings (ed.), *Principles of Visual Anthropology.* Berlin and New York: Mouton de Gruyter.

Collier, J. and Collier, M. (1986) *Visual Anthropology: Photography as a Research Method.* Albuquerque: University of New Mexico Press.

Concise Oxford Dictionary (1982) J.B. Sykes, (ed.). Oxford: Clarendon Press.

Connell, R.W. (1987) *Gender and Power.* Cambridge: Polity Press.

Connell, R.W. (1995) *Masculinities*. Cambridge: Polity Press.

Cooke, L. and Wollen, P. (eds) (1995) *Visual Display: Culture Beyond Appearances*. Seattle, WA: Bay Press.

Cornwall, A. and Lindisfarne, N. (1994), 'Introduction, in A. Cornwall and N. Lindisfarne (eds), *Dislocating Masculinity: Comparative Ethnographies*: London: Routledge.

Crawford, P.I. (1992) 'Film as discourse: the invention of anthropological realities', in P.I. Crawford and D. Turton (eds), *Film as Ethnography*. Manchester: Manchester University Press.

Crawford, P.I. and Hafsteinsson, S. (eds) (1996) *The Construction of the Viewer*. Aarhaus: Intervention Press.

Crawford, P.I. and Turton, D. (1992) 'Introduction', in P.I. Crawford and D. Turton (eds), *Film as Ethnography*. Manchester: Manchester University Press.

Crawshaw, C. and Urry J. (1997) 'Tourism and the photographic eye' in C. Rojek and J. Urry (eds), *Touring Cultures*. London: Routledge.

Crotty, M. (1998) *The Foundations of Social Research: Meaning and Perspective in the Research Process*. London: Sage.

Da Silva, O. (2000) *In the Net*, exhibition catalogue. Porto, Portugal: Rainho and Neves Lda.

Davis, J. (1992) 'Tense in ethnography: some practical considerations' in J. Okely and H. Callaway (eds), *Anthropology and Autobiography*. London: Routledge.

Devereaux, L. and Hillman, R. (eds) (1995) *Fields of Vision: Essays in Film Studies, Visual Anthropology and Photography*. Berkeley: University of California Press.

Devereaux, L. (1995) 'Experience, representation and film', in L. Devereaux and R. Hillman (eds) (1995) *Fields of Vision: Essays in Film Studies, Visual Anthropology and Photography*, Berkeley: University of California Press.

Edensor, T. (1998) *Tourists at the Taj: Performance and Meaning at a Symbolic Site*. London: Routledge.

Edgar, I. (1997) 'The tooth butterfly, or rendering a sensible account from the imaginative present', in W. James, J. Hockey and A. Dawson (eds), *After Writing Culture: Epistemology and Praxis in Contemporary Anthropology*. London: Routledge.

Edwards, E. (ed.) (1992) *Anthropology and Photography*. New Haven, CT: Yale University Press.

Edwards, E. (1997a) 'Beyond the Boundary: a consideration of the expressive in photography and anthropology' in M. Banks and H. Morphy (eds), *Rethinking Visual Anthropology*. London: Routledge.

Edwards, E. (ed.) (1997b) Special issue of *History of Photography*, 21(1).

Ellen, R. (1984) *Ethnographic Research: a Guide to General Conduct*. London: Academic Press.

Engelbrecht, B. (1996) 'For whom do we produce?', in P.I. Crawford and S.B. Hafsteinsson (eds), *The Construction of the Viewer*. Aarhaus: Intervention Press.

Evans, J. and Hall, S. (eds) (1999) *Visual Culture: the Reader*. London: Sage.

Fabian, J. (1983) *Time and the Other: How Anthropology makes its Object*. New York: Columbia University Press.

Fernandez, J. (1995) 'Amazing grace: meaning deficit, displacement and new consciousness in expressive interaction', in A. Cohen and N. Rapport (eds), *Questions of Consciousness*. London: Routledge.

Ferrándiz, F. (1996) 'Intersubjectividad y vídeo etnográfico. Holguras y textxuras en la grabación de ceremonias espiritistas en Venezuela,' in M. Garcia, A. Martinez, P. Pitarch, P. Ranera, and J. Fores (eds), *Antropologia de los sentidos: La Vista*. Madrid: Celeste Ediciones.

Ferrándiz, F. (1998) 'A trace of fingerprints: displacements and textures in the use of ethnographic video in Venezuelan spiritism', *Visual Anthropology Review*, 13(2): 19–38.

Fetterman, D. (1998) *Ethnography* (second edition). London: Sage.

Fischer, M. (n.d.) *Making Tradition in the Cook Islands*, http://www.lucy.ukc.ac.uk

Fischer, M. and Zeitlyn, D. (n.d.) 'Mambila Nggwun – the construction and deployment of multiple meanings in ritual', http://lucy.ukc.ac.uk/dz/Nggwun/nggwun_1.html

Flick, U. (1998) *An Introduction to Qualitative Research*. London: Sage.

Fortier, A. (1998) 'Gender, ethnicity and fieldwork: a case study', in C. Seale (ed.), *Researching Culture and Society*. London: Sage.

Freudenthal, S. (1992) 'La vidéo participante: un moyen pour les populations locales de faire entendre leur voix', *Journal des anthropologues*, 47–48: 153–58.

Fruzzetti, L., Guzzetti, A., Johnston, N. and Östör, Á. (1994) *Seed and Earth*. Video and Laser Disc. Middletown, CT: Wesleyan University.

Gledhill, J. and Harris, M. (n.d.) *Peasant Social Worlds and their Transformation*, http://res1.man.ac.uk/multimedia

Goffman, I. (1979) *Gender Advertisements*. London and Basingstoke: Macmillan.

Gold, S.J. (1995) 'New York/LA: a visual comparison of public life in two cities', *Visual Sociology*, 10 (1–2): 85–105.

Gold, S.J. (1997) (ed.) 'Visual methods in sociological analysis', special issue, *Qualitative Sociology*, 20(1).

Goldman-Segall, R. (1998) 'Gender and digital media in the context of a middle school science project', http://www2.ncsu.edu/unity/lockers/project/meridian/feat-3/gender.html

Grady, J. (1991) 'The visual essay and sociology', *Visual Sociology*, 6(2): 23–38.

Grady, J. (1996) 'The scope of visual sociology', *Visual Sociology*, 11(2): 10–24.

Hall, S. (ed.) (1997) *Representation: Cultural Representations and Signifying Practices*. London: Sage.

Hammersley, M. and Atkinson, P. (1995) *Ethnography: Principles in Practice*, 2nd edition. London: Routledge.

Harper, D. (ed.) (1994) *'Cape Bretton 1952: The Photographic Vision of Tim Asch'*, special issue, *Visual Sociology*, 9(2).

Harper, D. (1998a) 'An argument for visual sociology', in J. Prosser (ed.), *Image-based Research: a Sourcebook for Qualitative Researchers*. London: Falmer Press.

Harper, D. (1998b) 'On the authority of the image: visual methods at the crossroads', in N. Denzin and Y. Lincoln (eds), *Collecting and Interpreting Qualitative Materials*. London: Sage.

Harvey, P. (1996) *Hybrids of Modernity: Anthropology, the Nation State and the Universal Exhibition*. London: Routledge.

Hastrup, K. (1992) 'Anthropological vision: some notes on visual and textual authority', in P.I. Crawford and D. Turton (eds), *Film as Ethnography*. Manchester: Manchester University Press.

Heider, K. (1976) *Ethnographic Film*. Austin: University of Texas Press.

Henley, P. (1996) 'The promise of Ethnographic film', The Stirling Lecture, Fifth International Festival of ethnographic Film, University of Kent, Canterbury.

Henley, P. (1998) 'Filmmaking and ethnographic research', in J. Prosser (ed.), *Image-based Research*. London: Falmer Press.

Hesse-Biber, S., Dupus, Paul R. and Kinder, T. (1997) 'Anthropology: new developments in video ethnography and visual sociology – analyzing multimedia data quantitatively', *Social Science Computer Review*, 15(1): 5–12.

Hockings, P. (ed.) (1975) *Principles of Visual Anthropology*. The Hague: Mouton

Hockings, P. (1992) 'The yellow bough: Rivers' use of photography', in *The Todas*, in E. Edwards (ed.) *Anthropology and Photography*. New Haven: Yale University Press. pp. 179–86.

Hockings, P. (ed.) (1995) *Principles of Visual Anthropology* 2nd edition. The Hague: Mouton.

Homberger, E. (1992) 'J.P. Morgan's nose: photographer and subject in American portrait photography', in G. Clarke (ed.), *The Portrait in Photography*. London: Reakton Books.

Hoskins, J. (1993) ' "Why we cried to see him again": Indonesian villagers' responses to the filmic disruption of time, in J. Rollwagen (ed.), *Anthropological Film and Video in the 1990s*. Brockport, NY: The Institute Inc.

Howard, A. (1988) 'Hypermedia and the future of ethnography', *Cultural Anthropology*, 3(3): 387–410.

Hughes-Freeland, F. (ed.) (1997) *Ritual, Performance, Media*. London: Routledge.

Hughes-Freeland, F. and Crain, M. (eds) (1998) *Recasting Ritual*. London: Routledge.

Hutnyk, J. (1996) *The Rumour of Calcutta*. London: Zed Books.

Ihde, D. (1995) 'Image technologies and traditional culture', in A. Feenberg and A. Hannay (eds), *Technology and the Politics of Knowledge*. Bloomington and Indianapolis: Indiana University Press.

James, A., Hockey, J. and Dawson, A. (1997) *After Writing Culture: Epistemology and Praxis in Contemporary Anthropology*. London, Routledge.

Jenks, C. (1995) *Visual Cultures*. London: Routledge.

Josephides, L. (1997) 'Representing the anthropologist's predicament', in W. James, J. Hockey and A. Dawson (eds), *After Writing Culture: Epistemology and Praxis in Contemporary Anthropology*. London: Routledge.

Kulick, D. (1995) 'The sexual life of anthropologists: erotic subjectivity and ethnographic work', in D. Kulick and M. Willson (eds), *Taboo: Sex, Identity and Erotic Subjectivity in Anthropological Fieldwork*. London: Routledge.

Kulick, D. and Willson, M. (eds) (1995) *Taboo: Sex, Identity and Erotic Subjectivity in Anthropological Fieldwork*. London: Routledge.

Lakoff, G. and Johnson, M. (1980) *The Metaphors We Live By*. Chicago, IL: University of Chicago Press.

Larson, H.J. (1988) 'Photography that listens', *Visual Anthropology*, 1: 415–32.

Lister, M. (1995) *The Photographic Image in Digital Culture*. London: Routledge.

Loizos, P. (1993) *Innovation in Ethnographic Film*. Manchester: Manchester University Press.

Lomax, H. and Casey, N. (1998) 'Recording social life: reflexivity and video methodology', *Sociological Research Online*, 3(2), http://www.socresonline.org.uk/socresonline/3/2/1.html

Lury, C. (1998) *Prosthetic Culture: Photography, Memory and Identity*. London: Routledge.

Lydall, J. (1990) 'Filming *The Women Who Smile*, in P.I. Crawford and J.K.

Simonsen (eds), *Ethnographic Film Aesthetics and Narrative Traditions*. Aarhaus,: Intervention Press.

MacDougall, D. (1995) 'The subjective voice in ethnographic film', in L. Devereaux and R. Hillman (eds), *Fields of Vision: Essays in Film Studies, Visual Anthropology and Photography*. Berkeley: University of California Press.

MacDougall, D. (1997) 'The visual in anthropology', in M. Banks and H. Morphy (eds), *Rethinking Visual Anthropology*. London: New Haven Press.

Macintyre, M. and Mackenzie, M. (1992) 'Focal length as an analogue of cultural distance', in E. Edwards (ed.), *Anthropology and Photography*. London: Yale University Press.

McGuigan, J. (ed.) (1997) *Cultural Methodologies*. London: Sage.

McQuire, S. (1998) *Visions of Modernity: Representation, Memory, Time and Space in the Age of the Camera*. London: Sage.

McRobbie, A. (1992) 'Post-Marxism and cultural studies: a postscript' in L. Grossberg, C. Nelson and P. Treichler (eds) *Cultural Studies*. London: Routledge.

Marcus, G. (1995) 'The modernist sensibility in recent ethnographic writing and the cinematic metaphor of montage', in L. Devereaux and R. Hillman (eds), *Fields of Vision: Essays in Film Studies, Visual Anthropology and Photography*. Berkeley: University of California Press.

Martinez, W. (1990) 'Critical studies and visual anthropology: aberrant vs. anticipated readings of ethnographic film', *CVA Review*, Spring: 34–47.

Martinez, W. (1992) 'Who constructs anthropological knowledge? Toward a theory of ethnographic film spectatorship', in P.I. Crawford and D. Turton (eds) *Film as Ethnography*. Manchester: Manchester University Press.

Martinez, W. (1996) 'Deconstructing the 'viewer': from ethnography of the visual to critique of the occult', in P.I. Crawford S.B. Hafsteinnson (eds), *The Construction of the Viewer*. Aarhaus: Intervention Press.

Mead, M. (1975) [1995] 'Visual anthropology in a discipline of words', in P. Hockings (ed.), *Principles of Visual Anthropology*. The Hague: Mouton.

Mermin, S. (1997) 'Being where? Experiencing narratives of ethnographic film', *Visual Anthropology Review*, 13 (1): 40–51.

Metzgar, E. (n.d.) http://wings.buffalo.edu/anthropology/anthroglobe/field_experience

Miller, D. (1995) *Acknowledging Consumption*. London: Routledge.

Mitchell, W. (1995) *City of Bits*. London: Routledge.

Moore, H. (1994) *A Passion For Difference: Essays in Anthropology and Gender*. Oxford: Polity Press.

Morley, D. (1996) 'The audience, the ethnographer, the postmodernist and their problems', in P.I. Crawford and S.B. Hafsteinsson (eds), *The Construction of the Viewer*. Aarhaus: Intervention Press.

Morphy, H. and Banks, M. (1997) 'Introduction: rethinking visual anthropology', in M. Banks and H. Morphy (eds), *Rethinking Visual Anthropology*. London: Routledge.

Mulvey, L. (1989) 'Visual pleasure and narrative cinema' in *Visual and Other Pleasures*, Basingstoke: Macmillan.

Nencel, L. and Pels, P. (1991) *Constructing Knowledge: Authority and Critique in Social Science*. London: Sage.

Nuemann, M. (1992) 'The travelling eye: photography, tourism and ethnography', *Visual Sociology*, 7 (2): 22–38.

Nichols, B. (1994) 'The ethnographer's tale', in L. Taylor (ed.), *Visualizing Theory*. London: Routledge.

Okely, J. (1994) 'Vicarious and sensory knowledge of chronology and change: ageing in rural France', in K. Hastrup and P. Hervik (eds), *Social Experience and Anthropological Knowledge*. London: Routledge.

Okely, J. (1996) *Own or Other Culture*. London: Routledge.

Okely, J. and Callaway, H. (1992) *Anthropology and Autobiography*. London: Routledge.

Orr Vered, K. (1998) 'Plotting new media frontiers: myst and narrative pleasure', *Visual Anthropology Review* 13 (2): 39–47.

Pauwels, L. (1996) 'Managing impressions on visually decoding the workplace as a symbolic environment', *Visual Sociology*, 11 (2): 62–74.

Pels, P. (1996) *EASA Newsletter*, 18: 18, http://www.ub.es.easa.netethic.htm

Pink, S. (1993) 'La mujer en el toreo: reflexiones sobre el éxito de una mujer novillero en la temporada de 1993', *La Tribuna*, Spain, December.

Pink, S. (1996) 'Excursiones socio-visuales en el mundo del toro', in M. Garcia, A. Martinez, P. Pitarch, P. Ranera and J. Fores (eds), *Antropologia de los sentidos: La Vista*. Madrid: Celeste Ediciones.

Pink, S. (1997a) *Women and Bullfighting: Gender, Sex and the Consumption of Tradition*. Oxford: Berg.

Pink, S. (1997b) 'Visual histories of success' in E. Edwards (ed.), *History of Photography*. London and Washington, DC: Taylor & Francis.

Pink, S. (1997c) 'From ritual performance to media commodity', in F. Hughes-Freeland (ed.), *Ritual, Performance, Media*. London: Routledge.

Pink, S. (1998a) 'The "white helpers": anthropologists, development workers and local imaginations', *Anthropology Today*, 14(6): 9–14.

Pink, S. (1998b) *The Bullfighter's Braid: Unravelling Photographic Research*, CD ROM, University of Derby.

Pink, S. (1998c) 'Report on the Göttingen International Ethnographic Film Festival 1998' in *Anthropology Today*, 14(4): 23–4.

Pink, S. (1998d) *Interweaving Lives, Producing Images, Creating Knowledge: Video in Ethnographic Research*, CD ROM, University of Derby.

Pink, S. (1998e) 'Sunglasses, suitcases and other 'symbols': intentionality, creativity and 'indirect' communication in festive and everyday performances', papers presented at the ASA Conference, University of Kent.

Pink, S. (1998f) 'Students at the centre: non-lineral narratives and self conscious learning, in S. Banks, C. Graebner and D. McConnell (eds), *Networked Life Long Learning: Innovative Approaches to Education and Training through the Internet*. University of Sheffield, Division of Adult Continuing Education, Sheffield.

Pink, S. (1999a) '"Informants" who come "home"', in V. Amit-Talai (ed.), *Constructing the Field*. London: Routledge.

Pink, S. (1999b) '*Panos* for the *brancus*: interweaving cultures, producing cloth, visualising experience, making anthropology', *Journal of Material Culture*, 4 (2): 163–82.

Pink, S. (1999c) 'A woman, a camera and the world of bullfighting: visual culture, experience and the production of anthropological knowledge', *Visual Anthropology*, 13: 71–86.

Pink, S. (1999d) 'Students at the centre: non-lineal narratives and self conscious learning', *Journal of Computer Assisted Learning*, 15: 244–54.

Pink, S. (1999e) 'A Report on the Experience Rich Anthropology (ERA) Winter School, University of Kent, 15–17 January 1999, *Anthropology Today*, 15 (3): 20–1.

Pink, S. (2001) 'Sunglasses, suitcases and other "symbols": intentionality, creativity and "indirect" communication in festive and everyday performances', in J. Hendary and C.W. Watson (eds), *An Anthropology of Indirect Communication*. London: Routledge.

Pinney, C. (1992a) 'Montage, doubling and the mouth of God', in P.I. Crawford and J.K. Simonsen (eds), *Ethnographic Film Aesthetics and Narrative Traditions*. Aarhaus: Intervention Press.

Pinney, C. (1992b) 'The parallel histories of anthropology and photography', in E. Edwards (ed.), *Anthropology and Photography*. New Haven, CT: Yale University Press.

Pinney, C. (1994) 'Future travel', in L. Taylor (ed.), *Visualizing Theory*. London: Routledge.

Pinney, C. (1997) *Camera Indica: The Social Life of Indian Photographs*. London: Reakton Books.

Pitt-Rivers, J. (1954) *The People of the Sierra*. New York: Criterion.

Pollock, G. (1988) *Vision and Difference: Femininity, Feminism and the Histories of Art*. London: Routledge.

Poster, M. (1995) *The Second Media Age*. Oxford: Polity.

Pratt, M.L. (1986) 'Fieldwork in common places', in J. Clifford and G. Marcus (eds), *Writing Culture*. Berkeley: University of California Press.

Press, I. (1979) *The City as Context*. Urbana: University of Illinois Press.

Price, D. and Wells, L. (1997) 'Thinking about photography: debates, historically and now', in L. Wells (ed.), *Photography: a Critical Introduction*. London: Routledge.

Prosser, J. (1996) 'What constitutes an image-based qualitative methodology?', *Visual Sociology*, 11(2): 26–34.

Prosser, J. (ed.) (1998) *Image-based Research: a Sourcebook for Qualitative Researchers*. London: Falmer Press.

Prosser, J. and Schwartz, D. (1998) 'Photographs within the sociological research process' in J. Prosser (ed.), *Image-based Research: a Sourcebook for Qualitative Researchers*. London: Falmer Press.

Rapport, N. (1997a) *Transcendent Individual: Towards a Literary and Liberal Anthropology*. London: Routledge.

Rapport, N. (1997b) 'Edifying anthropology: culture as conversation; representation as conversation', in A. James, J. Hockey and A. Dawson (eds), *After Writing Culture: Epistemology and Praxis in Contemporary Anthropology*. London: Routledge.

Ratcliff, D. (n.d.) *Video and Audio Media in Qualitative Research*, http:// www.alltel.net/~ratcliff/qual.html

Reiger, J. (1996) 'Photographing social change', *Visual Sociology*, 11(1): 5–49.

Riches, G. and Dawson, P. (1998) 'Lost children, living memories: the role of photographs in processes of grief and adjustment among bereaved parents', *Death Studies*, 22: 121–40.

Robins, K. (1995) 'Will the image hold still', in M. Lister (ed.), *The Photographic Image in Digital Culture*. London: Routledge.

Rollwagen, J. (1988) *Anthropological Filmmaking*. New York: Harwood Academic Press.

Ruby, J. (1972) 'Up the Zambesi with notebook and camera or being an anthropologist without doing anthropology . . . with Pictures'. Paper presented at the 71st Annual Meeting of the American Anthropological Association, Toronto. Cited in Becker (1986).

Ruby, J. (1975) 'Is an ethnographic film a filmic ethnography?', *Studies in the Anthropology of Visual Communication*, II(2): 104–11.

Ruby, J. (1982) 'Ethnography as *Trompe L'Oiel*: Film and Anthropology', in J. Ruby (ed.), *A Crack in the Mirror: Reflexive Perspectives in Anthropology*. Philadelphia, PA: University of Pennsylvania Press, http://www.temple.edu./anthro/ruby/trompe.htm

Sanders, R. and Pink, S. (1996) 'Homage to "La Cordobesa"' in R. Wilk (ed.) *Beauty Queens on the Global Stage: Gender, Contests and Power*. New York: Routledge.

Schwartz, D. (1992) *Waucoma Twilight: Generalizations of the Farm*. 'Series on Ethnographic Inquiry'. Washington DC: Smithsonian Institution Press.

Schwartz, D. (1993) 'Superbowl XXVI: reflections on the manufacture of appearance', *Visual Sociology*, 8(1): 23–33.

Secondulfo, D. (1997) 'The Social Meaning of Things': A Working Field for Visual Sociology' in *Visual Sociology*, 12(2): 33–46.

Sekula, A. (1982) 'On the invention of photographic meaning', in V. Burgin (ed.), *Thinking Photography*. London: Macmillan.

Sekula, A. (1989) 'The archive and the body', in R. Bolton (ed.), *The Contest of Meaning*. Cambridge, MA: MIT Press.

Shanklin, E. (1979) 'When a good social role is worth a thousand pictures', in J. Wagner (ed.), *Images of Information*. London: Sage.

Silverstone, R. and Hirsch, E. (1993) *Consuming Technologies*. London: Routledge.

Simoni, S. (1996) 'The visual essay: redefining data, presentation and scientific truth', *Visual Sociology*, 11(2): 75–82.

Sixth International Festival of Ethnographic Film (1998) Festival Programme. London: Goldsmiths College.

Slater, D. (1995) 'Domestic photography and digital culture', in M. Lister (ed.), *The Photographic Image in Digital Culture*. London: Routledge.

Stirling, P. (1998 [1965]) *Turkish Village*. http://lucy.ukc.ac.uk/TVillage/StirlingContents.html

Stirling, P. (n.d) 'Paul Stirling's ethnographic data archive', http://www.lucy.ukc.ac.uk/TVillage/notes.html

Stoller, P. (1997) *Sensuous Scholarship*. Philadelphia, PA: University of Pennsylvania Press.

Strecker, I. (1997) 'The turbulence of images: on imagery, media and ethnographic discourse', *Visual Anthropology*, 9: 207–27.

Suchar, C. (1993) 'The Jordaan: community change and gentrification in Amsterdam', *Visual Sociology*, 8(1): 41–51.

Tayler, D. (1992) ' "Very lovable human beings": the photography of Everared and Thurn', in E. Edwards (ed.), *Anthropology and Photography*. London: Yale University Press.

Taylor, L. (1996) 'Iconophobia: how anthropology lost it at the movies', *Transition*, 69: 64–88.

Thomas, H. (1997) 'Dancing: representation and difference', in J. McGuigan (ed.), *Cultural Methodologies*. London: Sage.

Thoutenhoofd, E. (1998) 'Method in a photographic enquiry of being deaf', *Socio-*

logical Research Online, 3(2), http://www.socresonline.org.uk/socresonline/3/2/2.html

Tyler, S. (1987) *The Unspeakable: Discourse, Dialogue, and Rhetoric in the Postmodern World*. London: Academic Press.

Tyler, S. (1991) 'A Post-modern In-stance', in L. Nencel and P. Pels (eds), *Constructing Knowledge: Authority and Critique in Social Science*. London: Sage.

Urry, J. (1990) *The Tourist Gaze*. London: Sage.

Van Mierlo, M. (1994) 'Touching the invisible', *Visual Sociology*, 9(1): 43–51.

Wagner, J. (1979) 'Avoiding error', in J. Wagner (ed.), *Images of Information*. London: Sage.

Walsh, D. (1998) 'Doing ethnography', in C. Seale (ed.), *Researching Culture and Society*. London: Sage.

Woodhead, L. (1987) *A Box Full of Spirits: Adventures of a Film-maker in Africa*. London: Heinemann.

Wright, C. (1998) 'The third subject: perspectives on visual anthropology', *Anthropology Today*, 14(4).

Wright, T. (1998) 'Systems of representation: toward the integration of digital photography into the practice of creating visual images', *Visual Anthropology*, 12(1): 207–30.

Wright, T. (1999) *The Photography Handbook*. London: Routledge.

Filmography

Braun, K. (1998) *Passing Girl, Riverside: An Essay on Camera Work*. Documentary Educational Resources, USA.

Engelbrecht, B. (1993) *Copper Working in Santa Clara del Cobre*. IWF, Goettingen, Germany.

Getzels, P. and Gordon, H. (1990) *The Condor and the Bull*. National Film and Television School.

Henley, P. (1994) *Faces in the Crowd*. Granada Centre Productions (filmmaker Paul Henley, anthropological consultant, Ann Rowbottom).

Lydall, J. and Head, J. (1990) *The Women Who Smile*. BBC Under The Sun Series.

MacDougall, D. and McDougall, J. (1991) *Photo Wallahs: An Encounter with Photography in Mussorie: a North Indian Hill Station*. Berkeley, CA: Oxhard Film Productions.

Martinez Perez, A. (1997) *Cronotopo*. Taller de Antropologia Visual, Spain.

Pink, S. (1991) *Home from Home*. Granada Centre for Visual Anthropology.

Prelorain, J. Prelorain, M. and Saravino, Z. (1992) *Zulay Frente el Siglo XXI*, Department of Film and Television, University of California, Los Angeles.

Strecker, I. and Lydall, J. (1995) *Sweet Sorghum*. JWF, Goettingen, Germany.

Wendl, T. and Du Plessis, N. (1998) *Future Remembrance*. IWF, Goettingen, Germany.

Websites

http://www.muspe.unibo.it/period/MA/index.htm
   The Journal of Music and Anthropology an on-line journal.

http://www.socresonline.org.uk/socresonline/
  Sociological Research On-Line an on-line journal.
http://www.lucy.ukc.ac.uk
  The website of the Anthropology Department of the University of Kent at Canterbury. This has links to the *Experience Rich Anthropology* website, *The Virtual Institute of Mambila Studies, The Ascoli Project* (Colclough, Bagg, Hosking Coluccelli), *Making Tradition in the Cook Islands* (Fischer) and many other interesting examples of ethnographic hypermedia.
http://nimbus.ocis.temple.edu/~rchalfen/
  Richard Chalfen's page which contains examples of ethnographic hypermedia work and exhibitions of images as well as generally useful visual anthropology texts.
http://www.soc.surrey.ac.uk/sru/SRU11/SRU11.html
  Social Research Update, a set of on-line research methods guides.
http://www.rsl.ox.ac.uk/isca/
  The website of the Anthropology Department at the University of Oxford where links can be found to the Haddon Project as well as to papers on ethnographic hypermedia by Marcus Banks.
http://www.usc.edu/dept/elab/welcome/codifications.html
  Biella, P. (1994) 'Codifications of Ethnography: Linear and Nonlinear'.
http://www2.ncsu.edu/unity/lockers/project/meridian/feat 3/gender.html
  Goldman-Segall, R. (1998) 'Gender and Digital Media in the Context of a Middle School Science Project'.
http://wings.buffalo.edu/anthropology/anthroglobe/
  Anthroglobe, an on-line journal.
http://www.alltel.net/~ratcliff/qual.html
  Ratcliff, D. (n.d.) *Video and Audio Media in Qualitative Research*.
http://www.lucy.ukc.ac.uk/TVillage/notes.html
  Stirling, P. (n.d.) 'Paul Stirling's Ethnographic Data Archive'.
http://www.intergraphjournal.com
  Intergraph, an on-line anthropology journal based at the University of Hull.
http://www.temple.edu/anthro/ruby
  The website of visual anthropologist Jay Ruby. Contains links to a number of Ruby's publications on-line as well as a range of other useful texts.
http://www.copyrightservice.co.uk
  The website of the UK Copyright Service.
http://www.dacs.co.uk
  The website of the Design and Artists Copyright Society.
http://www.anthro-online.com
  Thompson Learning Anthropology website.
http://anthropology.ac.uk/Bhalot
  Lyon, S.M. (n.d) *Social Organisation, Economy and Development*.
http://lucy.ukc.ac.uk/dz
  The Virtual Institute of Mambila Studies.

Author Index

Subject Index